CARNEGIE'S CALL

Developing the Success Habit

MICHAEL MALONE

ARGYLL ✤ PUBLISHING

Argyll Publishing
Glendaruel
Argyll PA22 3AE
Scotland
www.argyllpublishing.co.uk

The author has asserted his moral rights.

British Library Cataloguing-in-Publication Data.

**A catalogue record for this book is available
from the British Library.**

ISBN 978 1 908931047

Printing: Martins the Printers, Berwick upon Tweed

To my son, Sam.
Every Dad should have one.

Acknowledgements

Writing is a solitary endeavour, made easier by those who offer unstinting support, insight and honest advice. In this regard I consider myself fortunate to count the following people as friends: Maggie Craig, Bill Kirton, Martie Hoover, Sara Bain, Angela Mathis and the woman whose generosity knows no bounds, Elizabeth Garrett. I would also like to thank the great Scots who generously gave of their time for this project.

"It's not about success, it's about happiness.
For me money is not the route of happiness –
how many billionaires are truly happy?
Getting more and more materials?
Ultimate success is being at one with yourself."

Graeme Obree

previous books by the author

Poetry

In the Raw Makar Press

Running Threads (with Sheila Templeton,
Rowena M. Love, Jim Hughes) Makar Press

Crime Fiction

Blood Tears (as Michael J. Malone)
Five Leaves Publishing

Contents

Introduction

> *'If you want to be happy, set a goal that*
> *commands your thoughts, liberates your energy*
> *and inspires your hopes.'*   Andrew Carnegie

I was on the way home from a MindStore conference at the Royal Concert Hall in Glasgow, when the idea for this book came to me. During the event, Jack Black, the wonderful motivational speaker, told the audience about the birth of the granddaddy of all self-help books, *Think and Grow Rich*.

Moments before he was due to meet with a young journalist called Napoleon Hill, emigré Scot and industrialist, Andrew Carnegie was looking down over the factory floor below his office. His attention was drawn to a man sweeping the floor, a man who shared a couple of similarities with Carnegie. This fellow was around the same age as he was and like him, he was an immigrant to the USA. There was also however, a major difference. Watching the man work with the broom, it struck Carnegie that while this man was sweeping floors, he himself was worth untold millions. What was the difference between the two men, he wondered?

When Hill arrived Carnegie asked him to forget about the interview. Instead, he set him on a course that would change the young man's life and take him twenty-five years to complete. Carnegie wanted Hill to write a book about success: he wanted him to interview five hundred of the most successful Americans and distil their abilities and attitudes into the form of a book.

Think and Grow Rich was published in 1937, has never been out of print and has sold in excess of 30 million copies.

With my hands on the steering wheel, my eyes on the road, my mind in the hall with Jack Black, my imagination was taking small steps into my future.

The inspiration for this book was a Scot. For such a small nation the Scots have been influential in so many areas of the planet's development. Scotland has given the world doctors, architects, engineers, entrepreneurs, innovators, writers; the list is long and makes hugely impressive reading. Yet why is the modern Scot so apologetic? Why are we so downbeat? Why are we so, dare I say it, negative? Why are we so suspicious of our fellow countrymen and women who are successful?

And why do so many of our people go abroad before their abilities are recognised?

How many of us are held back, in whatever sphere we wish for success, by such an attitude?

I explained to a few friends that I was interviewing successful Scots, and the reply from more than one person was, 'Did you find any?'

Yes, of course I did. There are modern day Scots who can match the achievements of the past, people who display a temperament suited to success, men and women who have the attitude and the ability to compete on a global scale. Perhaps it's time to be proud of that fact, perhaps it's time remind the world that Scotland is very much part of the global community.

Perhaps it's time to remind ourselves.

My aim with this book is not just to talk about how these individuals became successful. I also want to consider the 'why'. *Why* those interviewed performed so well in their chosen field. When you have a strong *why,* you can quite literally move mountains, you will bring to bear all your natural resources – desire, imagination, intellect, belief, determination, etc. – to achieve whatever it is you want to achieve.

Most books I've come across in this catogory are like manuals, laying out instructions on how to achieve success; they consider the mind and not the heart. This book examines through real-life examples the motivation behind the success and the obstacles that were overcome to get there. What's more, this book will demonstrate to you that successful people aren't any different from you and me. We all share the same physiology, and give or take a small percentage of the population, the same number of working brain cells.

The best lesson you can learn is one you learn for yourself and with this in mind, after each inspirational mini-biography I encourage you to examine what you have just read and to consider how you can make positive and lasting change in your own life. Also added are techniques and the suggestion of further research you can carry out to assist yourself in this journey.

Then there's the bad news message that is continually being pounded at our senses by the media. Just who came up with the notion that 'News' should exclusively be bad news? If there is any good news that the media deem to be worthy of our attention, it is tacked on, almost apologetically, at the end of the bulletin, lasts all of thirty seconds and is delivered with a wry, can-you-believe-it smile.

Watch a news channel for twenty-four hours and you could be forgiven for building a bunker in your back garden. Because your head will be filled with catastrophe, a hole in the ground will come across like a comfort in comparison.

There's good news out there, folks. Lots of it. Read the stories of these wonderful people like, Sir Tom Farmer CBE, Michelle Mone OBE, Jack Black, Margaret Thomson Davis, Dr. Robert Crawford OBE, Graeme Obree, Sir Tom Hunter and Muriel Gray and allow them to become your remote mentor.

Read and reflect and demand this of yourself: if they can develop the success habit, so can I.

Michelle Mone passes on her approach to business

Michelle Mone, OBE

A writer friend read the first draft of this interview which detailed Michelle's career to date. At the end of her reading, she paused, took a sip of her skinny de-caf latte, and with an expression that managed to convey puzzlement and embarrassment at posing the question, asked me – what about Michelle Mone, the family woman?

'Good question,' I answered, 'but having read a few of the other chapters, most of whom were about men, why haven't you asked that question before?' She struggled to give me an answer.

We all face the pressures of an aspirational society, so why are women still faced with this question, if the aspiration is a joint one? During the eighties and nineties women were empowered to have it all. You can have a successful career and a successful family life, they were told in the glossy magazines, in between dollops of fashion and skin care advice.

Following a number of stories in the press during the last few years about high profile males opting out of high level high pressure jobs to spend more time with their families, they could be forgiven for feeling cheated. Is it all it is cracked up to be? Are two holidays a year, flashy car and bulging wardrobes worth all the hard work? And what about the damage to the kids? What about the damage to the very fabric of society? Forgive the generalisation and the hyperbole, but the debate rages on.

The woman who is detailed in this chapter couldn't care about the questions, nor does she have the time to think about the answers, because she is **busy** – and loving it.

Michelle Mone grew up in the east end of Glasgow, experiencing what she describes as a very traditional working class background in Dennistoun. Home was a tenement flat of one bedroom, lounge, kitchen and toilet. She remembers it well.

'The flat had no bath. Remember this would only be about thirty years ago and I thought it was normal to go to the local swimming baths to get a wash two or three times a week.'

In the small rooms for hire where you could take a bath, Michelle would self-consciously share a tub with her mother: you could see over and under the walls. On other occasions where a head to toe wash was required she would have a wash in a big steel bath in the middle of the living room floor. It gives one a shock to consider that this way of life was still prevalent for many in Glasgow even during the seventies.

Family was Michelle, her parents and a baby brother, who tragically died when she was eight. The baby suffered from Spina Bifida. He didn't quite make his first birthday.

For many years she shared her mum and dad's bedroom, until her dad changed the broom cupboard into a single bedroom for her. Her father was a printer at a firm called Gibbons and after lowering the ceiling of the cupboard he brought home handfuls of sparkling stickers.

'So, we covered the ceiling with these stars and I just loved it. The room was tiny, but it was mine.' In fact the resultant room was so small; her dad had to saw a chunk off the end of the bed to make it fit.

'What I grew up with is really difficult to explain.' She smiles. 'It was fantastic, growing up in the east end. Dad used to come in from the pub most nights. Friday night was sing-along night and everybody would end up in our house and my mum would make them all a piece and fried egg to go along with their cans of Tennents.' Michelle paints a picture of a hard but simple life that most of us would have thought was consigned to the history books decades before. 'There would be no karaoke machine nor Pop Idol to keep a family entertained of a weekend, but the chant of "wan singer, wan song" kept the too loud, too enthusiastic and too drunk in line.'

Like the words from the folk song, Michelle remembers shouting up to her mother for a jelly piece and trying to catch the foil-wrapped sandwich that would get thrown down from the window. A simpler way of life perhaps, but not without its problems.

'I remember mum couldn't afford to get me anything for my birthday one year. She had a fiver left and she asked if I wouldn't mind if she went to the bingo to try and win me something.' Her mother won what would have been a huge sum of £300 and that afternoon she proudly escorted her daughter on a shopping trip.

'She paid cash. You never ever paid cash; you always paid with a provie check. And I got my stereo on my birthday.'

This is not an attitude to gift-buying that Michelle would advocate, but when you consider the risks she has taken in adulthood, it is a lesson that she has learned well.

It is a commonly held belief that entrepreneurs take more risks than the rest of us. Does the seed of Michelle's risk-taking lie in her mother's desire to buy her daughter just what she wanted for her birthday?

The behaviours that displayed her entrepreneurial tendencies also began at an early stage of Michelle's development. Many children play at 'shop' and enjoy it, however at the age of six or seven, Michelle remembers playing at such games, but she was always the boss – she was always the one giving the orders.

Within a few years she decided she was of an age when she should be earning some money. After she reached her tenth birthday she asserted her independence and began delivering morning goods like rolls, newspapers and milk.

With a wry smile, she remembers her young self. 'I used to get big crates from the dairies and run up and down the streets leaving stuff outside people's doors.'

Within a year Michelle realised she could earn ever more money if she took on some staff. Aged eleven, she divided up her area and took on some teenagers.

'This was a risk, because I had to buy the goods up front and then trust my delivery team to do the job and not run off with the milk and newspapers.'

The money she earned from this enabled her to buy things for herself, but also to give presents to her parents.

'I think I was 12, when I jumped on a bus on my own for the first time. I went into one of these catalogue shops in Sauchiehall Street and bought mum all this stuff for the house.' Among other things, Michelle remembers buying a toilet brush, a toilet roll holder and a toaster. 'I remember coming home in the bus with four huge bags.'

The next step in the progression of her career was to work in a shop and work at a till.

'I approached a guy we called George the Fruitie. He was having trouble because every corner in Duke Street had a fruit and veg stall.' Michelle felt that she was the one who could make a difference to his business. Armed with knowledge gained from reading business magazines she approached George and advised him that she could be his marketing person.

Quite predictably his response, as Michelle remembers it was, 'Don't be so stupid. You're just a wee girl. What can you do?'

But Michelle was ready. 'I can get uniforms for all you staff. Smarten up your image. Arrange a display outside your shop. Design proper posters with neat stencils instead of pencil.'

He asked her age.
'Twelve.'
'No way. Bugger off.'

Michelle, however, was determined. She wasn't taking 'no' for an answer. She offered her services for free for three months. And ended up staying three years.

'I belted down the road from school every day, started work at 4 and worked till 6:30 when I went home to do my homework. I worked the full day on Saturday, earning what I felt was great money.'

What was the reaction from your friends? I asked.

'They didn't say anything. In fact they used to come in to the shop expecting to get free strawberries and all that and I'd be like, no, where's your money?'

Michelle feels she did miss out on some of the more carefree aspects of childhood because of so much work, but her attitude of being self-reliant was more important to her.

'It was tiring, but I wanted to do it because I was earning all this money – I had this independence – all my friends had to ask their parents for the latest style of jeans when I could go into the shop and buy them.'

Impressed by the drive shown at such a young age, I asked if there was anyone who had a large influence on her as she grew up.

'I love my mum and dad equally, but I always wanted to make my dad feel proud. He's had such a hard life. As has my mum: she had to look after him. My family definitely are my heroes. I regularly meet people like Prince Charles, Rod Stewart, but I would place my family way up there against any of them. And although I look up to Branson, I wouldn't say he was the one to push me along.'

With this last comment Michelle tells me of the poster she put up on her bedroom wall. While her friends' pin-ups included Madonna and bands like Duran Duran, a certain bearded entrepreneur took up wall space in her bedroom.

At the age of fifteen Michelle was headhunted. A local sweet shop offered her more money and she moved on. This career move however, was short-lived due to developments in her family.

Her father had a bad limp for about 6 months, which doctors put down to a slipped disc. Then one day he woke up to find he couldn't walk. He was taken to hospital, where it was discovered he was suffering from a blood disorder, which damaged the blood vessels in his spine, leaving him paralysed from the waist down. Her parents had no savings and no insurance and when her father's employers found out what was wrong, he was out of a job as well.

Completely of her own volition Michelle elected to leave school, aged fifteen. She decided she needed to earn some serious money: the money from the sweet shop was not going to be adequate. Her first idea was to approach doctors' surgeries for work as a receptionist, however she was too young to have a national insurance number and no-one would take her on.

'But I was 5ft 10 so I went round a few model agencies and one of them decided to take me on. You should see my portfolio now,' she laughs with trademark honesty, 'looks nothing like me.'

For four years she trod the catwalks of Europe, but it wasn't what she really wanted to do. From as far back as she could remember all she wanted to do was run her own company and she refused to allow the glamorous world she was now living in to deflect her from her goal.

'A lot of the girls I worked with in those days were looking for men with big bank accounts. That footballer and this footballer, because they could look after you. I used to get all these players chatting me up, trying to impress me with their big cars, but I wasn't interested. That's *your* money. I don't want it to be mine. I want my own.'

Part of the vision that Michelle had for her life was a family. At eighteen she met Michael and within two years was married. Her first daughter, Rebecca, was conceived shortly after.

'I used to look at all the other models, who were a good bit older than me. I used to see them hanging around the town on a Friday night looking to see who had money. I decided I didn't want a life like that. And it was always, **always** on the back of my mind that my dad was getting worse.'

For someone with such progressive ideas as far as her career was concerned, Michelle was very traditional when it came to her family. She believed it was her duty to give her parents a grandchild.

'To be honest, I didn't want kids at 20, but I was worried that my dad was getting worse. I would wake up every day and worry that he would pass away before I gave him a grandchild. However, don't make the mistake of thinking I have any regrets, I don't regret one bit of it. When I'm forty, she'll be twenty: a pal.'

Knowing that pregnant models didn't get much work, Michelle secured a job with Labatt as a junior.

'I wanted business experience and there were so many A-levels you had to have. And I didn't have any because I left school at 15. So I told a few white lies here and there because I knew if I got in front of them they would give me the job. Because they would have no choice,' she added with a laugh.

Her career path was as dynamic and as focused as the actions of the younger Michelle might have suggested. Two years later, she was running their Scottish division and was instrumental in the launch of Labatt's Ice Beer.

'I worked my way up through 10 positions. I **knew** in order for me to get up there, in order for me to pay for childcare, a nice house, a nice holiday, I had to make it happen.'

As soon as the first promotion was won, she told herself she had three months to get the next one. After that box was ticked, she would tell herself she had four months to get the next one.

'Nothing was ever good enough. I'm not saying I was a greedy bitch. It was more like: ok, what's next? It's the same with this company. People think we've made it and I don't think we're even half way there yet.'

Just two years on, Michelle was made redundant from Labatt when they were taken over by Whitbread and as many people will testify, a forced change of life like this had a silver lining.

A few months later, Michelle was at a dinner dance in the Glasgow Hilton with her husband. The dress she chose for the event dictated that she wear a cleavage bra.

'I searched everywhere for a comfortable bra that would give me more of a cleavage. I found one that worked, but it was so unnatural and so bloody uncomfortable – during the dinner I had to run into the toilets and take it off. I came back to the table and complained to my husband, Michael, surely to god there must be a bra that could do the job.' She paused. 'And that was the start of it.'

Not everyone shared her early enthusiasm. She had to work at convincing her husband and her family and as if to help dirty the water a little, Whitbread who had bought Labatt, offered her old job back.

'You've got a mortgage and two kids,' she pursed her lips at the memory. 'To give up that salary was a big leap of faith. I think I would have gone for it eventually, but the redundancy made me take it sooner. And thank God, because when you get into that really secure stage where your bills are being met and you're relying on a monthly pay packet, it's hard to take that jump.'

As she recalls, everyone put her off. When she approached the banks they all but laughed at her, suggesting she commit to a business plan and return in 6 months, expecting never to see her again.

However, she was in her own words, 'bloody determined'. She wasn't going to let a small thing like banker's reluctance to put her off. 'I was thinking; you're not going to tell me when I **know**, because I can see. I can always see. I visualise things. I plan it all in my head and know it inside out. I just knew that this was it.

'It was like someone waved a magic wand and said after all these years (remember she was only 24) this is it. I knew they were all wrong.'

It took nearly three years of research and development, testing many different methods of cleavage enhancement to come up with the Ultimo bra: a bra which enhances the bust and cleavage without the discomfort normally associated with such products.

'We used every last penny: re-mortgaged the house. And every Christmas it was like, this is it. It better happen this year. It was scary, but I've since had even scarier moments when the business was bigger: when I had more to lose.'

Michelle admits that another driving force for her enterprise was that she felt strongly that she had to be her own boss. 'I couldn't bear someone telling me what to do, when I knew they were wrong. I'm not being arrogant. I cannot work for anyone. I can work **with** people; to battle for the result that they want, and the result I want. I can work with lots of people, but when someone tells me what to do?' She paused and grinned, 'Red, rag, bull.'

The fledgling company nearly folded before it had sold a single bra. Trusting the wrong individual, Michelle says she was conned by a distributor who disappeared with nearly £1m in cash and stock. Only by remortgaging the family home and using money left to Michael after the death of his mother did they fight off bankruptcy.

The culmination of 3 years work, the bra was launched in Selfridges in London in August 1999. The iconic store sold the pre-launch stock estimated to last six months within twenty-four hours.

'It was crazy. Over 60 photographers turned up. We were on CNN in America, Fox News, Japanese TV, German TV. Oxford Street came to a standstill. Everyone was shouting at me. We made the front pages of all the newspapers. It was the biggest bra launch in history,' she recalls with an energy and passion I would suggest hasn't waned one iota in the intervening years.

Michelle recalls the rollercoaster event. 'I had Bethany 2 weeks earlier. She arrived early. I actually went into labour in the boardroom; a 20 hour labour and I was back in office sitting on a rubber ring within 48 hours, with a Moses Basket at my side. It was a really emotional day. I was not long out of hospital. I was missing the kids, didn't know how my life was going to go.'

The importance of the moment is still fresh. 'I had three kids: it was all dependent on that launch.'

Michelle needn't have worried. The launch was a huge success and to cap it off, in April 2000, at a ceremony in the Epcot Centre, Florida, Michelle won the coveted *World Young Business Achiever Award* beating off top entrepreneurs from 14 countries.

Ultimo launched in the exclusive Saks Fifth Avenue store in New York in May 2000.

And in October of that same year, Michelle was the winner of *Business Woman of the Year* at the Corporate Elite Awards.

That however, was not the end of the story. As any student of life will tell, to be human is to experience ups and downs. Michelle contends that the biggest lesson for her in all of this concerns belief. She argues that if you really believe in something, when you can see it, and you're willing to give it 110%, you should do it. Not everyone can, not everyone wants to, but if you want to be there, you have to act. With a wry grin she adds that if other peoples' experiences are anything like hers it won't happen without some pain.

'It was like being locked up for 3 years and being used as a punch bag. It was horrific. And here's the important thing: I would never have gone through all that for someone else. Yes, I would do a good job for them, but at the end of the day the responsibility was entirely mine.'

The awards and accolades kept coming and Michelle could have been forgiven for thinking that her troubles were over, but in 2002 the business was 8 minutes away from being closed down by her bank. 'It was just like the beginning again: a rollercoaster ride. There's a good period, a bad period, a good period, then a disaster. That cycle just keeps on. As the company grows the highs may get higher, but the risks also get higher.'

When asked if it has all been worth it, her answer is an emphatic YES!

'With hindsight, it's good that we went through those lessons, because it made me a stronger person. I can cope with almost anything now in the business. I've had staff problems, bank problems, etc. The only way to learn is to go through all of these things first hand. This is not theory that can be taught.

'Out of Scotland's entrepreneurs, I won't be one of the wealthiest, but I certainly have gained so much experience. I've been beaten up. Taken it like a man. I've got balls of steel. I'm not frightened about taking challenges on.

'As long as you stay determined and focused you will win through. Even when it's over, it's not over. There is always a way. There is always a small, small chance. And thank God I had that in me. There's no way this company would still be here if I didn't have that.'

Despite her success, Michelle displays no sign of taking things any easier and her ambitions remain as intense as ever. Having lost more than five stones in a year via weight loss pills, she is now focused on turning her company into the 'Victoria Secrets of the UK'.

She is also keenly aware that there are other things in life and that a balance is required if an individual is to be truly happy.

Carol Craig in *The Scots' Crisis of Confidence* in the chapter titled 'Never Good Enough' quotes the words from the song by Fairground Attraction.

'Too many people take second best, but I won't take anything less. It's got to be perfect'. Carol goes on to say, 'Perfect or worthless, that's the see-saw most individual Scots are on.'

In a typical moment of candour, Michelle alludes to this very issue. As the interview wound to a close, I asked my last question. What would you have inscribed on your tombstone?

Michelle considered this for a long moment before answering. 'Oh. I've never been asked that before. You know I don't think about myself. It may seem weird. Everyone comes before me. It's like I'm punishing myself. It's always the kids, the business, the family. People say to me, away and have a day in a beauty salon and I'm like, you're joking, I could get this done and that done.' She counts off imaginary tasks on her fingers.

She confesses to being a worrier. 'I worry all the time. I lie up in my bed at night and worry; we'll never get the media interested in the next launch, we've had so much coverage recently. I worry about the staff, I worry about the warehouse.'

Many of us are frightened by our worries to the point of inactivity, but Michelle uses the energy this worry gives her in a hugely creative way.

'It makes me think of new products and if I wasn't worried I wouldn't be doing that. So although it's a pest, I use it positively for the business. I sit up in bed in the dark and set all these reminders in my phone for the next day. It's constant and I can't help it.'

At the time of the interview she has plans to launch a luxury beauty range and an Ultimo perfume. And if that isn't enough, this lady who relishes a challenge recently appeared in Celebrity

Masterchef and is in training for the London and New York marathons that she hopes to run.

Just like every chapter of her life, times are going to be busy and exciting one for Michelle Mone, OBE.

Mentoring with Michelle

Going out on a limb

That's where the fruit is after all. A common quality in the entrepreneurial mind is the ability to take risks, as is clearly evident from Michelle's story.

The turtle can only make progress if he sticks his neck out and it is fair to say it is often thought entrepreneurs are made from different stuff than the rest of us. It is posited that their different approach to taking risks is a result of traits that they were born with.

This can often be a get-out clause for the rest of us, but here's the bad/good news: there is little evidence for this. Every indication is that risk taking is a cognitive action and therefore something that can be learned and polished over time.

For Michelle Mone, even at a young age, it was a strong sense of dissatisfaction that drove her forward. It is a simple process to draw parallels from her early family situation to the desire to improve.

However, I'm guessing that there are a zillion people (give or take) all over the planet who have had a family situation just as, or even more trying than her's and how many of them began their entrepreneurial career at the age of 12?

So that's fine then. I'm in my (coughs) forties. It's too late for me. I'll just get back on the couch and exercise my thumb on the old remote control. Channel surfing is me. Until success comes a-knocking.

Except it doesn't, does it?

Think of the turtle.

Many of us don't take that move forward, which when you consider how many of us are miserable in our employment seems a little bit strange. On the other hand it can be very understandable. There's safety in our wee comfort bubble. A roof over our heads can mitigate the feeling of misery that comes from a job that sucks the joy out of our bones.

The downside of the climb out on the limb of the tree is that it might crash to the ground.

A fear of failure then?

While it is seen as a necessary part of the business world, risk taking is viewed negatively in relation to our everyday lives. We read/ hear/ say the word 'risk' and feel our self recoil. The hazard light comes on in our brain and the brake light joins it.

Has there ever been anything that landed on your lap that gives off the same taste of satisfaction as something you worked hard on? Perhaps we need to re-frame the word. View it as a positive activity relevant to all areas of life.

> 'If you are distressed by anything external, the pain is not due to the thing itself, but to your estimate of it; and this you have the power to revoke at any moment.'
> Marcus Aurelius

Fearing failure

There is no doubt that failure can be disappointing and discouraging. At the same time, it can help to build resilience. Few successful people achieve their success at the first try. It may take several attempts to gain the success you are looking for. It may happen first time! However it happens, flexibility in thought and attitude is key.

In any case, learning to deal with failure is as much a part of life as porridge. We all fail at something, don't we? Success and failure are different sides of the same coin. It's how you react to it that will decide if you continue moving on towards that goal.

Do you brood? Do you go into your shell? Do you run over all your recent failures and mentally give yourself a good kicking? Is any of that helpful?

Do you want to run for the hills and find a nice wee cave? Or do you run in the opposite direction and indulge in a spot of over-achieving? Do you work and worry yourself to a shadow, while at the same time dreaming up an escape?

Years ago, I was so miserable in my job I used to fantasise about having a car crash on the way home. Just a wee one. Enough to break a leg or a collar bone. And then I would get a couple of months off.

Seriously.

There was even a time when I was running on a treadmill at the gym when I realised the fantasy escape I was mentally working on was even more dangerous than the car crash. I was daydreaming about having a heart attack. You see I had a Critical Illness policy and if I had a heart attack of sufficient severity (we're talking muscle wastage) it would pay out and I could get rid of my mortgage.

I woke up to the nonsense I was allowing to run through my mind and soon after this; I got myself the hell out of Dodge and another job elsewhere.

Here's another approach. Fear of failure is a good thing.

Perhaps it gets you out of bed in the morning, or it forces you to do that report to your boss, or meet those targets. Note how in the interview, Michelle Mone talked about how she worries.

She uses the energy this provides in a positive sense. Instead of inhibiting her, it drives her to become more creative in her search for a solution.

Failure as your teacher

Sounds nuts, right? Life's most effective lessons come through failure. Fail often, fail hard is the old adage in business. Failure to a pessimist is the end of the road, whereas 'failure' to an optimist is simply a wee bump on the road.

Study after study has shown that if we are able to frame a failure as an instance of learning we are all the more likely to experience that occasion as growth.

There's the apocryphal story about Thomas Edison and his thousands of attempts to create the light bulb. When the next attempt didn't work, he didn't throw a wobbly; he took careful note of it, calculated why it didn't work, learned from it and made his next attempt.

The story goes that he made over 10,000 attempts. If he had sheltered a fear of failure, perhaps we'd be living in a quite different world right now. Edison took inspiration from his 'failures' and saw them as moving one more attempt closer to success.

As part of my journey as a writer I left my career in financial services in order to focus on my heart-purpose. To say that the money didn't exactly flood in is like saying cats have a fondness for those wee mouse-shaped things. At one point I had 5 jobs; bookseller, waiter, creative writing lecturer, among them. I was either preparing a lesson, delivering a lesson, selling books or serving coffee. How much writing did I get done?

Nada, zip, zilch.

Realising that writing and publication was still my goal, I had to find a way to keep the roof over my head, contribute to the family and still have the space to write and seek publication. (See that starving writer in the garret malarkey? It sucks.)

So, I found a job again in financial services in 2005 and got back to writing. In the last six years, I've written five books. Focus found: one part of the goal achieved.

I was chatting with my brother about my job changes recently and complaining that the outcome of this was to return to an industry I'd plotted for years to leave. He called me out on my attitude.

'At least you tried,' he said.

'Aye, but I failed,' I replied.

'Shut up,' he said. 'I really admired the guts you had in walking away from a good job to chase your dream. I wish I had your courage.' He paused. 'Did going back to your old job mean you've given up?'

'Hell, no,' I said. 'I'm never giving up.'

'That's when you fail, numpty-heid. When you give up. So, it didn't work out quite the way you planned it, at least you had a go.'

Thomas Henry Huxley said, 'Don't judge those who try and

fail. Judge those who fail to try.'

Do you see every setback as leading only in one direction: down? See the opportunity stitched into the moment. Energise yourself by seeing that value in life comes because of the setbacks, not despite them.

Fear of change

Or, metathesiophobia, to use its Sunday name.

> 'Change is inevitable – except from a vending
> machine.'   Robert C. Gallacher

In her book, *Feel the Fear and Do It Anyway*, Susan Jeffers, states that the real fear is the fear of not being able to handle it. This ties in with change; if change happens, we are frightened that we will not be able to cope with what that change might bring.

Another way of looking at it is that people fear change, because they focus on the possible negative impacts on their happiness and lives.

The man who launched a thousand quotes, Mark Twain once said, 'Courage is resistance to fear, mastery of fear, not absence of fear.'

Successful people aren't people who conquered fear; they're people who faced fear. They're people who, as it says in the title of the above book, were afraid and did it anyway. Like Michelle Mone.

Take a moment to consider your own feelings about change. When was the last time you changed something in your life – big or small? Did the local council add a one-way street changing your route to work? Was your favourite TV programme on at a different time from its normal slot? Did your favourite social network site change its settings?

Change is a constant in life: yes? So anytime you're struggling with the reality of a situation, take a moment and ask yourself some deeper questions. Like, what am I really afraid of here?

Beneath the situation, the things you see, feel or describe: within your reactions are real fears that are being activated. No event in life can bump against a hotspot of pain that doesn't already exist somewhere deep inside.

Success formula

Many books in the field of self-help assert that your brain is a success mechanism. A success outcome is built in (how else would you learn to walk/ talk) but we get in the way of it with our fears and our knack for self-sabotage.

The legend of Robert the Bruce and the spider is taught in all Scottish schools, and I would suggest is world famous.

In case it isn't, here's a wee précis. In the early days of The Bruce's reign he was defeated by the English and driven into exile. A hunted man, he sought shelter in a small dark cave and while he was brooding about his failure he noticed a little spider trying to make a web. As they are wont to do.

Time and time and time again the spider would fall and then without an apparent drop in effort, climbs slowly back up to try yet again.

If at first you don't succeed, try, try and try again.

Finally, as our Rab looked on, the spider got his strand of silk sticky enough to attach to the cave wall and the weaving began in earnest. Robert the Bruce was inspired by the spider and went on to defeat the English at the Battle of Bannockburn.

So at first you have to try.

If you try there's going to be a result, right?

The next step is to assess the aforementioned result. Get some feedback into your grey matter.

Your success mechanism (your brain) will then check the actions that caused the result and compare what actually happened to what your goal might have been.

You compare your performance against the intended outcome and for the next try, you make any necessary adjustments. You then go through the process (try, try and try again) until. . . Success.

No matter what you do, your brain is designed to succeed. Whether it be learning how to walk, or making yourself a coffee OR any number of life goals you might have.

We've all heard the saying, success breeds success. It means that once you have been successful, if you carry on putting the same effort and focus in, success will become easy and natural.

Speak to any number of successful people and ask them why, once they have achieved what we might see as success beyond our wildest imaginings, they still carry on.

Answer? Just as it has with Michelle Mone, success becomes a habit.

Margaret Thmson Davis

Margaret Thomson Davis

'For years I thought my father was Robinson Crusoe,' Margaret Thomson Davis, the award-winning novelist recalls. 'Then I thought he was Jim Hawkins.' She has many memories of her father reading to her and her young brother in her early years. However, her father changed the text slightly and told them all in the first person – as if HE were the hero. As any writer will tell you, this is a technique that makes a story more immediate, and for a child being told these stories it would make them much more realistic and frightening.

Other tales he told included Burke and Hare the body-snatchers and Sweeney Todd, the demon barber.

'I was ten or eleven and my brother was even younger, and we went to bed every night absolutely terrified.' As soon as her father left the room, Margaret's wee brother would plead to hear one of her nice stories so he wouldn't have any nightmares.

This childhood exercise strengthened Margaret's ability to tell a story. The seed of the desire to communicate to her fellow human beings also lay in her youth.

'Because it allows great insights into the human condition, I always say to beginner writers that an unhappy childhood is a great bonus to a writer or any creative person. . . and I was particularly blessed in this regard.' Her laughter at this comment is clear and without rancour. Which is remarkable when you consider the rest of her story.

'My brother was a delicate wee boy and my mother, quite understandably, lavished much more time, attention and love on him.' Throughout her childhood Margaret's mother left her father at frequent intervals. Sometimes she would take both children with her but more often than not she would leave Margaret behind. Consequently Margaret came to dread leaving the house for school in the mornings. She could never be sure that her mother and brother would be there when she returned.

'Every morning before I left for school I used to kiss my mother and then look up at her trying desperately to sense if she was going to leave me. Every single day I would shut the front door but couldn't bring myself to walk away. I had a compulsion to knock the door so she would reply and I could get another kiss.'

Once at school, Margaret simply existed through the day, not listening to the teachers or her fellow pupils, worrying desperately about what she might find when she went home. By the time she arrived at her door she would be on the point of nervous collapse. She would knock the door and pray to hear her mother's answering stride as she came to open the door for her. An early warning sign would be the smell of disinfectant leaking through the letterbox.

'If I peered through the letterbox and saw newspapers spread over the linoleum and smelled disinfectant, I knew she was gone. My mother had a cheerful disregard for housework, but whenever she left my father she would scrub the house from top to bottom, as if she was washing her hands of him forever.'

Eventually neighbours would see her sitting about the stairs in a state of shock and take her in, until her father returned from work. But he worked shifts and would often be out to work all night, so he was forced to find someone to look after his little girl while he continued to pay for a roof over their heads. Tragically, this trust was misplaced. Margaret was sexually abused at the hands of several people.

'It has taken me a long time to be able to talk about this part of my life,' she says. The mind often acts to protect the developing psyche when it is most at risk. Subsequently, Margaret's memories are mercifully patchy.

'One occasion that I wrote about in my autobiography, *The Making of a Novelist,* I asked, 'Where was I? Who was that woman who bathed me in the zinc bath by the side of an old-fashioned black range? The room was a pool of shadows. I see myself standing in the bath. The woman has gone out of the room. A man is sitting on a stool very close in front of me. There is something in the way he is staring at me. I remember his eyes with fear, even today. I see the vulnerability of my pink skin. I try to find some numb place inside my head where I'll see nothing. Feel nothing.'

As a result of all of this, Margaret was a very unhappy and introverted child desperate to reach out to people, to communicate and have friends.

Through the practice of making up stories for her brother she learned the very method that would bring her a substitute for her parent's affection: the attention of her peers. Margaret graduated to telling her stories in the playground.

'I compare it to the comedian who might tell jokes to other

children to get them to like him and not bully him.' During school playtime, children would gather round her while she beguiled them with her vivid imagination, and amazingly at such a young age, she instinctively caught on to another writing technique that would have her audience clamouring for more.

'Before the bell went to call us back into class, I would end on a cliff-hanger, and right enough at the next break they would all gather round me again asking what was going to happen next in my story.'

This desire to communicate and create strengthened as she grew older. 'But my parents and other relations thought that writers were a different breed from the rest of us. They lived in a completely different realm. Indeed it was hard for them to imagine that such creatures existed in flesh and blood at all.' When her parents asked her what she wanted to do when she left school, she told them of her ambition to be a writer.

'Don't be ridiculous. What do you want to work at?' was their reply. So she learned not to mention it again. The will to write, however, didn't fade.

'At first I just wrote small descriptions of things. Trees, people, buildings: whatever.'

While practising her craft in secret, Margaret left school and took a job to please her mother and father: she trained as a nursery nurse.

'But all the time I was observing other people and noting my experiences. I went into other jobs, all sorts of jobs with the intent to learn about all sorts of people and all different ways of life – that was my market study if you like – and while I was doing this work I was still writing away and gradually turned these descriptions into stories and eventually, novels.'

Things still hadn't improved at home. Her parents argued incessantly, and in those days a young girl could only escape through marriage. So she vowed she would marry the first man who asked her. A striking young woman, Margaret didn't have long to wait. A man duly obliged, and soon after, her son, Kenneth, was born. The marriage, however, didn't last.

'We were both far too young,' admits Margaret. With a child and no man to support her, Margaret needed a job that included accommodation and an employer who would be willing to take in a young woman and a toddler. Eventually, she found a position as a housekeeper for a widower. This not only gave her a roof over her head but a friend for Kenneth, as the widower had a young boy of his own.

Margaret married this man, who was quite a few years older than her, and she vowed to bring up his child as her own. However, she soon discovered her new husband was obsessed with the memory of his dead wife.

'There were photographs of her everywhere. He even forced me to visit her grave with him.' On learning of Margaret's desire to write, he was at first pleased, he even offered to help. Delighted and relieved that someone would show such interest Margaret followed his suggestions. Until she realised that the story her husband wanted her to write concerned an ailing young woman with a remarkable resemblance to his first wife. To make matters worse, he was persuading her to depict the housekeeper in the book as a cripple.

After so much upheaval in the young lives of the boys, she determined that she would endure her unhappiness for their sakes. But she soon discovered another difficult side to her husband's nature. He became abusive. This did not include physical contact, but the slow, subtle use of carefully chosen words, designed to erode her confidence. Like Chinese water torture, he dripped words into her mind that would have her believe that she had little worth and that she would never be able to manage on her own.

'He was terribly house-proud and to please him I would work my fingers to the bone. I even polished the bathroom walls, for goodness sake. But nothing would make him happy.' On top of this she also had to look after her husband's father who was by now living with them as he was suffering from Alzheimer's.

Writing would provide a release from all this tension. Margaret still nurtured the desire to communicate, but as yet she had nothing published.

'There comes a time when you have to make a choice. Either you remain a self-pitying failure with a closed mind and a huge chip on your shoulder. Or, you take a deep breath, gird your loins and try to learn where you are going wrong.'

Aware of the truth in the saying that it is madness to keep doing the same thing while expecting a different result, Margaret took a step back from her work and considered where she was making mistakes. By this stage she had five novels to her name, all of them unpublished. She decided to change her tactics and work the other end of the writing spectrum: letters and short stories. She wrote a letter to a woman's magazine and it was accepted for publication.

'I'll never forget opening the magazine on the street and

there was my letter, my very own words on the page.' All these years later and her face still shines at the memory of her first appearance in print. Next she decided to organise a campaign on the magazines of DC Thomson. She studied each of them, analysed their content from the letters to the problem pages to the short stories. This gave her an insight into what the readers of these magazines would prefer. It also gave her an insight into how to hook her reader's interest straight away, how to make sure that every word counted and how to tap into the emotions of her own life in order to give her characters depth.

Her work was accepted by the magazine and steadily published. Once she had established a working relationship with DC Thomson she began to have meetings with their editors. She was invited to one in Dundee dealing with a new glossy magazine and was terribly excited that she was to be involved at its inception.

'In those days DC Thomson was very strict about the morality of their heroines. Smoking and drinking were out. And any kissing or canoodling could do you a professional injury. But I thought that this new magazine might break new ground.'

Determined to find out if the new magazine had such taboos, Margaret set off for the meeting, armed with a pencil and a notebook to catch every note of wisdom that fell from the editor's lips. She was too early and sat in anxious contemplation waiting for the editor to arrive. When finally he did, she got straight down to business.

'About sex,' she burst out, 'how far can I go?'

'How far do you want to go, love?' he smiled in reply.

Margaret went on to have more than two hundred short

stories published, but her real goal in life was to be a novelist. Writing short stories helped to hone her craft, and bolstered a confidence that was sagging under the weight of her husband's cruel remarks.

She spurred herself on by thinking that if she could get short work into print then she could do the same with longer work. It was simply a matter of persevering in her daily writing practice and learning the appropriate techniques.

For years Margaret wondered if a better education would improve her chances of publication. So she attended extra-mural classes at university expecting to learn from the knowledge of her lecturers.

Initially, Margaret found the classes interesting. Then as books were endlessly analysed and dissected she became restless, bored and frustrated. She was learning nothing about the craft of writing.

'I found myself becoming more interested in the lecturer and my classmates as people. I watched them, noted their mannerisms and wondered what they were really like inside and what kind of lives they led.' Margaret's habit of observing her group didn't go unnoticed, however. A male student drew her to the side one day as she left the class and said, 'It might look as if there's something going on between me and Mrs Brown but I can assure you our friendship is absolutely innocent.'

Margaret allows at this point in her writing career that although her character descriptions in her short pieces were rooted in reality, her novels were not. 'They were about big houses in the country and at the time I'd never even been in the country.' A conversation with another writer was to prove the turning point for her. She discovered the Writers' Summer School in Swanwick, Derbyshire.

'One of the speakers was a best-selling writer at the time, Alexander Cordell. After he gave his talk I was so excited and overwhelmed by meeting all these writers, I went back to my room and wept with the sheer emotion of it all.'

Later, Margaret spotted Mr Cordell out on the lawn having afternoon tea. She plucked up the courage to speak to him and was soon explaining to him how she had already written five novels and how desperate she was to write books that would get published.

Very quickly he recognised Margaret's problem. He looked at her name badge,

'Where are you from Margaret?'

'Glasgow.'

'What's your background?'

'Oh, nothing interesting, just the Glasgow tenements.'

'Well my advice to you is to go home and with as much courage and honesty you can muster, write about Glasgow and about life in the Glasgow tenements.'

A career rose from that conversation. Margaret went home and wrote what was to become *The Breadmakers*, a trilogy that has sold over 100,000 copies.

But success still didn't come knocking: there was a lot more determination and perseverance needed. Margaret completed, edited and sent off the first book, *The Breadmakers*. It came back. Undeterred, she read it over again, edited it some more, and sent it off again.

'The publishers would keep the books for months and months and rather sitting and waiting in hope, I immediately started to write something else. And while the first book was bouncing around the publishers I started to write the follow-up, *A Baby Might Be Crying*. While the first two books were going the rounds of the publishers, again Margaret didn't rest. She started on book three.

'Then while all three were out there I wrote another two novels.' At one point, Margaret recalls, almost in disbelief at her own drive, 'I had ten novels in the house and not one word of them published.'

This was when she reached her lowest ebb. 'Right down to my soul I feared I was wasting my time, that I would never be a writer. But just at that point something rose up in me and I thought, dammit, I'll show them. If it takes me to the day before I die I will be a published novelist.' Now, re-living this memory she punches the table top with, I imagine, the same fervour.

Re-galvanised by this fire, Margaret set to work, packaging and posting her work. She informed her husband that she was going to work her way through the alphabet of publishers, starting at the very first one and work through them all. Her husband pointed out that the first publisher in the book was Allison and Busby and they had just sent back her trilogy. But Margaret was so in thrall of her regained determination that she sent them regardless.

Then she received the reply she had been waiting for all these years. Allison & Busby had changed their mind. Not only did they want the most recent two she had sent them, *The Prisoner* and *A Very Civilised Man*, but they also wanted her to return *The Breadmakers* trilogy to them. It was just a question of which of the five books they would publish first.

We can only imagine her excitement; five books accepted by a publisher at the same time. She danced around the house with joy. Then she realised there was no one at home to share her news with. So she phoned everybody she knew that owned a phone. No one answered.

'Then I remembered that mum was having the family round that afternoon. Wonderful. I'd be able to tell my glorious news to all the family at once. I rushed round. Burst into the house to find them all chatting happily in the front room. 'You'll never guess what's happened,' I announced. 'A publisher is going to publish all my books.' There was silence for a long moment, then someone said, 'I'm glad wee Tommy's cold didn't go into his chest after all.'

Although she can laugh at the memory now, it was painful at the time.

'I felt terribly ashamed. The unspoken belief had been confirmed that there always had been something odd about me. They didn't know any writers and didn't believe that it could be possible: these things didn't happen to the likes of us. They didn't know how to cope, so they just ignored me.'

This experience did nothing to put her off, and Margaret continued to try and make contact with her fellow human beings via the written word. The books kept coming. She has recently completed her 45th novel.

'For me it was the determination to reach out, to work it all out, to communicate, to find approval, and the only way I knew how was through my writing.' As she grew older and fought to make sense of her childhood through the lives of her characters, she experienced how cathartic the act of writing was.

'I could work through my problems safely, once removed through a fictional character. So although the abuse in my books might happen to a Victorian daughter in the slums or an Edwardian from a posh house, the truth of what happened to me is in the emotion expressed on the page.'

Research is a vital component of Margaret's books. She completes detailed research to ensure that her facts are accurate. The librarians at the Mitchell Library in Glasgow grew very fond of Margaret while simultaneously dreading her next request. Joe Fisher, the retired Head Librarian recalls with a smile, 'I remember her phoning up and asking what the smell of the inside of a carriage in the eighteenth century would be like.'

Her early attempts at research, however, were dampened by her lack of confidence.

'Although I could claim to be a published writer, I still hadn't the belief that I was a **writer**.' When researching *The Bread-makers* she felt acutely embarrassed at the thought of asking a baker about his job. She went to one shop and hung at the back of a crowd of shoppers, avoiding the gaze of the shop assistants. Eventually one of them spotted her and asked if she could help.

'I asked for half-a-dozen crumpets.'

Eventually after having bought enough cakes and scones to last her all week, she blurted out the real reason for her visit.

Now, more than thirty years after her first publication, Margaret is still producing on average a book per year. Her motivation to continue to strive for success doing something she loves is security and independence. This ambition more than any others keeps her going.

She is the first to admit that her career as a novelist has not made her 'rich' in financial terms; indeed she gets fed up with people assuming she is near the same income bracket as JK Rowling. She quoted from a survey commissioned by the Society of Authors which calculated that the average writer in the UK earns around £5,000 per annum.

'That's much lower even than the minimum wage. It's a good job we're not in it for the money,' she smiled. 'Mind you, a wee bit more would be nice.'

During the hours of drudgery spent keeping house for her husband and looking after his father, she instinctively employed a technique that many success gurus recommend: visualisation.

'That's what they call it nowadays, but I'd never heard of it back then. I used to imagine myself in a big house of my own. I used to imagine myself with all the furniture to fill it. I even visualised it down to the last teaspoon.'

Even in her dreams she didn't expect a thirty-year career. She didn't dream that the experiences of her youth would lead her to what she calls the best night of her life, being honoured by the City she calls home. She didn't dream of the hundreds of letters from fans all over the world who write to thank her for temporarily bringing the respite that only a good book can.

Her books have been adapted for the stage; she has worked in radio and sold over two hundred short stories worldwide.

Such is her popularity that in a recent review of the Scottish library system, she was found to be the most borrowed author in the country, apart from JK Rowling. In 2002 the City of Glasgow was awarded her The Provost's Award for Literature.

When she received the letter to tell her of The Provost's Award she phoned and asked a friend if she had to apply for it. 'No of course not,' was the reply. 'You've won the thing.' Even today, after all her success, Margaret doesn't fully appreciate how far she has come. That Scottish instinct to play things down remains with her still.

From a difficult and painful childhood Margaret has grown into a fine storyteller. The strength of character and sheer persistence that it took to turn a horrendous experience into books that would enrich our lives is humbling, as is her drive to continue doing so, well past a stage when most of us dream of retiring.

Many people with a similar experience to Margaret have been lost under its weight, but for her, an escape was finding a positive outlet for that negative energy. At an early age she found a means of validation, she found something she could do well and something that would bring meaning into her life. Perhaps, believing Robinson Crusoe was her father wasn't such a bad thing after all.

Mentoring with Margaret

Constancy of Purpose

There is nothing new in what I am talking about in this book. Benjamin Disraeli (a British Prime Minister during the latter half of the nineteenth century) is quoted has having said, 'The secret of success is a constancy of purpose.' In modern day idiom that might translate as 'keep your eyes on the prize'. Whatever language you prefer to use, the key to many people's achievements is perseverance.

Margaret kept on going until . . .

She analysed where she was going wrong; she sought advice from experts, she put in long hours perfecting her skills as a writer. And she kept on submitting her work and persevering until she received validation from a publisher. She freely admits that there were low points: times in her life when she was close to giving in, but she fought against the negative voice that chimes in us all and maintained a constancy of purpose. She *would* be a published writer if it took her to the end of her days to achieve it. Happily, for us all, publishing success came much sooner.

Calvin Coolidge (the 30th US President who served in office from 1923-1929) said, 'Nothing can take the place of persistence. Talent will not; the world is full of unsuccessful people with talent. Genius will not; unrewarded genius is almost a proverb. Education will not; the world is full of educated derelicts. Persistence and determination alone are omnipotent.'

The history of creative writing is littered with people who kept on going *until*. . . You'll have heard of some of them no doubt. *Watership Down* was apparently turned down by more than 60 publishers. JK Rowling approached about 20 or so before Bloomsbury saw her promise. One story that blew me away concerned Enid Blyton. I read a newspaper article years ago which reported that some time after her death, a letter to a friend was found in an attic. In this letter, Enid Blyton complained that she had just received her 500th rejection.

Who reading this would have given up at 99? Or even well before that?

Yet Enid Blyton persevered and became one of the most loved and celebrated children's authors in the world.

See it, hear it, feel it, taste it, smell it

Visualisation is a technique that Margaret Thomson Davis unwittingly used in her drive towards her goal. It is the focused engaging of your imagination in order to build a moving picture of something you want to manifest in your future. Effectively it is a daydream with purpose.

If you have ever spent time daydreaming then you can easily do this.

Before you start you have to consider what you would like to achieve. Get yourself a piece of paper. Now. Write down *everything* you would like to bring into your life. Don't put limits on it and don't give a thought to how it might happen. Simply write it down.

Be specific. Write down amounts, colours, places, types etc. Be concrete in your notes to yourself, this will be much more powerful in engaging your imagination.

This method works better if you are relaxed. There are many relaxation techniques taught on CD that can help you here. With practice the simple expedient of 'adopting the position' you assume when you begin your meditation will be enough to put your sub-conscious in the right place to listen to commands from your conscious mind.

The wonderful thing about visualisation is that it can be applied to any area of your life no matter the issue. Whether it be anger control, relationships, success, anxiety, self esteem or confidence, it can be brought to bear.

When using these techniques you will need to find a relaxed place and set aside some time every day when no one will disturb you. This has the added benefit of removing stress from your day to day life. It is recommended that you do this first thing in the morning and last thing at night. If you can only manage ten minutes, that is fine. Half an hour would be even better.

Find a comfortable position, close your eyes, take a deep breath and while exhaling relax your body from head to toe. Begin with the scalp and work slowly and carefully in time with your slowing breath, mentally name each body part and feel it relax.

Take another deep breath and while exhaling relax your mind by thinking tranquil thoughts.

Take another deep breath and savour this moment of deep relaxation.

It is time now to engage your imagination. In the screen of your mind, imagine that you have entered a room and with a sweep of colour paint one of the walls completely white. On to this wall you will project what is happening now when you achieve your goal.

Imagine it in widescreen, high-definition, surround sound. Bring all of your senses to bear. What can you see, hear, taste, smell, touch? Next amplify all of this by engaging your emotions. How proud are you? How excited? How fantastic do you feel right now?

Seeking advice/ help

One issue that is beyond the scope of this book is that of the abuse Margaret suffered at the hands of her supposed carers. If you have experienced similar issues and haven't yet done so, please seek help and support.

I'm sure Margaret's example will be of great comfort. She refused to be a victim and found a creative outlet and energy to help her deal with the morass of emotion that arises from such a life event.

Epictetus was a Greek sage and Stoic philosopher. Key to his teaching is the quote, *'It's not what happens to you, but how you react to it that matters.'*

He was born a slave at Hierapolis, Phrygia (present day Turkey) and his contention was that all external events are determined by fate, and therefore beyond our control. He thought that suffering arises from trying to control what is uncontrollable, or from neglecting what is within our power.

This attitude is also encapsulated in the Serenity Prayer by Reinhold Niebuhr:

> *God grant me the serenity*
> *to accept the things I cannot change;*

courage to change the things I can;
and wisdom to know the difference.

Another wonderful example of this kind of attitude is demonstrated by Katie Piper. She was a 26 year old budding model and TV presenter when she had acid thrown in her face. An ex-boyfriend took offence at being dumped and 'arranged' for someone to throw acid on this beautiful young girl's future.

The acid burned through four layers of skin and she's since had over 30 operations to rebuild her features. She is now going through a new form of treatment and wears a compression mask that is designed to help her injuries heal. Four years on and she is still going through the healing process. . . but she says she made a decision from the beginning not to give up.

I watched her on a news programme talking about the first time she looked in a mirror after the bandages were taken off. Her surprise at what faced her. 'You expect to see your own reflection. . .' When her words tailed off you could only imagine the horror that she would have felt at the time. She was articulate and cheerful while in front of the camera, but one can only guess at what goes on in her mind in the weak light and chill of a new day.

What Katie then went on to say gave me real optimism for her future and filled me full of admiration.

'In a split second my life changed forever,' said Katie. 'In hospital having the first stages of the surgery, it could go either way. Either I could let my attackers win and go into a shell, or I could rebuild a very different life, but still have an amazing life.'

Freewriting – Writing As Therapy

As evidenced by Margaret Thomson Davis, writing can be immensely cathartic. She used her experiences and the emotions these events elicited in her to inform and heighten her storytelling. But you don't have to be a 'writer' to enjoy the benefits of such an approach.

Have you ever written a letter to someone who hurt you? Once all the hurt is on the page – you ripped it up, but the simple act of writing everything down helped you move past that particular unhappy event.

Freewriting is a method of self-help. It involves writing for usually about 15 to 20 minutes in a spontaneous, free way.

Don't think about what you are writing.

Don't worry about style or how the writing might sound.

Write with your 'fastest pen' about your deepest thoughts and feelings. Once you start writing don't allow the pen to stop moving and don't lift it from the page. And don't be tempted to type rather and write. The action of working the pen across the page is much more effective in bringing our sub-conscious into play.

Write personally, without judgement and self-reflectively.

Write for your own use. The worry that someone else will read your work will affect how and what you write. It is important with freewriting that you write openly and honestly.

When can it be helpful?

When you have had a difficult or traumatic experience, either more recently or far in the past. Particularly if you find that thoughts, memories or dreams haunt you, but you don't talk about it.

When you are confused over some issue and you are not really clear what you want or what you should be doing.

As an educational aid, when you are learning or studying something, particularly if you are faced with loads of information, freewriting can help you organise and understand the material you are working with.

How does it help?

Freewriting can help by releasing internal stress. If we are holding onto powerful emotions without really expressing them, then the work involved in this inhibition produces internal stress on our bodies and minds. It can wear us down and increase our vulnerability to disease. Initially, it may prove difficult and upsetting, but it has been shown to reduce physical illness in the weeks and months after it has been used.

Freewriting helps us to understand what has happened. The simple act of putting thoughts and feelings into words is surprisingly powerful. The mind moves so fast that we may well be left with a mound of disorganised reactions that continue to churn inside. Speaking or writing slows us down. It's like being on a bike instead of in a car. You can see the world at an easier pace, and this allows understanding.

Freewriting gives us a sense of perspective. By using freewriting on a series of occasions, how we see and feel about an event or an issue gradually changes. The mind becomes less muddled and we can see what the real problem is. Less relevant aspects tend to drop away and the important lessons are highlighted.

Further points to bear in mind:
Freewriting supplements rather than replaces the value of talking to others.

It is not meant to be a chance to daydream about revenge or other potentially hurtful fantasies. Use it with positive intentions or it simply won't benefit you.

It aims to explore the deepest feelings in a self-reflective, questioning, open manner.

If you have a tendency to put yourself down or see things negatively, don't fall into this pattern when freewriting.

Here's a checklist to make your writing time more effective.

- Ask yourself, what can you learn from what has happened?

- How can the outer situation be improved?

- Or is it the inner state that is more important at this point?

- What small or bigger steps can you take to move forward away from past pain?

- How could you view what happened in a way that doesn't hurt you so much?

Once you've written down your thoughts and feelings, what can you do with it? Bin it? Hide it in a locked safe? If it is too personal this may be the right course of action for you.

I know people who have then gone on to show the writing to the people who caused the upset/ harm. They did so with love and affection and a determination to move beyond their hurt into a more equal relationship. Again, positive intent is the key because anything else won't give you the peace of mind you deserve.

An anchor to success

As you read Margaret Thomson Davis's story you see a trait emerge of someone who for a long time couldn't quite believe she had reached the levels of success she had. It was like she worried that she would eventually be found out to be some kind of fraud.

Does this thought ever enter your head? I know it does mine.

After interviewing Margaret we have become firm friends and she often phones me if she's going somewhere 'writerly'. On one of these outings I was able to witness an event that demonstrated despite her long career, she almost still can't quite believe it.

We were in the Royal Concert Hall, Glasgow to attend a 'Lunchtime Lecture'. The speaker was Sir Jeremy Isaacs, the guy who started Channel 4 and who was at that time in charge of the Royal Opera House at Covent Garden. He was a fascinating speaker and after the event there was a queue in the lobby to buy his book, which of course he would sign.

While I was waiting in the queue with Margaret, she spent the entire time wondering if she should introduce herself to Sir Jeremy. She was a great admirer of his and she had once been on a speaker's panel with him. Should she speak to him? Should she even wait in the queue or just go home? He wouldn't want to be pestered, surely?

I told her not to be daft and suggested she should stay and speak to him; he was bound to remember her.

At this point I spotted a middle-aged couple who weren't part of the queue, but who were facing us. I heard the woman say to her husband, 'There's Margaret Thomson Davis. Should I speak to her? She won't want to be pestered. I could just give her my book to sign.' The husband assumed a similar role I just had taken on with Margaret and he told her to say hello.

Margaret was of course delighted to speak to one of her readers and spent a good ten minutes chatting to the lady and her husband.

When it came to meeting Sir Jeremy, he stood up from the table as soon as he saw her approach and gave her a big hug.

Like Margaret, you may feel confident and 'successful' in one situation and mere moments later your feelings weaken and falter. You have no idea why, it just happens.

An aide to this situation is to set up an 'anchor'. This is a technique used in Neuro Linguistic Programming (NLP) and creates a stimulus that sparks a physiological or emotional state. The stimulus may be a sight, sound, feeling, taste or a smell. Your state is elicited by your sensory experience.

Employing an anchor changes your state or the way we feel or experience an event. For example if I'm driving and a certain song comes on the radio, I often dip back into a memory of hearing that song in an earlier period of my life and this will trigger the memory of thoughts or events that occurred while that song played before.

Anchors work on a sub-conscious level and are completely automatic. The sight, sound, feeling, taste or smell triggers an internal chain of reactions. Some of these may be beneficial: others can stop you from getting something you want.

The trick is to create and install a new anchor to disrupt a negative pattern that has become a habit.

Perhaps you have a fear of speaking in public and you associate something like that with a set of worrying symptoms: your voice wavers, your knees tremble, your face flushes or you become forgetful? Been there, done that, got a fractured patella to prove it.

Go back and refresh your memory about the visualisation technique I wrote about earlier. The screen in your mind that I suggested you use to broadcast your goals comes back into play.

Recall a time that you felt calm and confident and ON: an occasion when you are in your sparkling best form. Display it on the screen. Relive the experience with every ounce of your imagination. Brighten the colours; make the sounds clearer, your emotion sharper, make the memory on screen as vivid as you possibly can. You are back there. You are in The Zone. Your sense of satisfaction cannot be beaten and you feel the energy of this move to every part of you.

Now squeeze your thumb and forefinger together. This small physical action serves as an anchor to the positive sensations coursing through your mind and body and every time you squeeze your thumb and forefinger together you will experience the sensations you have just created.

With anything else like this, practice solidifies the habit. Just as it does when you form a negative pattern. Except this time we are forming something that will help rather than hinder. It only takes moments to go through this process. Go on, try it now. Create the pattern and practise it over and over again until it sticks. Then go and face that presentation/ meeting/ whatever with well-placed confidence and a vibrancy that gets everyone involved on your side.

Robert Crawford

Dr. Robert Crawford, CBE

The atrium at Scottish Enterprise Head Office in the Broomielaw, Glasgow gives one a strong sense of space and openness, as if to represent the mindset of the people who work here. This impression is strengthened when I tell the receptionist that I'm here to meet Robert Crawford, the then Chief Executive. He picks up the phone, speaks to someone and then smiles at me.

'Robert will be with you shortly.'

Robert. In my experience heads of large organisations tend to have receptionists who give their boss the honorific, *Mr.*

Once on the floor where Robert has his desk, I am shown through to an office already set out with refreshments and as I go in I notice the man himself at his workstation. This is a man with nothing to hide. How many people, in his position would need the ego-balm of a room all to themselves with the requisite imposing desk and chair? Not Robert Crawford, who at the time of our meeting was the highest-paid civil servant in the UK.

He may not be the most prepossessing physical specimen, being of slim build and around average height, but foolish would be the person who let this influence them. For this is a man from his clothes, to his posture, to his intellect, to his gaze, who is *sharp*.

Robert Crawford was appointed to this post at Scottish Enterprise in 1999. His appointment was welcomed by CBI

Scotland, which underlined his experience of both business and government as being important to the role. As head of SE he oversaw a budget of £500million and the duty of the office is to increase award investment and back Scottish firms. He turned his boundless energy in laying what he hoped would be the bedrock for the future prosperity of Scotland.

His vision of a 'Smart Successful Scotland' is one that he chased at no small personal cost. He lives on the Ayrshire coast, one hour's travel from his office, yet he is at his desk by 7am each morning. Then, his evenings are regularly taken up with the black-tie dinners that abound in the world of business.

So how did a boy who left school at 15 become one of Scotland's most influential people by the age of 50? Sheer hard work, limitless drive and a finely tuned intellect is the short answer. For some detail, read on.

An only child, he was brought up in a respectable working-class family. For an early clue as to the people who might influence the young Robert we can look to his father. He was a butcher with IBM and in due course became a test engineer. Quite a career progression in itself.

School was St Michael's in Kilwinning, an institution that Robert was keen to leave as soon as possible.

'It was a dire place,' he explains. 'I couldn't stand it.' Robert's story at school is one that perhaps many overly bright children might identify with. He was widely read at this age and cites people like Marcus Aurelius as being his literary heroes and yet he was bottom of the class.

'From my perspective, the school system now and then is a disaster. It doesn't make allowances for the fact that we are all unique, we are not going to be across-the-board good at everything. . . or few of us are. It doesn't seek out the unusual or gifted. It seeks out the average and the norm. . . it tries to pigeonhole everyone. I can understand why. There has to be some form of mechanism to educate the numbers. The problem with it in my view is that is reduces people to a series of assumptions about performance and capabilities. I simply couldn't identify with what I was being told.'

Being seen as a failure led to Robert having very little sense of self-worth.

'I guess I became something of a loner. I had friends, but none who were particularly close.' But he knew there was more to Robert Crawford than poor exam grades. 'I came to believe that despite appearances and my current reality, that I was actually pretty smart. I did suffer from low self-esteem, but in my view this came from being bottom of the class and intellectually isolated.' He struggled to connect his performance as measured by school standards with what he thought he could actually do.

'There was always a sign that I had more. I definitely knew more than my peers.' To boost his confidence Robert would enter general knowledge competitions, secure at least in the knowledge that this was something he could excel in.

At the age of 15, the headmistress 'invited' him to leave school on the final day of term. Here was a young man marked as a failure, by the system that failed him. What could he do with little education? He got a job as an apprentice printer with a firm in Ardrossan. A job he hated with a passion. This lasted for four years before he followed his father into work at IBM.

The feeling that there was more to him as a student stayed with Robert and with the need to gain some intellectual self-respect, he went back to school.

'At 19 I was going to night school every night of the week.' By now he was an assembler at IBM. 'To their credit, IBM gave me a day off. I got 6 Highers in the one year and I did it by getting up at five in the morning, studying until seven, going to work and from work I went straight to night school.' Oh and he worked weekends as well.

From there he went to Strathclyde University, studied Politics and loved it. Finally doing something he enjoyed without distraction, was an important time for Robert and he began to regain his confidence. So well did he do at university that at the end of his third year he was approached by his professor who suggested that he was in with a chance of winning, if he applied for a Kennedy Scholarship.

An appeal had been launched in the UK in 1964 to enable British people to contribute to a fund that would commemorate the assassinated President. Since the first Kennedy Scholars travelled to the USA in 1966, twelve scholarships have been awarded annually to British post-graduate students to enable them to study at Harvard. Robert was the first Scot to win this prestigious award.

'That was just fantastic,' he recalls. 'I'd never been further west than Ireland before and here I was studying at Harvard. It was a startling experience . . . a transformation occurred. A driver for me through my young adulthood was intellectual respectability. Getting a real education transformed my life. I will always be grateful to the three universities who taught me. The great thing about university life for me was structure, and learning the ability to understand argument.'

A glutton for knowledge and not sated with his studies, Robert read voraciously. He read every piece of classical literature he could get his hands on. 'I read all the time, I read while I walked. . . bumping into lampposts. I even discovered I actually liked science though I hated it at school. What reading did was give it a context in which it actually meant something to me.'

His experience at Harvard changed his whole outlook on life and its possibilities. Here was a young man who left school at 15 with little or no formal education and yet nine years later he was walking through the doors of Harvard as a Kennedy Scholar. He had grown from someone with little self-worth to someone who *knew* that he was capable of doing extraordinary things.

'America is a society we in the UK often deride for its ambition but for myself, expansion intellectually, spiritually and in health terms is something I feel very strongly about and in this regard America struck me as a very palatable place.'

After his year in the States was up, Robert intended to return to Scotland to finish his PhD, but a friend called him to say that the Scottish National Party was looking for a researcher.

'I enjoyed aspects of the job, I enjoyed research, but what I discovered was that I did not like politics one bit.' He stayed for two years and left to finish his PhD at Glasgow University. The next stage in his progression was to work for the American corporation, Citibank. He was by now a married man with a child and on finishing his PhD sent off literally hundreds of job applications. Citibank hired him for their Corporate Development Programme.

'They were great. . . and if I have one regret in my career it is what I did next.' Although he enjoyed working with Citibank, he missed the world of academia. So when the head of the Fraser of Allander Institute phoned and offered him a job, he jumped at the chance.

'Looking back, I should have stayed, but there was the niggling thought that someone from my background doesn't end up as an Investment Banker.' Citibank were hugely disappointed. At one point the President of the Bank called Robert to say that he had regarded him as a future member of the board.

'I wobbled slightly at this.' His smile is flavoured with irony. 'No one had given any indication that this might have been the case.' In any event, a man of his word, Robert had made a commitment. So back to Scotland he went.

What happened next seems slightly strange, even to Robert. Although he was enjoying work with the Institute, he had become accustomed to the cut and thrust of the world of high-level banking. He realised with some regret that the world in which he was now working was too slow for him.

'While I was on holiday in Spain, I had a dream, an incredibly forceful dream where I was crossing a bridge. I've never had a dream like it, before or since. It was so focused and so positive. I realised it was some form of Jungian symbolism. I just had to do something else.'

That 'something else' was revealed to him within an hour of waking. That morning at breakfast, his wife happened to be reading a Scottish newspaper. She spotted an advert from the

Scottish Development Agency (SDA), which was setting up a Management Development Programme.

'The advert coming on the heels of the dream told me that I had to act upon it. But there was something else. . . and it's difficult to articulate this without sounding silly, but years earlier I had cause to visit the old SDA Headquarters and I remembered standing in the main reception, looking around me with this sense, this *feeling* that I was going to end up working here.'

The Scottish Development Agency was of course the predecessor to Scottish Enterprise (SE). Here Robert worked his way through the ranks till he became director of *Locate in Scotland* in 1991 after leading its operations in the US for three years. This was work that he relished and it was with mixed feelings that he accepted the number 2 post in SE, becoming managing director of operations.

'As far as career goals go I was never driven by making more money or by attaining the next step up the ladder. I did set out clear educational goals. I was determined to attain a PhD. I was more interested in making a difference than making money.'

A year later he was back in America on a secondment with the World Bank.

'I realised that I missed America and by a series of circumstances met a fellow Scot who worked there. He opened some doors and to my predecessor, Crawford Beveridge's credit, I was allowed to go on secondment.'

Settled in the US and sure that he was there to stay, he received a call saying that Ernst & Young were looking for someone of his calibre. He agreed to consider it if they made him partner.

'I heard later that Ernst & Young hoped that I would see the advert and apply for it, but for some reason they didn't want to approach me directly.' Robert had what he describes as an excellent two years with Ernst & Young and asserts that if the Chief Executive position at SE hadn't come up, he would be there still.

'I'd had my eye on the job for a while. It just came around sooner that I thought.' Robert was delighted with the opportunity to be at the helm of an organisation he saw as being crucial to Scotland.

'I always believed passionately about a development agency for this country. I feel strongly about the contribution an organisation like this can make. This was never about money. It was about making a difference. I took a huge drop in salary when I left Ernst & Young. . . it dropped by more than half.'

Where does this desire to contribute come from I asked?

'Like a lot of Scots, I have a love/hate relationship with the country. I think it could be much better than it is. I'd love to see the country ambitious for itself. I'm very patriotic and I want to leave my footprint in the sand and make this society a better place.' He warms to his theme and leans towards me.

'If I could pass something on it would be the view that if you want to climb the tree, just go as high as you possibly can. Don't believe that you can't go any higher. I believe that we are under an obligation to make the most of any skills, talents or opportunities that we are given and I absolutely believe that you shouldn't engage in anything unless you can give it 100%.'

Football is one of his passions outside of business and he

uses it to drive home his view.

'When you see these footballers that earn huge amount of money, who don't have any heart for it and who have clearly given up on the game. . . it ticks you off. In my view that's the reason why Roy Keane survived so many culls at Old Trafford. He gave 150%. Sir Alex Ferguson loves that commitment to the cause.'

One of the problems he sees with a percentage of his country-men is the unwillingness to make an effort, to take action and change.

'Scotland's health stats aren't simply an outcome of bad marketing and bad teaching, they are an outcome of something fundamentally worse than that. . . an absence of self-respect that runs through many people in this country. When you go abroad and reflect on the way they live, it saddens me when I consider the amount of alcohol people in Britain drink comp-ared to other parts of the world.'

While he speaks about Scotland and his part in its future, he is sitting forward in his chair, his hand slices through the air and his eyes flash. This is a job he feels passionate about. One he worked long and hard for. So why was he leaving? How does the man feel about leaving an organisation he has bled his heart and soul into? From his body-language and tone, the least I expect is regret.

'I've had enough. I'm relieved to go actually. I have become increasingly disillusioned with life as a public figure in Scotland. We have a tendency to self-destruct. There is a growing disconnect between public and private life and I'm tired of that. I want to go back into anonymous private life.' He doesn't entirely blame the media and cites a destructive gene he thinks runs through Scottish society.

'This is a country that doesn't like Tall Poppies. I'm reminded of the aphorism by Gore Vidal which says that a little bit of him dies every time a friend does well. I've *never* had that attitude. There can also be a communal joy in other people's failure that I find immensely distasteful.'

Robert returned to SE at a time of considerable industrial change and uncertain economic growth. His tenure was marked by some major plant closures among some of Scotland's new-generation technology industries. It was the end of an era for inward investment and the US financial giants, among others, were licking their wounds from the sustained battering the world's economy was taking. The organisation itself was slack and over-staffed, more than 500 jobs had to go.

He didn't have far to look for his enemies. Some ex-members of staff were angry at their jobs being terminated and began to leak stories to the press. Project Atlas, a scheme to help Scottish firms receive cheaper broadband access had its problems. Not least of which were complaints to the European Union from the huge commercial players in this field who claimed Project Atlas was illegal.

Other critics have included the Scottish National Party, the Conservatives and what has been described in some quarters as the 'Anti-Scotland Axis' of the *Scotsman's* then editor Andrew Neil and the columnist Bill Jamieson. Indeed, this newspaper claimed in May 2003 that SE was at risk of missing nine of its twelve targets and that key projects were on the verge of collapse. A claim that was easily rebutted by SE. In a self-penned article in *The Herald* in June 2003, Robert himself supplied the facts.

'Two years ago we met 15 of the 20 targets we set out to achieve. The following year, we improved our performance to 18 out of 21. This year we succeeded in 21 out of 22. These are the facts, pure and simple. This is not the record of an organisation that's failing. It's the record of an organisation that is focusing its efforts very firmly on delivery. And it's a record that I'm particularly proud of.'

Ian Gray, the Enterprise Minister until May 2003 was cited in the press as saying, 'His departure is very regrettable and a real shame. It's another example of Scotland eating its own.'

Sir Ian Robinson who stepped down as SE chairman in December 2003 is quoted in the same article in *The Herald*: 'Somehow Scotland needs to give people a chance to show that they can deliver against an agenda. If you're on a 10-year agenda, you cannot be delivering every five seconds.'

So what next for this man of action?

'I want to lead a quieter, more balanced life. I am devoted to my family and have come to realise that there is more to life than a 16-hour day.' He feels that he has one more, big job in him, but he is keen to balance that with the needs of his family. Perhaps his favourite spots on the planet, Arran and Tuscany will see more of him?

He has had some offers as you would expect, but prefers to concentrate on his current purpose for now. He will continue to give 100% until the new man or woman is in the hot seat.

When the interview is over, Robert walks me to the lift,

warmly shakes my hand and turns back to his workstation. As he purposefully strides back, I watch his retreating figure and consider the man I have just spent an hour with.

To be in his current position when you consider his modest upbringing is remarkable. He is man driven by his need to grow, to study the forces of change in human development, to contribute. He is a man of purpose. A man who gets things done. A simple phrase, but how many of us can lay claim to it?

The words of his literary hero, Marcus Aurelius sum him up.

'Death stands at your elbow. Be good for something while you live and it is in your power.'

Mentoring with Robert Crawford

The Pygmalion Effect

*'Treat people as if they were what they should be,
and you help them become what they are capable
of becoming.'*   Johann von Goethe

During his interview, Robert Crawford stated his views on our education system. By sheer force of numbers our schools are forced to seek out the norm: the average and those children who, for whatever reason, are unable to meet that yardstick are set aside. In Robert's days that meant being asked to leave the institution. I would like to think that we have moved on from that scenario but a part of me worries that we are still seeking and studying for the average and in that case we are rarely going to exceed 'average'. I don't know about you but I'm looking for more than that for our next generation.

There is a Burmese saying: 'Who aims at excellence will be above mediocrity; who aims at mediocrity will be far short of it.'

The term Pygmalion Effect, highlighted above, refers broadly to the effects of interpersonal expectations, that is, the finding that what one person expects of another can come to serve as a self-fulfilling prophecy.

Robert Rosenthal in *The Corsini Encyclopedia of Psychology* demonstrates how this can be used for the benefit of our pupils, and by extension our dealings with other people in our lives.

In his now famous study he set out to learn how a teacher's expectations might impact on his or her pupils. All of the children in one study were given a nonverbal test of intelligence, which was disguised as a test that would predict intellectual potential. The test was given the entirely bogus title of The Harvard Test of Inflected Acquisition.

There were 18 classrooms in the school, three at each of the six grade levels. Within each grade level, the three classrooms were composed of children with above average ability, average ability, and below average ability, respectively.

Within each of the 18 classrooms, approximately 20% of the children were chosen at random to form the experimental group. Each teacher was given the names of the children from his or her class who were in the experimental condition. The teachers were told that these children's scores on the Harvard Test of Inflected Acquisition demonstrated that they would show strong gains in intellectual competence during the next 8 months of school.

The truth of the situation was that the only difference between the experimental group and the control group children was in the mind of the teacher. An expectation of promise had been raised.

At the end of the school year, 8 months later, all the children in the school were retested with the same 'nonverbal test of intelligence'. The children from whom the teachers has been led to expect greater intellectual gain showed a significantly greater gain than did the children in the control group.

The study was then broadened to take in other areas of human endeavour and after another dozen years, the overall mean effect size of 479 studies was found to be that a teacher/ leader's expectations changed the proportion of people performing above average from 35% to 65%.

So, how did this expectation on the teacher's behalf translate to the mind of their pupils? Non-verbal communication. You may well be aware that speech as a method of communication only carries about 3% of the intended impact of the communication and that the remaining impact is carried through by body language and tone. If you didn't, you will appreciate now how powerful non-verbal communication is.

The researchers were effectively tapping in to this phenomenon. Teachers appeared to create a warmer socio-emotional climate for their 'special' students. This warmth appeared to be at least partially communicated by nonverbal cues.

Teachers appeared to teach more material and material that required more effort to their 'special' students.

Teachers appeared to give their 'special' students greater opportunities for responding. Opportunities that were offered both verbally and nonverbally, e.g. for giving a student more time to answer a teacher's question.

Teachers also appeared to give their 'special' students stronger feedback, both verbal and nonverbal, as to how they had been performing.

As I read through this I wonder how many people of my generation were impacted by the negative impact of this effect. How many of us heard the words, 'you'll never amount to anything' and went on to live down to them? It is to Robert Crawford's huge credit that he found his own way.

Jack Black

Jack Black – MindStore Founder

The first time I saw Jack Black he was on stage at the Royal Concert Hall in Glasgow, doing his stuff. Boy was he good. Passionate, inspiring, moving, he was all of this and more. Not only was I captivated by him, I was captivated by his message. I didn't have to settle for what life gave me. I had a choice. I could improve my life for me and those I care for. All I needed was the desire, the belief and the expectation.

Why wasn't everybody doing this stuff?

Jack was like a colossus on that stage. So I think I hid my surprise well when I met him, because he's actually about the same height as I am. He must be about 5 feet 7 and all of 11 stone dripping wet. But in common with all of the successful men and women I've met, physical stature is no mirror of mental capacity and physical energy.

'My childhood was very happy,' Jack began. 'My mother in particular stands out. My father like any other father at that time was working hard, but my mother brought us up. I've got lots of happy memories of good times.'

Until Jack was two they all lived with his father's mother, then the family managed to get a house in Easterhouse.

'I must have been around two and a half and I can remember sitting up in the front of a big lorry – must have been the removal van. Great childhood, happy memories. I suppose I had lots of constants, constantly being loved, constant in myself, constant in the support and affirmations that my parents gave me. Looking back I've got nothing but good memories of my childhood.'

Jack is the eldest of three siblings; his brothers still live in the west of Scotland, while his sister now lives in Australia. In common with many families, his mother was the 'tock' in the family clock. She ran the show, looking after four kids, she made sure they were fed and watered, happy and healthy. They had what Jack describes as a 'normal' family life until his mother took a stroke when he was sixteen. His sister who was the baby of the family was only eight.

'It was a massive stroke. This incredibly vibrant, wonderful human being was, if you like, taken out of the picture. We weren't allowed to see her for six months.

'The doctors thought that it would be too upsetting for us to see her the way she was after the stroke. My father tried to prepare us for the shock. She had turned into this old, old woman. It was horrific to see. She fought back to a tremendous place for five years when she fell right back again and sadly died.'

Their mother's illness and subsequent death had a strong impact on the family dynamic. Jack's sister appeared to handle it well, but the brothers struggled. Jack, being the eldest took it upon himself to try and help his family cope, but his mother's illness affected him profoundly. He began to have serious doubts about his own health.

'At only sixteen or seventeen, the slightest wee twinge and I was at the doctors. I developed these psychosomatic situations which all joking aside were pretty severe.' If he felt a pain in his chest he was convinced a heart attack was on its way. He persuaded himself he had other equally worrying conditions.

'I was certain I had cancer. I was forever going to the doctor for tests and refusing to believe the results. I thought the doctor was lying to me, telling me I was okay when I was actually dying. I suffered quite badly with migraine headaches for a while and I was convinced that this was much more serious. I also developed quite nasty coughs, which in my mind also became much more serious. If ever there was a twinge in my head I was about to suffer a massive stroke. This was all part of me trying to deal with my mother's illness and subsequent death.'

It is with a strong sense of irony that Jack suggests that if he hadn't gone through this experience, which lasted well into his adult life, he would never have learned the amazing power of one's own mind.

'This was all evidence of the power of thought. But up to that point in my life it was all negative. It was the power of this that allowed me to see the amazing possibilities of using this same power of thought in a positive way.'

Like many boys who grow up in the west of Scotland football was a major influence in his life.

'I was into football in a big way, so my earlier influences were footballers. I was into people like Jim Baxter. Surprisingly in this part of the world being a Catholic, as a kid I was a Rangers fan. There was always a bit of the rebel in me. Then later on I fell into the Celtic thing. When you go into a Catholic secondary school you travel further to school, make new friends and I began to conform.'

Blessed with huge reserves of energy Jack says that he has always lived life with passion.

'I got stuck into everything and anything that was going. I've always had energy and enthusiasm for creating things and doing things.' One particular game of his devising he remembers well. He lived in Cumbernauld and during wet summer's days he and his friends all hung around underpasses to escape the rain.

'I must have been 10 or 11 and I created this whole thing like a bus route and made timetables and everything. I was running a bus company with bikes. There were bus stops and I would make sure the timetable was running smoothly, 'Right, you're number 47,' I ordered another boy. 'You need to go now.' The guys would all go away and run their route and come back again.'

Man from Uncle was a major TV programme at the time and happily for Jack and his pals Cumbernauld was one big building site. They would 'appropriate' all the materials they needed and build their own dens. They would build these dens miles apart from each other and designate them 'Man from Uncle' centres, pretending that they were actually in different countries. Jack was the boy who organised all of this.

'I think this sort of creativity comes from dissatisfaction with your current reality. I've always been a futurist. What have we got? What do we want? You create it in your mind first and then somehow or other it would happen.' Jack contends that creativity comes from the vision. If you have a vision that is big enough, the ideas come.

'As soon as you take ownership of it all the creativity comes.

The interesting thing is, the further you place your vision from your current reality the more creative you will be. If you commit to the vision. Unfortunately the vast majority of people don't do it. They tell you that life's no like that.'

An intelligent boy, first in his class who achieved seven 'O' grade passes out of seven, he feels that he and his friends were let down by the school system. Instead of being encouraged to consider going further into the education system, they were fed through career counselling to think about a job.

'At no time were my friends or myself encouraged to consider higher education. It was a good, normal comprehensive school and I don't remember any of us being encouraged to go further into the education system. But I kicked against that.'

Fortunately Jack also had an aptitude for technical subjects particularly technical drawing, engineering and mechanics. His teacher took a shine to him and encouraged him to become a technical teacher.

This was during the time of the teachers' strikes and it was impossible to get a placement as a student teacher. It wasn't until the second year of his studies that he found himself in front of class full of kids.

'By coincidence I started helping out at a youth club at night and I did a course in youth leadership. The organiser sent me to a school as a youth trainer and it turned out it was the same school I was doing my teacher training in. It was a bizarre experience.' During the day Jack was working with the kids in the classroom as Mr Black and in the evening he was 'Jack' working with the same kids in the youth club.

'I was getting tremendous results with the youth club. I was helping and encouraging them. They took a shine to me. I took a shine to them. But in the school I had to maintain an element of distance, I couldn't talk to them in the same way; I had to return to being the more traditional 'teacher'.'

Jack realised with some regret that this set-up wasn't working for him. The kids were by and large almost adult and he had a huge conflict with the duplicity of the situation. He decided to get out of the classroom and concentrate on youth work. He returned to college to complete a Youth and Community Course, qualifying after three years and went into Social Work. He then worked for ten years with children at risk, primarily within the age group of 8 to 18.

While he enjoyed working with and helping these children, the itch to do something else persisted. A need to stretch himself into other areas.

'I was always a budding entrepreneur and got myself into some messes.

'I noticed that the *Glasgow Herald* used to have ads for auctions on a Monday and I used to go to these auctions and try to work out what was happening.' After a few visits, he felt he had a hang of it and decided to have a go at making a bid himself.

'So I went along with some money and I spotted this great big carton with Adidas/Puma training shoes in it. It was high on a shelf and I had to reach in and pull a few out. I thought: I could sell these.' He bid for the box and to his surprise and delight, he won it. It was only when I got the box home that he realised that the shoes were all for left feet.

At another auction Jack spotted a box of jeans. He raked through the box and kept coming up with the Wrangler label. So again he thought: that'll do for me.

Once home he opened the box only to find out that they were all 28-inch waist and bell-bottoms.

'Everyone was wearing drainpipes at the time.' He laughed at the memory. 'I tried to salvage something from the operation by finding a woman who could reduce the width of the legs, but eventually could only get rid of them by giving them to a jumble sale.'

The need to work for himself; to become more entrepreneurial persisted probably in part due to the hopelessness that pervaded his professional life. He was a social worker in what was at that time one of the most underprivileged areas of Glasgow: Easterhouse. Every day he was working with people, who were living without hope, who felt they had no future. The realisation that despite his best efforts and his initial determination to make a change, that he had in effect done nothing, was a painful one. He remembers working hard and trying his very best but has described the situation as trying to bale out a ship with a tea strainer.

On top of this almost every week he felt that he had contracted a life-threatening illness and suggests that at the time he almost had his own seat in the doctor's waiting room. Every ache, every twinge, every mark on his skin was cause for deep concern.

His financial situation was also something of a worry, so in an effort to make ends meet he started a second career and set up his own travel business. Working an 80 hour week, he saw little of his family, but the business was bringing in the much-needed extra cash. He started off with ski holidays and grew to the extent that he felt the time was almost right to give up his paid employment. But life had other plans for him.

'There were three sudden deaths of people close to me within a fortnight. All were stress-related, heart disease, cancer and stroke. . . and that changed everything. I was a hypochondriac remember. This was a big lesson.' A lesson that was hammered home when he became ill himself.

'I was working flat out on the business while still doing the day-job. I hadn't yet made the move to self-employment and I was overworking.' He was in the hairdressers when he collapsed. He slumped from the chair and blacked out.

'I realised that this was a big warning. Maybe my first, maybe my last and what was I going to do about it?'

Once he came to, surrounded by the faces of worried hairdressers, he knew he had to make a change to his life and he had to do it right away. He left the shop and walked to what was then John Smith's bookshop in St Vincent Street. He asked the assistant if they had any books on stress.

'I walked round to the section I was directed to and a book fell off the shelf and landed at my feet. And that was the start of an amazing journey. The book was called *The Silva Method*. Amazingly enough, all these years later, the woman who works closest with me in the organisation was looking for help when she quite literally tripped over the same book, in the same bookstore some years later.'

He read the book that same day, sitting in the car until it was finished.

'I didn't go to work. Ten o'clock that night I was still in my car reading that book. I found that it instantly made sense to me and I wondered, why don't people know about this?'

He made contact with the Silva organisation and found that he was in the right place at the right time.

'At the point of my first contact they were looking for someone to look after Scotland.' He trained with them and eventually worked for them for three years, building up their operations in Scotland.

A man not to go into things lightly Jack had various passions for different things and when the Silva Method popped up, his then wife Norma, no doubt thought, 'Oh here we go again.' She worried that Jack jumped like a butterfly from one thing to another.

'But this one really stuck in a profound way. So initially she resisted it. I took her along to the Silva course but she fought against it as lots of people do initially when they come to my own *MindStore* courses. Then the resistance fell away and she realised that there was something in this. As a teacher she started to experiment with it in the class and being passionate about kids she was thrilled when the results were shown to be pretty impressive.'

Because of these results she argued that *MindStore* techniques ought to be taught in schools. Jack encouraged her in her vision. He reminded her not to worry about the 'HOW', because that just gets in the way. Make your mind up what you want to do and do it. The Learning Game was born, a system that has now been taught in many schools throughout the country.

Things however weren't going to well for Jack with the Silva people. His relationship with them ended acrimoniously.

'They had a control freak working for them; call it a clash of personalities. I was trying to build things and he was trying to hold me back. . . and eventually he sacked me. A lot of people reacted to that because I was teaching the method fairly successfully and people were saying to me, you can't just walk away after getting us into this.'

A man Jack held in high regard saw how affected he was by this turn of events and offered him one of the best pieces of advice he has ever received.

'If you believe in what you are doing, set a date six months from now and tell the world that you are going to teach your course that day. Work with your creativity. Do your research and you will make it happen.'

'I knew he was right, but it was a frightening proposition.' Jack recalled. So he wrote to everyone that he had worked with previously, explained that things hadn't worked out with the Silva people. He let them know that he was going to present his course on the 19th May 1990, six months exactly from that point. . . and he never looked back. *MindStore* was launched to 13 people in a conference suite in Ibrox Stadium. An address that will tickle those who know that Jack's preferred football team wears green and white hoops and who play at the other side of the city.

MindStore is now a many layered organisation and Jack is no longer at the helm. He has taken a step back from the management of the company and concentrates on what he believes he does best, delivering the course.

Research that Jack completed with Strathclyde Business School helped him solidify his thinking. In this research people were asked to describe their ideal job. Then they were asked if they were in it. . . 94% of people said no.

'What I've been looking at is matching myself to my unique ability. I realised quickly that I'm not good at managing people: I haven't got the patience for it. And I realised fairly quickly that it is not relevant to what my unique skills are. You get bogged down with things that are totally irrelevant. If I'm up on stage or working with clients then I'm doing what I'm meant to do, but if I'm in the office worrying about Jeanie's sore foot or wondering about the dynamic in the office. . . it's not for me. Then there are the figures. It just does my head in. So I set up a management team.'

This didn't work either for Jack. He realised he had to manage the management team. Convinced that he needed to step away from management altogether he offered one of the management team the business, as it stood.

'I offered them everything. Share the profits of each course with me, and you can run the business, was the offer. And now I get to just turn up and deliver the course.'

The next step in the business's progression was modelled on one of Jack's heroes, Richard Branson. He decided that he needed to start developing the brand. Partnerships were formed where appropriate and licensed agreements given where people could use the *MindStore* brand in similar areas.

'We have MindStore Coaching, MindStore for Women, Mind-Store Active and MindStore Legal, which looks at Employment Law training with a MindStore bent to it, with an amazing lawyer.

We are also looking at creating a retail empire called MindStores. We will continue with the Life Programme, as it's important to me.'

Having worked exceedingly hard over the years, another lesson that Jack has learned is one about balance.

'I'm a firm believer in the Wheel of Life,' he leans forward in his chair, '. . . that every area of your life is worked on equally – work hard, play hard ethic, if you like, and that's what I apply to my life.'

He also contends that this form of work doesn't end life's difficulties. To be human is to face challenges, but what this mindset does is help you work your way through.

'Like everyone else you go through the same old stuff. I've come through some great challenges, worked with some great people, got great kids. I've travelled the world, shared meals with some pretty famous people. Every single person has their ups and downs and it's largely a matter of degree. You can dwell on them or take them as lessons and see what the solution is. I live and breathe what I do – I practise what I preach.'

Jack then goes on to echo every single successful person I've had the good fortune to meet. 'Like everyone else I have my fair share of challenges, things that go wrong and setbacks, but I just pick myself up and go after them again.'

Mentoring with Jack

I would urge you to go and check out the materials that Jack has published over the years. The *MindStore* website (www.MindStore.com) is full of information about courses and other learning materials (CDs, books etc) you can have access to in order to help you make the change in your life that you are looking for.

His weekend courses are held throughout the UK and once you are a member you are able to repeat the course at a heavily discounted rate.

Fantastic!

One of the first lessons I picked up on during a *MindStore* weekend was the use of the above word.

Take note of your response the next time someone asks you how you are. Will you answer with one of these – och, ok thanks – aye, no bad – could be worse – gettin' there – fair tae hellish?

We like a moan don't we? Fair tae hellish. What's that all about?

Actually, it's part of that Scottish mindset that says we have to blend in, keep our head below the parapet, and not get ideas above our station. After all, misery loves company and if we appear as miserable as everyone else we can never be accused of getting too big for our boots, can we?

Just who is that kind of mindset helping?

If someone were to ask you about a restaurant you'd visited, a movie you'd watched or a book you'd read and you answered – aye, ok – do you think they would want to repeat your experience? Don't think so.

Words become action ...

If you answered – fair to hellish – consider how your body shaped as you spoke. Did you have your hands in your pockets, shoulders slumped? Did you feel yourself shrink as the words slipped from your mouth? Did you feel a little of your energy leak through the ground?

Here in the West we don't pay much attention to the mind/body link, but in the East they are much more cognisant of how these two elements make a whole.

As I discuss in another chapter, the mind doesn't know the difference between the real and the imagined world. If through long years of habit your mind has become programmed to focus on the negative, then that is what your sub-conscious will seek out. Conversely, if you have a positive inner dialogue your mind will look for the good stuff.

Words become action. If you met one hundred people in the one day (extreme, I know) and you answered each question with 'fair to hellish', guess where your mind is going to send you? A version of your own physical hell, perhaps. At the very least I'd think you would have a humdinger of a headache.

There's a friend of mine I bump into from time to time. Let's call him Wullie. 'Cos that's his name. Wullie is without fail, positive, enthusiastic, smiling and shining with good vibes.

Two minutes in his company, I'm smiling, my energy is up and my mood is elevated. I don't know much about his personal life (like everyone else, I expect he has his ups and downs) but judging by how he faces the world things are going along very nicely, thankyouverymuch. Ask Wullie how he is and he'll answer – great – magic – fantastic!

What sort of energy would you like to be in the world? The fair-tae-hellish dude, or someone who gives an energy and mood lift to everyone they speak to?

An instant lift. . .

Again with the mind/body link. . . where the body goes the mind will follow.

Next time you're in a bit of a mood check out your body language. Are you sitting slumped, arms crossed, frowning? Are you wearing a scowl that would send milk prematurely past its use-by date?

Ok, everyone has their troubles, but does that have to affect NOW? (I will allow that if you are suffering from stress/ anxiety/ depression the following technique offers little relief. But a little is better than nothing, right?)

So try this instead.

Sit up straight. Shoulders down, chest out – and plant a huge smile on your face. Push those cheeks up and get your eyes and teeth flashing.

Now how do you feel? You have introduced what NLP practitioners call incongruence. Your mind and body don't match: the mind will take note of this and catch up quickly with where the body is. Result? An immediate lift in mood.

Entering the flow

Many self-help programmes available today advocate a system where you enter a state of what is effectively guided meditation.

We all perform at a higher level when we are relaxed and these systems encourage you to enter a state of mind and body where your success mechanism (your brain) can turn of the chuntering, unhelpful chatterbox (you know the one that groans in a high pitch in your ear telling you that you are too fat/ skinny/ stupid/ weak/ undeserving/ unworthy). Then you can listen to and programme in a more helpful thought process.

Meditation has for centuries been practised within religious traditions. Today much of what is considered meditation in the West is secular in nature, for instance mindfulness-based programmes. Mindfulness refers to a psychological quality that means bringing your complete attention to the present experience on a moment-to-moment basis.

It is a form of non-elaborative, nonjudgmental, now-centered awareness in which each thought, feeling, or sensation that arises in your attention is acknowledged and accepted just as it is. (Remember the non-judgemental part?)

In common parlance, this means when you are cooking the dinner you are focussing on preparing the chicken breasts, instead of worrying about what someone meant by saying you were looking 'more prosperous these days'.

In some cultures the very word 'meditation' comes burdened with all kinds of off-putting connotations. If you read/ hear the word and it causes a negative reaction, consider it as a form of prayer or a time of reflection.

Make time to meditate

Stress means you are unable to respond adequately to mental, emotional, or physical demands, whether actual or imagined.

Let me repeat that: actual or imagined. Your brain doesn't know the difference. You crank up the fearful imagination and the brain processes it as if it were real.

Our brains are cranked up to work to 'Expectancy Theory' and this expectation created brain patterns just as real as those created by events in the real world.

Signs of stress may be emotional, physical, or behavioural. Symptoms include poor judgment, a negative outlook, excessive worrying, moodiness, irritability, inability to relax, feeling isolated or depressed. Then there's the bun-fight that is aches and pains, diarrhoea or constipation, nausea, dizziness, chest pain, rapid heartbeat, reaching for the mega-packet of crisps or eating barely enough to feed a midge, sleeping too much or not enough, hiding behind the couch when there's a knock at the door, procrastination, bingeing on alcohol, nicotine or drugs, etc, etc, etcetera.

The autonomic nervous system (ANS) provides a rapid response to stress commonly known as the fight-or-flight response. When animals get this they, guess what? Fight for their lives or run for the nearest high, bumpy ground. Humans nowadays are rarely in that kind of situation. Instead triggers are often an uncaring/ bullying employer, excessive debt, worry about job prospects.

Fight or flight? Fighting would be inappropriate and excessive. Flight would make you look like you need to be administered a straitjacket and, like, now.

Your body releases all the required hormones to assist in your flight/fight, but they have nowhere to go.

Which means you'll get sick.

Thankfully, we have an answer for this.

Meditation.

Meditation is a process where we give the nervous system, the brain and the senses a chance to re-calibrate. Meditation gives your body the time and space to do a wee spot of healing.

Is sleep not enough, I hear you ask up the back?

A scientific study (the science community is all over this stuff) evaluated three key indicators of relaxation and found that meditation provides a far deeper state of relaxation than simple eyes-closed rest.

The benefits of developing this habit are many and varied (one website I came across listed 100 of them) including stress management, weight management, lasting positive change in the immune system, increased fertility, improved sleep, improved circulation, lower heart rate, lowering of blood pressure, decrease in the thickness of artery walls, improved self-esteem, a higher level of creativity, reduced migraine and headaches, reduced dependence on drugs, a higher level of pain tolerance, improved tolerance of exercise, improved sport performance, improved capacity for intimate contact with a loved one (you get me?), improved relationships with family, friends and colleagues.

In several studies worldwide they even proved that when a certain percentage of the population of a given area was meditating regularly, the crime level in that area dropped.

Why are we all not doing this? It should be made compulsory, like wearing a seatbelt in a car. You could have a wee card you get your doctor to stamp – after they check your cortisol levels – and you could produce it to get a tax reduction.

How to do it. . .

There are many methods of meditation and if you are interested (and why shouldn't you be?) you should go on a wee search and find a method that suits you. As I said earlier in this book, I believe the most effective lessons are the ones we learn for ourselves. The same thing can be said for books, courses and methods of meditation.

In the generic methods there are two steps:

1. Repetition of a word, sound, phrase, prayer, mental image or concentrating on your breathing.

2. Passive disregard of everyday thoughts that inevitably come to mind and the return to your repetition.

Pick a word or short phrase that is rooted in your belief system, such as 'one,' 'peace,' 'our father who are in heaven', or, 'I love me, who do you love?' (Nah, I'm only joking about that last one.)

Sit calmly in a comfortable position, somewhere you can relax knowing you won't be disturbed. (When he was a lot younger, my son seemed to know I was meditating and he would come find me and curl up on my lap.)

Close your peepers.

Relax your muscles, moving from your feet to your calves,

thighs, abdomen, shoulders, head, and neck.

Allow your breathing to happen naturally, and as you do, say your word, sound, phrase, or prayer in your mind as you exhale.

Allow yourself to be passive. Don't worry about how well you're doing. Just let what happens happen. (It takes practitioners years to quieten the monkey mind.) When other thoughts come to you, simply accept them and return to your word/ sound repetition.

Go with it for ten to 20 minutes.

When the time is up continue sitting for a minute or two. Then open your eyes and sit for another minute.

Some people will then take a note of the thoughts or images that arose while meditating – like a dream journal – and later on consider what the sub-conscious was pushing out.

Get the habit of doing this once or twice a day. Good times to do so are either side of your working day – giving you a cleansing experience and separating your work from your home life.

Too busy? What, you can't find ten minutes a day? This is me doing a horse impression with air being blown out from between pursed lips.

Taking advantage of the placebo effect

Jack's early experience of ill health demonstrates the power of the mind to cause harm. The negative side of this mind process has been termed the 'nocebo' effect. Thankfully, he woke up to the possibilities if he switched from an all-consuming worry to the expectation of a positive outcome.

This power of the mind has been baffling the medical community for years. Big pharmaceuticals are also trying to work out what is going on. When billions of dollars are at stake and a sugar pill is proven to be just as effective as your carefully researched compound, wouldn't you? Prozac, anyone?

As a wee aside – the Public Library of Science Magazine published an article in 2008 which stated 'Drug–placebo differences increased as a function of initial severity, rising from virtually no difference at moderate levels of initial depression to a relatively small difference for patients with very severe depression, reaching conventional criteria for clinical significance only for patients at the upper end of the very severely depressed category.'

Let's repeat that – 'clinical significance only for patients at the upper end of the very severely depressed category'. So a wee dod of sugar in a pill-shape is every bit as effective for most patients, except for those at the upper end of the scale. Wish I'd known that before I started pill-popping. Of course Big Pharma came out the blocks in a rush to poo-poo the research and highlighted their own scientific findings.

Don't know about you, but when those doing the 'finding' have a vested interest to the tune of billions of dollars, I get just a touch more cynical.

Taking these drugs HAS helped millions of people throughout the world. That is undeniable. But what is also undeniable is that the biggest share of the effect of the pill is the patient's expectation that the pill is going to help.

The research into this situation continues apace and the scientific community is concerned about how widely this research should be shared.

Doctors are also in a bind. They know that a combination of exercise, diet, therapy, time-out, a dollop of sunshine, life-style change and mindfulness programmes is the best way to find a lasting solution, but they have all these people with their hand out for a prescription, seeking a cure NOW.

It's an easy option for us all, but wouldn't a better option be to give people the information and to help them seek help that doesn't come with major side effects and huge costs? (It is estimated that in 2008 the NHS spend on anti-depressants was over £300 million. That could fund a whole army of Cognitive Behavioural Therapists.)

I have to add at this point if you are reading this and you are using any form of anti-depressant DO NOT SUDDENLY COME OFF THEM. That can cause serious withdrawal symptoms, including twitches, tremors, blurred vision, and nausea – as well as (ironically) depression and anxiety.

A placebo effect happens when a treatment or medication with no medical value (a placebo) is given to a patient and their symptoms improve. The patient believes and expects that the treatment is going to work, therefore it does. (Jack Black's message is chiefly that of bringing to bear the power of desire, belief and expectation.) The word placebo comes from the Latin 'I shall please.' It could be argued that for most of medical history, the placebo effect was the main treatment doctors offered their patients. Reassurance, attention and someone with a white coat and a stethoscope worn at a jaunty angle and belief in treatment, would mobilize patients' internal powers to fight their conditions.

Apparently, the most effective part of the placebo effect is your doc's bedside manner, but the colour and size of the placebo pill are also important. For example, yellow pills make the most effective anti-depressants and white ones are more effective as an antacid even if they contain nothing but lactose.

Muriel Gray

Muriel Gray

'Why do you want to interview me then?' asked Muriel Gray with genuine surprise when I told her I was interviewing successful Scots. 'I don't think I am successful. I think I'm mediocre and that's a great source of discontent. I don't want to be mediocre. I want to be brilliant,' she laughs with a self-deprecating tone. 'Brilliant in everything I do. I'm just going to have to accept that I'm simply not talented enough, and I'm not looking forward to that day.'

We are in the lounge of her Glasgow home on a bright winter's morning. Muriel is suffering from a heavy cold and wrapped in a blanket. All I can see of her is the trademark white, spiky hair and her tired, pale, sharp features.

She coughs. Then laughs. Two sounds that are to punctuate our meeting. More coughing, 'Oh, god have you chosen the wrong day.' Then she hoots, cheerful in her germ-filled misery.

'How would you describe success?' I ask.

'Success is all about being happy. I would much prefer to be happy than to be minted and miserable.' She laughs, pauses and considers her next words. 'When will we be happy?' Cough. 'Next year?' She contends that for most people the easiest thing in the world is to get what you want. 'The difficult part, in my opinion, is to decide what you actually do want.'

'How would you describe happiness?'

'I know some people who are so happy, they just don't care. They have tiny lives – tiny in that they don't aspire to change anything, don't want to grow, they're not curious about anything, they don't examine, they don't self-criticise. I just can't live like that. On the other hand, how delicious. How fantastic, because that's where happiness lies. I'm a restless spirit, not blessed with that sort of attitude.' Pause. Rueful grin. 'I'm never happy, Michael.'

For those of you who watch little TV and don't read newspapers or horror novels, Muriel has been a colourful part of our media for the last thirty years. She first brightened our screens as the mouthy, witty, passionate, enthusiastic presenter on *The Tube* and is now a businesswoman, occasional TV presenter, a writer of classy horror novels, wife, and mother to three children.

She still balances her varied career in the media, in production, presenting, journalism and novelist, so where I wondered does she have a quibble with the 'S' word?

Perhaps it is her refusal to be content; the continuous search for improvement and her 'restless spirit' that ensures that whatever she turns her hand to would work out well. The daughter of a merchant seaman, she says she had a lot of positive influences in her life and one of the most important was while she was at school.

'I was just about to go off the rails,' she laughs. 'Because I liked being a bad girl at school . . . and just by mistake, I wasn't quite paying attention . . . I ended up getting As in English.' Naturally gifted with words, she read voraciously as a child.

'There's only one way to become a writer and that is to be a reader.'

Despite her best efforts to fail at school, when she 'wasn't paying attention' her facility with language brought her to the attention of a teacher called Morvern Cameron.

'She treated my rebellion with delight. Every time I argued to try and irritate her she would just throw it right back at me and ask, why do you think that? She would argue with me and she always won because she was in her forties . . . and crafty.' She laughs loudly and then grows still as she considers the impact this woman had on her formative years. 'And I think she saved me from a downward spiral.'

Muriel counts herself hugely fortunate that Morvern came into her life at just that moment. She was immensely fond of and grateful to her and on the occasion of Morvern's recent death had the privilege of writing her obituary.

'She was a fantastic individual – a poet – really inspiring – a huge influence.'

A woman who is never short of an opinion or two, Muriel then continues heatedly on the subject.

'Good teachers can save anybody. There are just not enough of them – and those that are get their morale broken by poor resources, lack of appreciation and deep fatigue from being a political pinball. They're saving a whole generation of kids right now from ending up serving burgers – like Gray's Elegy in a Country Churchyard – and what thanks are they getting?'

Painfully introverted as a teenager, Muriel had a life changing moment of clarity that Buddha himself would have been happy with, although he might not have expressed it in the same terms.

'I don't know where it came from because I was always so shy when I was young – very self-conscious about how I looked – gangly. Although it's fashionable now, it wasn't then. I'd be a supermodel now. Always out of time and place.' She laughs. And coughs.

She was going up an escalator in a Glasgow shop, gaze fixed on the metal tread of the stairs, avoiding eye contact with the strangers surrounding her when a thought rose in her mind. Why did she care what these people thought of her? She then went on to turn the question around. What did she think of them?

'I remember thinking, these people don't care about me, so why do I care what they think about me?'

Her attitude changed in an instant and she saw that for her, shyness, insecurity and being too self-aware were really a form of vanity: if you believe that other people really care how you look. She learned that it was much more interesting to be interested in other people than to be continually projecting her thoughts and judgements.

'And then you become automatically invisible. From that moment on I never suffered a crisis of confidence at all, because as far as I was concerned, in the big scheme of things, I didn't matter. You can really make yourself invisible by judging other people – not harshly, nor in a pejorative way – they are just more interesting than you. As a consequence your own over-worked sense of self diminishes and you can relax.

'In other words, I just became a pair of eyes and ears on a

stalk,' she hoots. 'That, for me, is the secret of self-confidence. Lack of self-awareness. A good tip. A fiver if you use it.' Smile.

Muriel is an incredibly busy woman, juggling her various roles and fans of her TV programme, *The Munro Show* will have no surprises when they learn how she re-charges her batteries.

'I have a passion for the Highlands. The fact that they exist stops me from ever thinking of emigrating. I think I would just curl up and die if I couldn't visit them regularly.'

Most of her holidays as a child were spent camping there with her brother who recently turned his back on the rat-race and moved to Wester-Ross. An action that delights Muriel and fills her with pride.

Her favourite place on the planet?

Without a pause, she answers, 'Assynt.'

I admit I haven't been.

'That's terrible, Michael.' She smiles by way of a warning that she's about to pull my leg. 'That's 'cos you're from Ayrshire. They don't go anywhere.' Then she laughs/ coughs. 'You have to go there before you die. It's this mad, flat moorland with a crazy mountain sticking up out of nowhere. Astonishing. If I don't go into the Highlands every couple of weeks I get withdrawal symptoms.

'It reminds me that I'm solar dust. I am of no importance whatsoever. They have been here for millions of years and will still be here after my tiny, little mayfly existence. It makes me feel privileged to have some cognitive understanding and appreciation of it just now.

'You think you are so pivotal to everything around you and simply to walk up one of these ancient pieces of rock puts you right back in your place. It has a nameless, spiritual quality . . . you recognise it in your heart . . . that you are returning to it . . . that you are made of the same stuff.' Her voice is low with awe, her gaze turned inward. And it makes me want to go to the nearest outdoor store and stock up with boots, water-repellent clothing and a map.

This love of the outdoors has recently resulted in her agreeing to become the patron for *Trees for Life*. With only 1% of the original Caledonian Forest remaining in Scotland, *Trees for Life* is dedicated to restoring the forest to an area of 1,500 square kilometres in the Highlands, west of Inverness. The organisation's first trees took root in 1991 in Glen Affric, and as part of her duties as patron, Muriel planted the half-millionth tree in Scotland's newest National Nature Reserve, managed by Forestry Commission Scotland.

After being set on the straight – and not so narrow – you simply can't imagine Muriel having such a limiting word as 'narrow' in her lexicon – by Morvern Campbell, the next step in her life was university. Given her ability with language she was accepted to study English, but because that came too easily to her she didn't view it as a sensible option. Instead, she chose a subject that would stretch her – that would force her to invest more effort.

'To get into art school,' she recalls, 'you had to submit a portfolio of your work. Making it the more difficult and testing option.'

This decision was to prove crucial in how Muriel's life

developed, but her path into the bright lights of the TV world was not instantaneous.

After she successfully completed her art degree she went to work as an illustrator for an old family firm called Terstons. Muriel saw this as an excellent start in her career, but not for the reasons you might expect.

'I hated that job,' she laughs. 'Which was fantastic because I was able to think that nothing could ever be that bad again.'

Then came a job at the National Museum of Antiquities in Edinburgh as Assistant Head of Design. She sees this as the best job she ever had.

'Absolutely loved it. Loved the people. Loved working with all these beautiful things and all these academics who were so unstressed and charming.'

While working there, Muriel was also pursuing a career in music with the punk band, The Family Von Trapp. Although the band didn't reach the dizzy heights of musical fame it led to her being noticed by TV producers at Channel 4, and she was invited to present on a new music show called *The Tube*.

In these early days of her TV career, she was still able to complete her duties at the museum. The lead-up to an exhibition took so much time – meaning a work day that ran well into the small hours – that she was given days off in lieu of increased wages.

As Muriel recalls it, Channel 4's coverage in Scotland at that time was patchy and she was therefore able to maintain a degree of anonymity while at home in Glasgow.

'It was great. My ideal job, presenting a TV show. Got paid quite well and no-one that I knew got to see it.'

Of course, this didn't last and once Channel 4 improved their coverage in Scotland, Muriel began to be recognised in the street.

'I have a peculiar ego. I hated, hated, *hated* being recognised as a famous face and yet I loved getting fan mail for what I saw as doing absolutely ****-all. TV presenting is chimpanzee work.'

She doesn't think she is a particularly good presenter but found it came easily to her. And like anything she had a facility for, she treated it with disdain and a healthy dollop of suspicion.

'I hated doing it and saw it as money for old rope.' She makes a face. 'I'm never really happy, Michael. I get bored and I want to move on to something else.'

Being creative is very important to Muriel and she contends that you can bring creativity to everything that you do. 'You can be a creative property developer, a creative cook – just do what you're doing with flair.'

How have you changed over the years? I ask.

'I'm not as angry as I used to be, but I still get annoyed at stuff. I can't bear stupidity. I am still passionate. Too passionate for my own good. They don't like it in girls – neutrality on TV and print is what is required. Misogyny is almost like a biological requirement – it's built in to every mainstream religion on the planet. What makes us different is that we've been trying to combat it since the turn of the last century – and we've been quite successful till lately, when religion started to rise again.'

A driving force for Muriel is that she never feels she does anything particularly well. She feels that to be successful – and here she echoes all of my interviewees – you have to work hard and take risks.

'I would go further than that and say that you have to be honest and decent. You have to be kind to people. You need to remember why you are doing it. There's no point in running a business if you're not contributing to make other people's lives better. For me that's what it's all about.'

Muriel was first struck with this when her TV company became very busy and it occurred to her that the work she was involved in was helping to keep a roof over peoples' heads.

'My first assistant bought a flat and I thought: I did that. Just by thinking up a TV programme idea and then a better one and always by trying to be better. And don't be cruel.' She pops back to an earlier point. 'People think you have to be ruthless. What does that even mean? The only person you should be ruthless with is yourself. I think people base that whole approach on 1980s soap operas. It just doesn't make any sense in the real world.

'How I have changed. . .' she gets back on topic, 'is that I'm far more tolerant. Mind you, it doesn't read like that in my columns, but as you get older you realise that nothing is black and white. Then there's the questions I ask myself. What are you trying to prove? What is life really all about? What does it matter if you go to the grave having written a bunch of not so great books? Does it really matter? Does any of it matter? What's the big deal? Are you happy? What is your day-to-day life like? How are your children?

'Why do I keep going? I'm still trying to prove it to myself. Don't know why. I need to get to the bottom of that.' She makes a face and laughs. 'But I can't be arsed spending money on a therapist.'

TV production became a larger part of her life and she admits that there was no big plan, simply a lot of energy, creativity and plenty of spirit. 'We were a wee bit mad and that possibly led to our success. An element of rebellion that worked terribly well for us. That's certainly true for *Gallus Besum*. Thereafter we'd learned the craft and turned that angry imagination into just straightforward creativity. But probably a business plan would have helped.' A shrug. 'Every risk or decision we made turned out well for us.'

She's referring to the growth from her initial production company Gallus Besom to Ideal World Productions and popular TV shows like *Location, Location, Location* and *Bricking It*.

'*Location* was a huge achievement for us: a Scottish company making such an impact on the TV landscape. *Bricking It*, as well. We helped poor kids get a job. Our wee TV programme changed people's lives and I'm so proud of that.'

Being a writer myself, I'm keen to know more about Muriel's career in that area. She completed her first novel – a horror – when horror as a genre was almost completely out of favour. 'It became a bestseller – and it was wonderful. A professional highlight for me was meeting Stephen King and him giving a quote for the cover of my book.' She laughs. 'Stephen King thinks I'm great, what can I do now?'

She complains that she has several projects on the go and they are all late. 'I used to wait until ten o'clock at night to write. I'm too knackered now. My first book about the Munros, I did that in five weeks. Every morning before I went to work, from 6 am till 10. Couldn't do that now. I'm old and shagged,' she laughs. 'Keep thinking I need to get young and healthy again.'

The subject moves on to that of a legacy and Muriel says she is not interested in leaving a pile of work for the world to remember her by. 'I only want my family to remember me. Nobody else. For them to know I loved them, was kind to them and put them above everything else. That's enough for me.'

It's evident in Muriel's change of focus that she turns down a lot of work to be at home more with her children. This change in focus was a long time coming but happened following an accident in a neighbour's garden where her daughter almost drowned and was left with permanent brain damage.

'Having a disabled child knackers you. And it gets harder and harder, trying to keep the energy levels up. That's why I can no longer work into the night. And that's why I need to get more energy: I'm working for her. To protect her – first and foremost. I keep asking myself; what happens when we die? And secondly I don't want to let any of my family down. I've worked since I was 14. I can't imagine never working.'

Muriel feels that a work ethic is ingrained into her. She says that at a deep level she fears that if you don't work: you don't eat. 'When I see women in Buchanan Galleries with huge hat boxes, doing lunch, I think who are you? What's going on here? I don't get it. What kind of bargain has been struck?'

I wonder if Muriel is envious of these women. Her answer is as forthright as I've come to expect.

'I'm envious if they are happy. I'm always envious of happiness.' Pause. 'I am quite happy.' The word quite is invested with an almost apologetic air. Like she can't quite accept it. 'I have an adorable family. I'm living where I want to live. I'm pretty well off and all that stuff. But I could do without the restlessness and the drive. So if people are truly content, not curious and not discontented at not knowing the secrets of the universe . . .' she bursts into laughter at the grandiose choice of words. 'I'm guessing these women I talked about earlier out shopping are not too bothered about those kinds of issues. On the other hand, they may well be suffering from a deep discontent. We'll never know.'

She leans forward, pauses and smiles. 'I'm not all girl. I'm partially man. That's part of my problem. Too much testosterone.' And that's a cue for more laughter and coughing.

'That's it really.' She makes a small smile of apology. 'Nothing else to say.'

My turn to smile. 'Aye. Right.'

Mentoring with Muriel

Being too others-conscious

Speaking to Muriel Gray the first thing that resonated with me was her Shyness Epiphany. Please excuse the hyperbolic term, but that was what effectively happened. She moved from ten out of ten on the 'affronted' scale to a zero – with the speed of a thought. It occurred to her that to the people she was trying to hide from she had little or no importance. So what was she worried about?

'Humility does not mean thinking less of yourself than of other people, nor does it mean having a low opinion of your own gifts. It means freedom from thinking about yourself at all.' William Temple

Like the words above, Muriel became free from thinking about herself and felt a whole new freedom of thought and action. How many times have you wanted to do something and stopped because you were afraid someone might say you were mad, sad or too big for your boots? How often have you been offered an opportunity you would have enjoyed but stepped back from it because you were worried how it might look to other people?

If what you were about to do was in your interests and no-one was going to get hurt, haven't you allowed this fear of others to rob you of something vital?

As someone who when a teenager, would have rather drunk a tub of acid than speak up in a classroom, I can fully identify with Muriel's pre-epiphany state of mind. And I'm guessing many people reading this will be nodding in agreement.

If you feel too self-conscious when all eyes are on you and you want to shrink and dissolve until you are nothing but a puddle of sweat, could you learn from Muriel's example?

To look at other people is human. People-watching is practically a hobby for some. We are all aware of our environment when we are out and about. We look at the things around us and continually take in feedback in relation to our own needs at that particular point. Are we safe and dry? Hungry or sated? Where is the public toilet if I need it?

We might be looking at the people around us, but the question is – do we actually see anything? For most of us our eyes move to someone's face, their clothes, who they are with – but it is only for a second because then our minds move back to whatever is going on in our life, we go back to our own internal dialogue.

How do you really see yourself?

Now we're talking about self-awareness, as opposed to being self-conscious.

How well do you know yourself? Do you lurch from one internal crisis to another, never understanding why? Do you have a limiting belief system that has you questioning or even sabotaging, every positive act in your life – and you don't know why?

Knowing who you are, what you want and why you want it gives you the ability to bring those wants into your life. Otherwise, you will forever get caught up in your own inner dramas and uncertain beliefs, allowing indeterminate thought processes to decide on your feelings and actions.

How can you make wise decisions and choices if you don't really know why you want what you want? Is it not a wee bit chaotic to not know why this stranger, who is me, is acting the way he/she is?

Many people sneer at those of us who want to improve on our 'self'. After all it's easy to be a cynic. You just pick your point of view, remain blind to everything else and knock down those who make an effort to improve. Socrates wrote 'the unexamined life is not worth living'. What he missed out was that it takes real courage and stamina to carry out that examination. So give yourself a big pat on the back if you are reading this with a view to putting in the work.

Feeling daft? Smiling? Good.

A cynical stance, as I said above is an easy stance, the path of least resistance, a get-out clause, but when I meet people like that it always surprises me that they will sit exams, broaden their knowledge, polish physical skills and yet leave the mind untouched.

The mind-body link has been largely ignored in our rush towards a scientific age. If science can't rationalise it, we don't want to know. And so far the brain is largely un-mapped. We don't know what is really going on in vast areas of that grey stuff.

Going deep

The subconscious mind is where you want to address your efforts. Via the conscious mind. The former is a mass of functions and parts that make up our behaviour and personality. These subconscious parts can even hold opposing beliefs, because those that you formed in the early episodes of your life grew to understand, respond and survive in a certain reality that is very probably no longer of relevance.

These old subconscious parts can continue to alter, even distort our perception of reality. These old beliefs were formed by our child mind as a reaction to events both out of our control and out of our understanding and are often the root cause of our present conflict, guilt, fear, limiting ideas and even, dare I say it, our physical complaints.

What other people think of us can hurt us emotionally. This

false assumption is what the mind uses to work in a fear of emotional pain. However, do thoughts in another person's head really establish our feelings? Surely, what **we** believe about ourselves determines how we feel.

When you look at it like that, it all becomes a bit nonsensical, doesn't it. We can't possibly be what other people build in their minds. And I don't know about you, but I can't read another person's thoughts.

Here's more good news: when you fully grasp your negative beliefs you instinctively lose your belief in them. This shift happens just through your growing awareness. Just by identifying your beliefs you facilitate change in your feelings, reactions and behaviour.

Run through the above process again. We are too quick to believe the opinions other people have about us. We often do it without realising. Get into the habit of scrutinizing your thought process and this starts to fall apart.

Stakes in the ground

I remember a few years ago watching a documentary about elephant handlers (mahouts). The first thing the mahouts did with the baby elephants was tie one of their back legs to a small stake planted in the earth. The fact that the young animals could not move away once tethered like this was reinforced each night. Each and every night after a day of work, they were tied to the small stake. So strong was this lesson that when the elephants were adult and could have plucked the stake out of the ground as if it were a blade of grass, the simple act of being tethered to the stake was enough for them to believe that to try and move forward was futile.

It made me wonder, what false lessons do we learn as children? You drop a glass. Your parents tell you off. Another broken glass, another row. You're told that you are clumsy. The idea takes root in your head and you start to look for evidence that backs this up. I'm clumsy, therefore I must drop stuff all the time. Everyone actually does it – lack of concentration, whatever, but many don't let the idea take root in their heads. But you do – and you see yourself as being clumsy for the rest of your life.

You write your first poem. Your mum loves it. Everyone else tells you that you are rubbish. You tell yourself you are a rubbish poet – you can't write poetry. But have you really tried? Did you study your craft, learn from masters, read as much about poetry as you could, write loads of poems. No. You take that singular situation and turn it into a life failure. Do you recognise yourself in this scenario?

What negative beliefs have you set up for yourself when it comes to your life? What is your habitual self-dialogue like? I'm not good enough? People will ask, who the hell does he/she think she is? Who am I kidding, I'll never succeed.

Real growth will happen in your life when you realise the connection between your limiting thoughts and the areas of your life in which your results are disappointing.

Happiness is smile shaped

A recurring theme of my conversation with Muriel Gray was happiness. When talking about the hypothetical women doing lunch, she said, 'I'm envious if they are happy. I'm always envious of happiness.' She then admitted to being 'quite' happy, citing family and home as being crucial.

What makes us happy? What makes you happy? Do you ever seek it out, or wait for it to happen, or are you blessed?

Happiness is a choice

> *'Two men look out the same prison bars; one sees mud and the other stars.'*   Frederic Langbridge

Which would you choose to see? Is it really a matter of choice?

> *'We who lived in concentration camps can remember the men who walked through the huts comforting others, giving away their last piece of bread. They may have been few in number, but they offer sufficient proof that everything can be taken from a man but one thing: the last of the human freedoms – to choose one's attitude in any given set of circumstances, to choose one's own way.'*
> Viktor Frankl

On September 25, 1942 Viktor Frankl, along with his wife, and his parents was deported to the Theresienstadt concentration camp. There he established and maintained a camp service of psychic hygiene and mental care for those who were sick and those who were drained of life. Then, on October 19, 1944, he was moved to Auschwitz where he was processed and moved to Türkheim, a Nazi concentration camp affiliated with Dachau, on October 25, 1944. Here he was to spend 6 months and 2 days working as a slave-labourer. Meanwhile, his wife and both his parents died under privations enforced on them.

In his seminal work, *Man's Search for Meaning*, Frankl describes how despite the near-certainty of death, the beatings, the hunger, the cold, he found a reason to go on.

This is the core of the human spirit, according to his study of the mind. If we can find something to live for – if we can find some meaning to put at the centre of our lives – even the worst kind of suffering becomes bearable. He observed that by being determined to preserve some measure of their humanity, in spite of the Nazis' efforts to rob them of it, many were able to survive the concentration camps.

I remember reading John McCarthy's account (*Some Other Rainbow*) of being held by terrorists in the Lebanon for five years. His fellow prisoner for much of his ordeal was Brian Keenan and often as part of their suffering their jailors would separate and beat the men. By way of mutual support, when one man was being dragged off to solitary confinement, the other would whisper two words as a reminder: 'Choose joy.'

In common with Frankl's learning, these two men realised that despite everything their captors could inflict on their physical state, they still had control of their minds – and therefore rather than choose a state of anger, resentment or to harbour feelings of revenge, the practice of finding a state of joy would mean to them a better chance of survival.

Control is a key element here. These two men found a way to retain some form of control when to all intents and purposes they were completely control-less.

It is noted that a perceived lack of control is a contributory factor in depression and other mental health issues. Unhappy people tend to believe they are life's toys and conversely, the more an individual is able to find a way to control their environment or even an element of it, like Keenan and McCarthy, the more happiness becomes an attainable position.

Tom Farmer makes a point

Sir Tom Farmer, CBE

The phone rang just as I was about to leave the house. It was a friend. I explained to them that I was on my way to Edinburgh to meet Sir Tom Farmer and I didn't have time to speak. This was one of the first 'names' I had managed to arrange an appointment with and I was keen to make a good impression. To my friend's refrain of 'You can't get better than a Kwik-Fit Fitter . . .' I hung up and made for the car.

With this song bouncing around in my head, I considered what an excellent piece of marketing that little song was. Not only was the song instantaneous when my friend heard Tom Farmer's name, but the connection between the two was still very strong, although Tom is no longer with Kwik-Fit.

There are many businessmen and entrepreneurs in Scotland, but how has this one individual managed to become a household name? Is it his modest upbringing that has captured people's imaginations? Is it the huge sums he is reputed to have earned? Is it the time he devotes to charity work? Whatever it was, I was about to meet the man himself.

His office is in a beautiful nineteenth century villa. It's shiny, light and spacious. Tom strides towards me in the reception area, his hand extended towards me in welcome. The words of the song persist as I return his smile.

In his office we sit on long, brown leather suites and talk

begins easily over a cup of coffee. I explain what I would like from him.

He pauses before saying, 'What you've just asked there is impossible. In fact, I wouldn't even try to give you the answer. If you want to find out about me as a person then you'd have to ask someone else. There is a danger it would come over as vain, or hesitant to tell the actual truth. To talk about yourself . . . there is a danger that you just say what you think people want to actually hear. I don't think that I would be able to give a straightforward answer. What I **can** talk about is the things that have influenced my life.'

Tom was born in Edinburgh and brought up in Leith, the youngest of seven children.

'I was so lucky. I was born into the greatest family in the world. I had the greatest parents in the world.'

He was also brought up in a community in the real sense of the word; where even as a young boy he could recognise that people were attentive to those around them.

'When people ask me what I remember about life as a boy, all I can remember is this feeling of total security. Not financial security, but knowing that you were surrounded by people who actually cared about you. They would give you a clip over the ear when you needed it. Or encourage you when you needed encouragement.'

Tom feels blessed to have had this background and believes that it gave him a concrete, solid base to begin his life from. In effect, he argues, it shaped his destiny.

'I was also blessed with a great deal of energy. If you are

born with high levels of energy it is a tremendous asset. You can drink as many bottles of Lucozade as you like, but it won't give you the energy to make a difference to your or anyone else's life.'

This level of energy was apparent in Tom from a young age. Even before he left school he had a job cleaning cookers. Observing his mother cleaning the cooker after cooking for her husband and seven children, Tom realised that people would pay good money to a young, enthusiastic boy who was willing to do this for them.

'I worked out I could charge 5 shillings a time and clean two cookers a night.' This meant that as a thirteen-year old Tom could earn £3 or £4 per week, at a time when a working man's wage was £6 per week.

When he left school, he joined a local firm as a mechanic. A firm that took on the mantle of guardians.

'I joined a great company. I didn't realise it at the time, but the people I worked for really looked out for me. I worked long hours and during that time they effectively replaced my mother and father.' In this job, Tom learned a few valuable lessons that would stand him in good stead when he came to run his own business.

'These people were very good to me. So I worked really hard. I didn't work for the £1/10 that I was earning – I didn't want to let these good people down, because at the end of the day, I **knew** they wouldn't let me down.'

This was a huge learning curve for Tom in how to deal with people. He was associating with people he respected, people who were always encouraging him and his workmates to always try that bit harder.

'They didn't set you targets that were outwith your control, because then you would get despondent when you struggled to make them. They didn't tell you to go climb Mount Everest, but what they did tell you was to go run up and down Arthur's Seat a few times, then you'll be able to climb Ben Nevis.' For Tom it was a steady progression, a ladder of achievement that he responded to very positively.

Next in his career progression was the position of van driver, a job he relished. He was able to get out and about on his own and meet people. Tom was a self-starter long before that particular phrase was coined.

'This is a job where you have to use your own initiative. From eight in the morning, you are on your own all day. You can sit in a lay-by, or you can sit in a cafe, **or** you can get on with the job. I enjoyed it, so I got on with it.'

Another job change, another important lesson.

'Then I became a sales rep and I learned very quickly that a good salesman isn't anything another than someone who has good interpersonal relationships. Having the right techniques to sell, to my mind is a myth.' The job of salesman is one that raises negative connotations to many people in this country, but Tom asserts, nothing ever happens unless you sell something.

'The first thing we've got to sell is ourselves. It's as simple as that. And that comes out of your ability to interact effectively with other people. How can I develop a relationship with you whereby at the end of the day you'll say, "Aye, Tom Farmer, he's a decent guy." If I can achieve that then I've opened the door and I can come back and speak to you later on.' He also learned that when dealing with the public you don't have to be servile. Build a relationship with someone where you are seen as a person of integrity, someone who is reliable and trustworthy; someone who carries out his promises.

He also learned the power of activity.

'For every ten calls I made I got three orders, so if I made 20 calls I got 6, if I made 30 calls I got 9. I just made more calls than anybody else and I got more orders. I was top salesman.'

Tom knew that at some stage he would work for himself. He knew, as if it were written. Events however, gave him a wee push.

'The company I was working for got taken over by a large organisation and I found that I wasn't enjoying the job.' What's more, he wasn't getting paid his commission.

'They didn't pay me so I decided I ain't ever going to work for anybody else again. I was determined to control my own destiny as much as I could.'

At this time Tom was seeing a young lady, who later became his wife. He had known her most of his life. They grew up in the same street, went to the same school, attended the same church.

'We shared the same upbringing, came from that same environment, so when I went into business for myself I had no pressure from her. I had her full support. There was nothing holding me back.'

This business was a tyre and exhaust shop and the support was such that she didn't pass as much as a whisper of complaint when after nights out together, Tom would go back to his shop in order to make sure the batteries were charged up for the next day's work.

This tyre and exhaust shop became very successful, but he would never have known this level of success, he asserts, if it hadn't been for the people he surrounded himself with.

'People say I was a one-man business. Rubbish. I've been able to achieve whatever it was I achieved because of the team of guys I was working with. Young guys, high energy, enthusiastic. If there was one quality that we had, which I didn't realise at the time, it was total trust in each other. No matter what happened we wouldn't have let each other down. What's more we worked hard, really hard . . . and enjoyed it.'

The way he describes his team in those days sounds like a marriage made in business heaven. 'We worked so hard and we all had a similar nature. We all met our wives at the same time; we all got married around the same time.' He laughs in recollection, 'We all had babies around August and September because the only holidays we would allow ourselves were at Christmas and New Year.'

His first shop had a corner site in Edinburgh, 'Tyres and Accessory Supplies'. It had a problem that any businesses would struggle with, let alone a discounted tyre shop. It had very little parking; indeed it was burdened on both sides of the corner by double yellow lines.

An acquaintance of mine, who shall remain nameless in case the book on parking violations is timeless, lived in Edinburgh in the mid 60s and remembers the parking problem well.

'You had to wait until the traffic warden had moved on before you could stop and get your tyres changed.'

Tom and his team were not going to allow such a situation to hamper them.

He smiles, 'You can overcome any problem.'

They successfully built the business up and sold it for a reported £450,000 four years later to Albany Tyre Services.

'It wasn't until I sold it that I realised how much money I'd been making.' This he sees as a blessing, because it kept him focused on the job, providing a service that people would come back for time and time again.

'Everyone in the team took home the same amount of money, £12 pounds a week. Then it went up to £17 per week. Every penny we made after that was put into buying materials for the business. We used to measure our profits by how many tyres we had in stock.'

In those early days, life was very simple. They didn't focus on things like depreciation and cashflow.

'Five year plans? Didn't have them. Our planning was very simple; short term plans were what are we doing tomorrow morning, medium term was what are we doing tomorrow afternoon and long term plans were what are we going to do tomorrow night.'

That is a statement that would have many business gurus choking behind their well-tailored collars and ties. But don't make the mistake that Tom was naive; he simply had a vision and a work ethic, and a team that ensured his success.

'My life has been about being in the service industry. It's not difficult dealing with customers. It's the easiest thing in the world. What do you want as a customer? You want a fair price. You don't want me to be servile. You want to go away and think – that was an enjoyable experience.'

Having sold the business Tom decided to 'retire' to America in 1970 at the ripe old age of thirty. Typical of the man it became a working holiday.

'I would go and visit tyre and exhaust centres and see how they set out their shops, see how they dealt with their customers and think, there ain't no secret sauce here. In the UK we were exceptional – no bragging – whereas in a lot of cases in the US that sort of service was the norm.'

The 'S' word enters the conversation. Tom sits forward on his chair. 'Success' is clearly a subject that fascinates him.

'When you read all the books, cut through all the buzzwords and clichés, you come to one thing: the successful person is able to see the opportunity and grasp it.' His hand punches out and he holds on tight.

'Entrepreneur. This is a word that is bandied about a lot these days. But what does it even mean? For me it is somebody who sees an opportunity and is able to reach out and grasp it for his or her benefit, for the benefit of their family, the organisation they're part of and more importantly to me, use it for the benefit of the community they are actually involved with. **That's** what an entrepreneur is.'

The danger here as Tom sees it, is that people only think of success in business in financial terms. This is something that was reinforced following a conversation with one of the most important people in his life: his son. He breaks his train of thought and asks me.

'Have you got a son?'

'Yes'

'Well, when he's about 20 take him away and do something together for about 5 weeks. My son and I went backpacking in China. What a wonderful experience. That cemented our relationship. Wonderful.'

'Anyway, one day my son pulled me up on the subject of people's comfort levels. He felt that I was a little harsh about this. That I talked about someone who had reached his or her comfort level in a negative way.'

His son argued firstly that when it comes to 'comfort levels' there is a world of difference between being comfortable and being lazy. If someone wants a semi-detached house, a Ford, a holiday in the Isle of Man, and they get it, then they've cracked it.

'Who is more successful,' Tom's son asked him. 'A guy like that who has achieved everything he wants out of life or a guy like you, who could have anything, but is continuously striving for more and doesn't really know what he wants'

'It was a sobering thought. I still want to be achieving things. I'm always looking out for an opportunity. But that's my nature. So if someone else wants a simpler life and they're not doing any harm to society, well good luck to them.'

Following his 'retirement' in America, Tom returned to Scotland and in 1971 he established the first of the Kwik-Fit Tyre and Exhaust centres. The company grew very quickly. Such rapid business expansion however didn't come without its challenges.

'This was almost foolhardy, on reflection,' he mused. 'We went from 50 sites to 200 in seven months. We had to take what we refer to now as a 'profit sabbatical'. We never ever made a loss, but our profits took a tumble.'

Able to recognise their own strengths and more importantly at this point in the business, weaknesses, Tom and his team set about boosting their management. They recognised that they didn't have the necessary skills in terms of managing the finances, marketing or property. With the maxim, never go for second best to the fore in their minds, they brought in the best people they could find in all of these areas.

'We brought in the best and that enabled us to concentrate on what we were good at and that was operating centres. We knew intimately what that game was all about.'

As well as bringing in the finest people you can find, Tom reasons that you shouldn't be afraid of bringing in people who are better than you, nor should you be afraid of making a mistake.

'What really annoys me is a reluctance to do anything in case you get it wrong. In that case I say forget it. You can plan out everything to the last detail and still you'll never know how it is going to turn out. But I'll tell you what, if you have confidence in your abilities and in what you are doing, sit on top of it and if it's not right do something about it. Sit on top of it and change it.' He snaps his fingers.

'Change it.'

Snap.

'Change it.'

Snap.

As the business grew, so did Tom. From the guy who ordered the tyres, to the guy who managed, to the guy who had to employ other people to manage. He developed from the man who was doing it all, to the man who took on the mantle of leader. He realised quickly that leadership was what was required, not simply a manager.

'I created a culture where people could earn money and where they had complete trust in the organisation. My employees could trust that we would train them how to do their job, allow them to do the job and when their success was measured it was measured fairly and in a way that they understood.'

'A leader's role is to ensure that programmes are in place to encourage self-motivation. And as well as the trust issue, money plays a big part in the commercial world. We all want the opportunity to earn enough money to give us the quality of life that we want for our families and ourselves.'

From being such a hands-on person, Tom had to learn one of the hardest skills of all, delegation.

'That was unbelievably difficult. It wasn't enough to say I want you to do that and then walk away. That's not delegation, that's abdication. You have to say this is what I want you to do. This is what I'm going to give you to enable you to do it and by the way, this is how I want you to tell me how you are getting on with the job.'

At several times in our conversation Tom has used the phrase 'secret sauce'. If there was such a thing, the key ingredient as far as he is concerned is how you deal with people.

'To me interpersonal relationships are the be-all and end-all.' He then goes on to advocate patience with those who work directly with the public. 'The next time you go into a shop and the assistant is not relating to you in the manner you would like, stop and think. Maybe they're having a wee bit of a problem. So I ain't going to allow that to beat me. I only ever get the best of service wherever I go, because I won't allow you to give me bad service. When it's not right I'll say to you. I'll ask you, is there something wrong? Have I done something to offend you?'

He then recalls an occasion when he was dining with his wife in a new restaurant. The waiter was more than distracted and less than friendly. Tom decided to have a wee word with him.

'Excuse me, do you not like me?'

'Why are you asking that?' the waiter replied, somewhat taken aback.

'Because from the minute I came in here, you've thrown the menu at me, you've taken my order as if it's a real hassle for you. If you don't want me here just tell me. If I've done something to offend you, just tell me. I've come here to have a nice pleasant evening with my wife and I can't have you spoiling it for me.'

The waiter apologised and explained that he'd been having

problems. Tom left his chair, brought a spare one over to the table and asked the waiter to sit down.

'I'm going to ask you to sit there for 5 minutes and listen to my problems. Then you can have 5 minutes to tell me yours. Then we can start the evening from scratch.' The waiter burst out laughing. The service from that point on was exemplary.

All of the influences in Tom's life seem to be in the past. Is there anyone who has influenced him in more recent times, I wondered? He pointed to a photograph on a side table,

'I've had the privilege of spending time with that woman there.' The photograph shows him and his wife with Mother Theresa.

'Talk about success, that's one of the most successful people who ever lived. She was someone special. I've been fortunate enough to have met loads of wonderful people. There's another nun down in Leith, a Sister Margaret. An unbelievable lady who will never receive the recognition she's due. Night and day she does things for other people. She's in her 80s and she has spent the last few years working with the people in Bosnia and Croatia. Talk about success, Sister Margaret is an unbelievable success.'

Having achieved a huge degree of success himself, both in financial terms and in terms that Mother Theresa herself would have appreciated, what keeps Tom going?

'You can get carried away with the whole issue of success. You keep going because you don't want to be seen as unsucc-essful. People ask me why I'm still doing all of this and the truth is that I'm doing it for the recognition. It's nice to be recognised that you have achieved success and because of that recognition you have to keep going.'

'My passion is business; it's about being involved in doing things that are successful. I'm not passionate about things like golf or art, but I'm passionate about being involved and making things happen. The day I lose that is the day I walk away.'

Another area that he has more than a passing interest in is football.

'I got involved with Hibernian FC because I was brought up in Leith and Hibs were part of that environment I loved as a boy.'

He has no involvement in the day-to-day running of the club, but he attends matches regularly. He has a fear though, that if he goes too often he'd want to be on the touchline with the manager. He'd want to be there telling them all what to do. He realises as a fan that he needs to keep a distance and not interfere.

'Football has such a high profile now and you can easily get dragged into it. Spending money on that player and this player. But how I am interested in the club is as more of a focal point for the community.'

'When I was a boy in Leith, our whole life centred round the church. Not solely from a spiritual point of view, there were the social activities: the Boys' Club, the Girl Guides, the dancing etc. That's all gone and I think the football club could replace that. People should have a lot of pride there. They could send their boys there because they can learn all about the game. They can meet their heroes. There could be social clubs. . . we should involve the whole family. It could be a total package. That's the side of the football business I would like to get involved with. Creating a community.'

It's this part of Tom's nature that earned him a CBE in 1990 and a knighthood in 1997. Following his work on behalf of the Catholic Church he was appointed a papal knight of St Gregory the Great.

His work in community activities and charities helps keep Tom grounded after all the success he has earned and helps him appreciate the fruits of his hard work over the years. Success at his level can be a corrupting force, but Tom has managed to keep his feet on terra firma through helping others. With his usual candour he adds weight to the argument that says there is no such thing as the completely selfless act.

'I must also say that being in a position to help others has played a considerable part in my own feel-good factor.'

As he accompanies me down the stairs, out of the office, across to the car park, the famous advert starts its merry jingle in my head. But the lyrics I'm hearing in my head have changed.

'Aye, Tom Farmer. He's a decent guy.'

Mentoring with Tom Farmer

Aye, but.

Often we look at other people and the actions they take and a wee voice chimes in our head – 'Aye, but that was him. I cannae do that.'

Am I right?

Over the years I have coached many clients and ran a number of creative writing workshops and there has been a multitude of times when the response has been similar.

'Aye, but.'

This tells me the speaker can see the sense of what I'm saying, but for whatever reason they don't want to listen. Can you think of a time when 'aye, but' stopped you from getting something you wanted?

I can't remember how many years I have harboured the desire to see my name in print. I would walk into bookshops, pick books from the shelves, admire the covers, read the blurb and wish that my book was among them. I'd look at the ranks of novels and think, how the hell am I going to get published when there's all these great writers out there?

Then one day, something switched. Completely unbidden, the thought that rose in my mind was, 'If they can do it, why can't I?' I went from what was effectively a position of 'aye, but' to 'I can do that!'

The successes you read about in this book and many others have been brought about by people much like you and I. Composed of heart, lungs, gut, brain, eyes etc. If they can do it, so can you.

Still saying, 'aye, but'?

During a creative writing workshop I challenged my students to consider their writing goals. I wanted to reassure them that if their goal was simply to be taken up by the pleasure of pouring words onto a page and never to seek an audience, that this was fine.

Similarly, if their goal was seek publication or even earn a living from their writing, I wanted to encourage them to take the steps to make it happen.

One woman cited the success of J.K. Rowling as the reason why she didn't want to be published. This lady couldn't bear the scrutiny that would come with being a public figure.

In my view, this response was a smokescreen. The real 'aye, but' here was a fear of success.

Let's examine where a fear of success might originate.

Fear that you will accomplish all that you set out to, but that you still won't be happy.

Belief that you don't deserve all the good things that come into your life as a result of your success.

You fear success because you fear being recognised and honoured.

The worry that no matter how much you are able to achieve or accomplish, it will never be enough to sustain success.

Belief that there are others out there who are better than

you, who will replace you if you do not maintain your performances. So why bother, right?

Fear that you will find no joy in your achievements: that you will forever have a sense of dissatisfaction with life.

Do you recognise yourself in any of these?

The court of public opinion puts the brakes on your goals. It stops you from daring to put yourself out there, to try your best at what you're passionate about.

And here's the rub. Take a moment. Be completely honest. Do you find yourself indulging in the odd bout of tall poppy pruning? If so, you are contributing to the very thing that is holding you back.

In her excellent book, *The Scots' Crisis of Confidence*, Carol Craig debates this point much more eloquently than I could. She borrows two lines from the poem by Alexander Scott.

Scotch Equality
Kaa the feet
Frae thon big bastard

In other words, he's getting too big for his boots, knock (kaa) him off his feet – bring him back down to size.

And yes, if I'm being honest this is a thought that has entered my own head from time to time, but as soon as I am aware of it, I quash it ruthlessly. In my view there is no room for such a sentiment in a society that wants to see its entire populace achieve its potential.

Here's an alternative point of view taken from Marianne Williamson's book *A Return to Love*:

'Our deepest fear is not that we are inadequate. Our deepest fear is that we are powerful beyond measure. It is our light, not our darkness that most frightens us. We ask ourselves, who am I to be brilliant, gorgeous, talented, fabulous? Actually, who are you not to be? You are a child of God. Your playing small does not serve the world. There is nothing enlightened about shrinking so that other people won't feel insecure around you. We are all meant to shine, as children do. We were born to make manifest the glory of God that is within us. It's not just in some of us; it's in everyone. And as we let our own light shine, we unconsciously give other people permission to do the same.

'As we are liberated from our own fear, our presence automatically liberates others.'

During my meeting with Tom Farmer, he introduced an important point that his son raised. Success: what does it mean? Is it health, wealth, two cars in the drive, two holidays a year, being able to afford to put your children in private education, keeping up with the neighbours?

His son challenged him. 'If someone wants a semi-detached house, a Ford, a holiday in the Isle of Man, and they get it, then they've cracked it. Who is more successful? A guy like that who has achieved everything he wants out of life or a guy like you, who could have anything, but is continuously striving for more and doesn't really know what he wants'

While carrying out goal-setting workshops a regular question I am asked is – what if you don't know what you want?

Fair question. We are so caught up in the stuff of modern

life – the newest gadget, the latest diet fad, paying the bills, how many hours we've had to put in at work, finding work, are the kids in the right school, do the kids have the right friends, buying a lottery ticket, going for the shopping, cleaning the house, doing the garden, do I have time to go to the gym, my clothes are getting too tight, watching TV, surfing the net – searching for a distraction that will allow us to take our minds off our worries.

Think of the experience you might have while walking through a wood and compare it to what it would be like if you were driving through the same place. While walking all of your senses will be engaged and you will see, hear and smell things that you wouldn't experience while driving. The breeze on your face, a squirrel darting up a tree, the smell of grass after it has been raining, the rustle of leaves in autumn. If you're in the car you will get to the other side faster, and you might startle a few wild animals, but how much do you miss?

Clumsy metaphor, I know, but we all need to slow down, take stock and examine if we are living the life we really want to. But if you don't know what that looks like try this exercise.

Make yourself comfortable in a soft chair. Place both feet on the ground and your hands on your lap. Close your eyes. Take a deep breath (feel your stomach rise, not your chest) to a count of nine. Exhale to the same rhythm. Do this three times and each time you exhale, imagine that all of your negative thoughts are being expelled with your breath.

Now imagine that you are aged 99 – sitting in a place where you are safe, warm and comfortable. You have achieved everything you ever wanted and the symbols of this success surround you. Savour the moment. Feel the joy of it warming every cell in your body.

Now open your eyes, pick your paper and pen and write down the things you saw: the symbols of success that surrounded you.

Any surprises?

Look through your list. Are you making the steps now that will bring these elements into your life? If you are, congratulations. If you feel there are areas you can improve on, write down what is missing and take action now.

Graeme Obree

Graeme Obree

'I'm in agony by the last quarter of the ride – feet, ankles, genitals, hands, face and scalp all numb. Every fibre of muscle in my thighs is on fire. My eyes are a flickering blur, lungs rasping air in and out like bellows – I'm losing the ability to think or focus – when I reach the line I can barely see it.'

So writes Graeme Obree in his autobiography *The Flying Scotsman* as he describes his experience on his way to the monumental achievement of beating the record of one of cycling's blue riband events: The Hour.

Graeme emerged from relative obscurity, as an amateur cyclist, with no financial help, on a bike he designed and built himself to beat a record that had stood for some nine years and one that many people thought would never be broken.

When I met with him, I recalled the passage above I had just read in his book and asked him to put this into context for someone like me who was a non-athlete. He collected his thoughts before speaking.

'Imagine running from a burning building with your baby in your arms and you've GOT to get out that building.' He punched the table in front of him for emphasis. 'You can't breathe and your legs won't work but you HAVE to get out of that building. That's what it felt like.' He laughed. 'What was I thinking? This was extreme, not normal effort. It was awful.'

Yet he kept going. His motivation he recalls as being total fear and total belief. 'It sounds like arrogance,' he says, 'but it was a belief based on something I hadn't done yet. I told myself I can break that world record. I will do this.' At the point of committing to the action he knew he wasn't good enough, but he knew he could build towards it. 'The record holder has two arms and two legs like me,' he smiles, 'so by a basic limb count we have the same qualifications. But I'll suffer more pain than he did and spend more effort than he did.'

When he announced his plan to those closest to him, the response as he remembers wasn't universally welcomed. 'But as far as I was concerned, I had broken that record. I just had to physically do it. It wasn't like I was thinking I'm just going to crack out and try. The word 'try' implies failure. I was like, as far as I'm concerned, I'm going to break that record. It's mine.'

To understand the mindset required to expend such epic effort I wanted to go back to his childhood and any influences he might have had growing up.

'I didn't have any heroes growing up,' he shrugged, 'I lived in a forest; climbing trees to hide.'

Graeme's battle with depression, his diagnosis of bipolar disorder and his 'coming out' as gay have been well documented in the press in recent times, but less well known is the terrible bullying he and his brother suffered on an almost daily basis as children.

Home for the boys was a small Ayrshire town and as children of the local policeman and newcomers to the town they became targets. He remembers that barely a week went by without the teachers strapping him for fighting. He had done everything he could to avoid the fights, but was deemed to be the common denominator and therefore guilty as charged.

The physical attacks on him were a regular occurrence but apart from the worst incidents he feels that the violence didn't leave an emotional impression. It was the less overt actions of his peers and even his teachers, the social exclusion they visited upon him that had the biggest impact.

As a seven year old boy he remembers the feeling that he could not live and be a part of the world because it held too much pain for him. He asserts that his time in school built damaging core beliefs: that he was inherently unlikeable, that he was apart and fundamentally different from everyone else. As a means of protection, his sub-conscious mind forced him to form the mindset of an observer. Anything that hurt the shell of the little boy, couldn't reach him because he was only a witness. A habit that grew into an acute feeling of isolation and a visceral fear of social situations.

Strangely, the kicks and punches in the playground were almost bearable by comparison and in his book he describes the fear, beauty and adrenalin rush of violence. But in one physically harmful incident he recalls himself and his brother being taken at knifepoint, aged around nine and ten, to a derelict house by three older boys. There, the boys urinated on his brother and forced them to touch each other's genitals.

This incident was reported to the police and taken to court, but Graeme was too young to give evidence and his brother was so traumatised he fainted in the witness stand.

Cycling became a way to escape. Quite literally. When walking through the town felt like he was running the gauntlet;

being on a cycle meant a fast way past the bullies and a freedom of movement that gave the small boy a glimmer of something other than pain.

As teenagers, Graeme and his brother, Gordon, started to explore the surrounding area on their bikes, sometimes travelling as much as sixty miles in a day. Not 'real' cyclists yet, just two boys on bikes. On his biking adventures, Graeme took to riding through forests and along dirt trails and once in the safety of a wood, he would climb a tree, spending hours deep in the foliage, safe from harm.

At the age of fourteen a classmate suggested to Graeme that he should go along to a cycling club in Kilmarnock. With a strong sense of trepidation he did so, but apart from the initial silence and what he describes as like walking into a bar in a Western movie, he was welcomed with a 'come away in' by one of the club organisers. What followed surely laid the foundation of his future cycling success. He passed the early 'tests' proving that although he was green, he had a strong work ethic and along with a couple of other young cyclists he was soon racking up incredible distances.

His first time-trial, 10 miles on an open road at the age of 16 was hardly an auspicious start as he mis-judged the end of the race and came in second to last. But undeterred, his need to cycle continued. He continued to build up his experience, entering as many races as he could and going away for days at a time on huge journeys.

He began to perform well in races and this provided motivation for him to continue.

Serious lack of funds however meant that Graeme soon

experienced the proof in the saying that necessity is the mother of invention. He was able to pick up parts discarded by other cyclists and re-use them. This brought about a familiarity with the mechanics of the machine that was to reap spectacular benefits in the future.

He was seen as a maverick even in the early part of his career and gained experience and titles on a regular basis. He won Scotland's first mountain biking title, several TT races, was Scotland's first ever sub-50 minute cyclist and became the British mile record holder. One cyclist who appeared on his radar time and time again, was to become one of his greatest rivals: Chris Boardman.

Problems with his mental health continued to affect him. He explained his ongoing love/hate relationship with the sport. 'One day I'd be happy riding, then the next I'd be feeling that I hated it, that there was too much pressure. Then I'd never want to get on a bike again.'

With words that were to come back to me just days later with the news of the footballer, Gary Speed's death, he continued. 'There's a higher incidence of depression among elite sport people than the general population,' he says. 'We have a weird level of contentment. Think about it, if you have to win every race then there's something not right about you. It's not a healthy obsession, not the sign of a balanced, self-fulfilled person, happy in their own skin.'

The desire to earn a living was also beginning to play a part; there were a couple of business ventures that didn't come off and a short stint working on a mushroom farm. In one of these business ventures, he and the co-owner of his business miscalculated their cash flow and initiated a false insurance claim. This was uncovered and the boys were charged, tried and given a criminal record.

The events of those difficult days are summarised in just a few words, but this affected Graeme so badly it resulted in his first suicide attempt. Fortunately, his father came home from work early that day and his intervention saved Graeme's life.

Then came an even more pressing need to earn a living when Graeme married and became a father and his ongoing love/ hate relationship with the sport continued to the extent that by 1992 he was convinced he would never ride again. His mood and his form took a dip until a cyclist by the name of Chris Boardman won a gold medal at the Barcelona Olympics.

Strangely, the fact that his main competitor proved his worth against the best in the world, gave Graeme perspective. He was able to see how good he really was. But while Chris had a team of experts around him and quality funding, Graeme had little but his own determination.

He said, 'After Chris won the Olympic gold it made me realise we were both cycling at a very high level because we rode against each other many times and sometimes I would beat him.'

At the time, Chris Boardman was the golden boy of the sport with a team of sports scientists, psychologists and bike builders. Graeme was largely on his own and his finances were so perilous he couldn't afford to have a phone in the house (this is pre-mobile phone days) and he used to walk to the local phone box at the end of his street if he needed to phone someone.

His parents used to bring food to his house: what they all jokingly referred to as 'Red Cross Parcels' and he recalls a time when only the fact that he found 19p down the back of his sofa meant that he could eat that night. It was enough to buy a cheap loaf of bread at the local supermarket. 'We live in a material society so of course money is important, and you don't know how important it is until you run out and you've none left. That 19p down the sofa,' he shrugs. 'I was starving. We literally had nothing to eat. When your back is against the wall and you feel the cold weight of concrete . . . 'have to' is a great motivator.'

Of course, he had mixed feelings about the charity of his parents and his parlous financial situation. On the one hand it made him feel that he was a failure both as a father and a husband, but on the other, it allowed him to focus on his training – at this point he had re-engaged with the sport and his desire to beat the hour record was all-consuming.

His mental health was fluctuating; he was fighting against an inferiority complex, self-hatred and an utter lack of confidence. So how, I wondered did he manage to get on the bike and race in front of people? How does he tie up the two sides of his personality: the competitor and the part of his psyche that was still effectively hiding up a tree?

'Escapism,' he answered. 'When you are cycling well, legs and heart pumping, you're an albatross flying, soaring. You're in total control, you're the best you can be, and you're winning that race.' He pauses and considers his next words. 'In truth, the hour record for me was not about glory or money, but about justifying my next breath.'

Of course, the bike that Graeme built to beat the record became almost as famous as he did. He has said since that he regrets mentioning the provenance of some of his materials as journalists tended to focus on the quirky side of it. But for anyone who takes the time to understand his actions, they can see that it was ingenuity and inspiration that allowed him to innovate in a sport that had seen very little change in over one hundred years.

Being intimately familiar with the workings of a cycle he was able to take his unique approach and formulate something that would make more effective use of the scientific factors involved, both in terms of the machine itself and how it related to the human being powering it along. Instead of traditional dropped handlebars it had straight bars like those of a mountain bike. He placed them closer to the saddle than usual and rode with the bars under his chest, his elbows bent and tucked into his sides like a downhill-skier.

Studying a washing machine spin at 1,200rpm he realised that the ball-bearings were of a higher quality than the ones normally used in cycles, so he dismantled the machine and fitted them to his bike.

'Old Faithful' as Graeme named it, has a narrow bottom bracket, around which the cranks revolve, to bring his legs closer together, as he considered this to be a more natural position. He thought a tread of 'one banana' would be ideal. The bike had no top tube, so that his knees did not hit the frame. The chainstays are not horizontal so that the cranks can pass with a narrow bottom bracket. The fork had only one blade, shaped to be as narrow as was possible.

And this is where the genius of Graeme Obree lies. He visualised every element of the bike – 3D mental imagery if you like – over a three week period before he even considered getting his tools out. 'That was instinctive for me. I always had the ability to imagine things like that,' he laughs at a memory. 'Playing with plasticine when I was 14 till mum threw it away. I was always making things. I lived in my own wee world of escapism. Life wasn't good and I developed abilities that might not have happened.' A shrug of acceptance.

Thinking about the design of the bike he continued. 'It's the concept of concept. What does it have to do? We're talking about functionality: purpose. With that in mind you can design anything. Then comes the simple question: how can I make it better? Next you consider limitations and possibilities and then it becomes a simple matter of logistics.'

Obree went for his hero, Moser's record, on 16 July 1993, in Hamar, Norway. He failed by nearly a kilometre. Eddie Merckx who beat an earlier record in 1972 with the advantage of altitude, it has to be noted, declared it the hardest thing he had ever done. He climbed off his bike and said 'never again'. Graeme Obree had booked the track for 24 hours and decided to come back the very next day.

He said of day two of his attempt, 'I was Butch Cassidy in terms of swagger. I didn't want any negativity. This was blitzkrieg. I'm going in there. Let me do it. I'm not going to be the timorous guy from Scotland. That's what the difference was. Purely mental state. The day before, I had been a mouse. Now I was a lion.'

Visualisation was also a technique Graeme used to help him in his quest for the physical action of cycling to win. Understanding that he was riding to what he termed, annihilation, and acknowledging the power of a winning mentality, he programmed his mind to expect success. He visualised being in 'the groove', imagining the pain, the numbness, the hyper-ventilation and his body telling him he couldn't go any further and how he would carry on beyond this point. He carried this process on through the night, seeing himself at the exact rate and pace of pedalling. He recalls, 'the fear of failure was more powerful that the allure of victory.'

When the hour signal sounded on the second day of his attempt, Graeme Obree had established a new record of 51.596 kilometres, overcoming Moser's record by 445 metres. Cycling commentators of the time were astounded by this man, an amateur who had come from nowhere and achieved incredible things. Chris Boardman, his great rival of the time said in a documentary made following this event, 'Graeme doesn't know what he's capable of.'

The press tried to make much of the rivalry between the two men, but from footage made at the time it is clear to see that they held a deep respect for each other. Chris Boardman was nicknamed 'the appliance of science', while Graeme was working on his own, armed with a formidable imagination and an intuitiveness that is rarely seen in the world of sport.

After little activity on this event for decades, what happened next was an almost unseemly clatter of attempts to beat the same record. First, Chris Boardman beat the record just a matter of weeks later and then Francesco Moser, whose record Obree had beaten, adopted Graeme's riding position, with the addition of a chest pad. He recorded a veterans' record of 51.84 kilometres, and again he did it in the altitude of Mexico City as he had for his earlier record, whereas Obree and Boardman had both ridden at close to sea level.

Graeme retook the record on 19 April 1994, using the Bordeaux track that Boardman had used. He rode 52.713 kilometres, a distance which was beaten a few months later on 2 September 1994 by the Spanish Tour de France winner, Miguel Indurain.

The world governing body, the Union Cycliste Internationale grew concerned that the innovations being brought into cycling by Obree were making a disproportionate progression on their records. They decided that they should take action and among other measures, they banned his elbow-tucked riding position. This 'rule' was not relayed to Obree until an hour before he began the 1994 world championship pursuit in Italy. He was disqualified when he refused to obey the new rules.

Undeterred, he set his formidable mind on a solution and the now equally famous 'Superman' style, with arms fully extended in front was born, and he won the individual pursuit at the world championships with this and 'Old Faithful' in 1995. Petty officialdom won out and that position was also eventually banned, but not before a host of other riders adopted it.

Graeme lists his victory in the pursuit at the World Championships in Colombia in 1995 as the one that brought him the greatest pleasure in his career, not simply for winning the rainbow jersey but as a settling of scores with the president of the UCI, cycling's governing body, Hein Verbruggen, who most observers felt unfairly disqualified him in the previous year's competition with a rule change passed the night before Obree was due to ride. Verbruggen was present at the track in Bogota.

Despite his ongoing success, Graeme's state of mind was not entirely positive. While training for the Atlanta Olympics in

1996 he noted an old feeling of detachment creeping up on him. 'It wasn't just cycling,' he said. 'Everything was affected. My depression and sense of isolation made everything seem so pointless.' Out on a training runs he could only push his legs to a touring pace and he began to think again about suicide. He even took a detour into a wooded area on foot with the hope of finding the toxic *foxglove digitalis*.

'I wanted to be immersed in alcohol. I would have taken anything; lighter fuel, glue, hash, cocaine . . . anything to add a spark of colour.'

The twisted logic that his mind presented to him at this point was that despite knowing his wife and sons would be deeply affected by his death, living with such a terrible person as he was would be even worse and that he should do what was best for everyone. Of course, this state of mind caused great difficulty on the track and he performed abysmally by his own standards. A small consolation was that most of the gold-medal winning riders on the Olympic podium had adopted his 'Superman' style of cycling.

He was now firmly in the 'hate' swing of his relationship with the sport and elected to retire, which brought about fresh pressures on his mental health. He had previously allowed himself a value based on what he could achieve in cycling. Now that he was retired, the absence of this left him feeling almost naked and emotionally vulnerable.

A late night cycle run to the stables where his wife kept a horse ended in an attempt at hanging himself. He was saved by a young girl visiting her own horse and ironically, his unusually large lung capacity.

As he considers his career, more than the frustration of having his riding position banned not once but twice, Obree regrets that he never followed Chris Boardman into the professional peloton and a missed chance to ride the Tour de France prologue. He was hired by French team, Le Groupement in late 1994 but was fired after two days in mysterious circumstances, having not ridden one race for the team.

'I would have loved to have ridden the prologue and I think I would have had a good chance of winning it.' He pauses and adds, 'I now have no involvement in the sport. I think I'm seen as dangerous because I say what I think. I was a distraction from what was going on. I said to *L'Equipe* that more than 90 per cent of the riders were on drugs.'

Fellow professionals accused him of bringing the sport into disrepute. When he was invited to events he couldn't get changed in the changing rooms because he was worried he would be attacked by other cyclists. 'The animosity was that bad,' he recalls. 'I had huge resentment about it. My career was effectively blocked because I refused to take drugs.' But for his own peace of mind, Graeme has had to let it go. 'I now see that the riders were all victims of a system. And my belief is that the sport has now cleaned itself up. It had to.'

Now from a remove of years he is able to appreciate his achievements and to place them into perspective. 'It's not about success, it's about happiness. If you're happy doing very little, lying in bed reading the Sunday newspaper, that is success. For me money is not the route of happiness – how many billionaires are truly happy? Getting more and more materials? Ultimate, success is being at one with yourself.'

He contends that as a society we knew how to be happy thousands of years ago and argues that we've lost our way. 'Being in the moment, being content with what we have is where happiness lies. I realise I don't fit in with modern society. I don't have this or have that. I don't have a car. I don't have the aspiration to own a car. Or a garden for that matter.' He looks out of the window at the beach and points and smiles. 'I don't need a garden. I've got two beaches and the local council very kindly look after them for me.'

He continues. 'Much of our mental health issues come where people are not connected to the way they live in our modern society. They fill their lives with 'stuff', TVs, cars, gardens. The less you own the better. I have my wee flat and this is enough. I don't feel the weight of ownership.'

In the documentaries I watched and material I read before I met with Graeme, I noted how at the time of his achievements he was lauded in other countries, where he was a seen as a true sporting legend. How does he recall being received at home, I asked him.

'The Scottish mindset,' he smiles. 'It can be quite negative and positive. Two extremes at the same moment. When I broke the hour record, people were saying to me, but you just live round the corner. You can't do that. And they'd repeat – you just live round the corner. We're useless. You can't go breaking world records.' He paused. 'They were incredulous that someone from their environment could be so successful.'

'But for some,' he continued. '. . . the negativity can be a springboard to push themselves forward. I think the younger generation are better than we were. I had no positive influence of any kind. I was so miserable; I was wishing the Russians would press the ****ing red button and blow everyone up. That the bombs could drop any minute was for me a ray of hope. So maybe I'm not the best example,' he smiles without self-consciousness. 'But I do see the younger generation as seeing that they have more possibilities.'

'I am worried that they want to be famous for the sake of being famous. That's not good. What does that even mean? Famous. Wouldn't recommend it,' he laughs. 'The important thing I've found is the people around me. Family, friends, other cyclists, my peer group. They respect what I achieved. This is what matters, really.'

Having experienced the extremes of mental health and great sporting success, Graeme now feels that he is in a position to contribute. He has learned some valuable lessons and if he can use them for the benefit of others that makes him a happy man.

Talking about lessons, I say, what advice would you give now to your younger self.

Without hesitation and wearing a large smile he answers, 'Get a real job. We're not going to get blown up. So do your homework and get a job. I would advise my younger self to give that guy a good kicking. He deserved it.' He laughs and slaps the table. 'Getting into trouble would have been worth it.'

'Truth is if I could go back, which of course you can't, I wouldn't change a thing. Great things come from adversity. I'm going through to Edinburgh later on to speak to a group of young people and I'm going to tell them that from my perspective things are fine.'

'I feel that if I hadn't gone through all of that stuff, I wouldn't be in a position that I am now to give a positive message to young people. I am fortunate, I can pass on to people the truth that out of negativity can come positivity.'

'Even when I was World Champion I would go to a party, or a wedding and hide behind my pint. But now? We're only on this planet once, well, that we know of. At a recent wedding I was the first up on the dance floor drinking my council juice (water) and orange. It's like I have a responsibility to be a positive influence.'

I remark that this is a huge difference in outlook and ask what has made the difference between then and now?

'After I tried to kill myself, my therapist told me I had the emotional age of a 13 year old, and I was 30.' He paused. 'Because I was locked in, closed. I didn't know who I was, because I wasn't there. I was hiding.'

Therapy has been effective for Graeme, but a pivotal point was allowing himself to recognise the fact he had broken a world record. 'The result of that went against every inner belief I didn't recognise, or couldn't articulate. People would say to me, you're amazing, I would say, no I'm not, I'm a piece of shit.'

Initially, breaking the world record went against everything he believed about himself. He now had incontrovertible proof. He had achieved something of greatness. 'I had to challenge my beliefs. That was the point. My earlier strong belief was that I wasn't destined to be successful. I was useless, remember. The feedback from that success, with people telling me I had done well was the point when I started to improve. But I had to get a lot worse before I got better.'

'I couldn't handle a compliment. "It was nothing – don't mention it," I would say and just brush it off, not allowing myself to even hear it. Now I take any compliment that's going,' he mimes accepting a compliment with a wave of his hand, 'Oh, thanks very much.' And laughs.

Next for Graeme is the promotion of a training manual he has published, The Obree Way, and to carry on with charity work. He's also writing a survivor's guide to depression with his ex-wife.

Current cycling success stories queue up to say how he was their childhood hero. His great cycling moments happened well over a decade ago and yet he is still in demand as a motivational speaker and a positive example to people wherever he goes. Sir Chris Hoy, arguably Britain's greatest ever Olympian quotes Graeme as his hero and inspiration. He said of him, '. . . in spite of his demons and without huge financial backing, he has managed to change the face of his sport and bring joy to countless fans around the globe.'

The word 'hero' itself comes from the Greek and literally meant someone who was semi-divine and born from one mortal and one divine parent. Eventually Greek society went on to view sporting champions as 'born of the Gods'. But today experts say heroes not only sell newspapers and magazines, they also perform a vital psychological function in helping us cope and come together as a nation and a people.

Against a background where many of us seek our heroes through the medium of television, gossip magazines and find those individuals who have a skill merely for being noticed, Graeme Obree is a reminder that a celebration of talent, courage and character is the more meaningful pursuit.

Mentoring with Graeme

As you read through the events of Graeme's life and how he reacted to them, there are a number of qualities that emerge. Courage is one of them. Courage on many levels. Courage of his convictions, courage to face any number of demons. And one of the most endearing aspects of the man when you meet him is his complete lack of awareness of this fact. I just did it, he says.

He felt he was outside of society and yet he strove to achieve things that would bring great delight to many people who were within that very community. He was one man. He made a huge difference to lots of us.

One thing I am hearing more and more recently as I talk to friends and discuss the world we find ourselves living in is, 'But what can you do?'

They are of course talking about the ongoing economic situation as reported in the media and the collective inability of our elected leaders to do anything about it. As I write this, the state of play has become chronic and sees no sign of abating.

But what can you do?

Two stories spring to mind to evidence the extremes of what you as an individual might do.

The first relates to a friend of mine who visited a client in her capacity as financial adviser. This gentleman lived in a modest, Glasgow tenement flat. He had a very good income and a sizeable portfolio of assets; in the region of £300,000, much of which was locked in to safer types of investments. He wasn't earning much in the way of capital growth, but he was happy with this as his capital sum was constant. Inflation was a worry, but what could you do? So far, so understandable, yes?

His flat had five bedrooms. He rented them all out to students. His own bedroom was like an antique furniture store with heavy wooden chairs, tables, wardrobes, sideboards and beds all pushed against the wall. My friend felt she was in a store-room rather than the man's living quarters. The only thing that was given importance in the room was his giant TV. My friend visited this man three times. The TV was never off and it was always locked on to a 'news' channel.

This man talked about a wee house he'd dreamed about owning in a suburb of the city. It was a bungalow. The street was lined with trees. Everybody knew everybody. But the world was going to the dogs so why should he bother? As he said this his eyes never left the screen and the constant images of a world on the edge of eating itself. Death and disaster were his constant companions and my friend realised that this client of hers was frozen by fear. He had filled his mind with so much dark material that he simply couldn't see anything else.

His dream was permanently on hold in the vain hope that the news people might report on a brighter world. He was stuck in his bunker and storing up for better times.

What else could he do?

An alternative way of thinking when faced with a problem is

one espoused by Loren Eisley in her apocryphal story about the starfish. Her story goes like this. . .

One day a man was walking along the beach when he noticed a boy picking something up and gently throwing it into the ocean. Approaching the boy, he asked, 'What are you doing?'

The youth replied, 'Throwing starfish back into the ocean. The surf is up and the tide is going out. If I don't throw them back, they'll die.'

'Son,' the man said, 'don't you realise there are miles and miles of beach and hundreds of starfish? You can't make a difference!'

After listening politely, the boy bent down, picked up another starfish, and threw it back into the surf. Then, smiling at the man, he said, 'I made a difference for that one.'

Engage your creativity

'Creativity is just connecting things. When you ask creative people how they did something, they feel a little guilty because they didn't really do it, they just saw something. It seemed obvious to them after a while. That's because they were able to connect experiences they've had and synthesize new things.'   Steve Jobs

One of Graeme Obree's qualities, as Sir Chris Hoy puts it, is to see things differently. This has its seed in his creativity. I would contend that most of us see this word and think about the arts and artists who seem to be able to tap into that side of their psyche at will. Painters, poets and musicians lead a creative life. Theorists, artists, scientists, inventors, writers can be creative. Nobody else can be. And certainly not teachers, shopkeepers or athletes.

Let me challenge that way of thinking. A neighbour's mother. She was uneducated, she struggled financially, she was at home with the kids round the clock. She did none of the actions that we acknowledge as being creative and yet she regularly cooked up a feast, her home was always clean and, even to my young mind arranged with art. She was great fun and arranged inventive play for her kids. As I look back, with the benefit of maturity, she was novel, ingenious, unexpected and inventive. And we kids were lucky to have her around.

I would say she was a creative, wouldn't you?

Are you in touch with your creative side? It could have huge benefits to the quality of your life. Studies have demonstrated that, compared to a control group, creative people enjoy the following benefits:

• They stay healthier for longer.

• They need fewer visits to their doctor.

• They use fewer medicines.

• They are more outgoing, more enthusiastic and their self-esteem is improved.

• Creative types are more socially active and therefore less lonely.

The reason for the above assertions is that people who engage with their creative faculties experience more sense of control. They are proactively involved in living and therefore less reactive. Imaginative people are more socially engaged. This is of particular help in retirement.

For every year that passes, it appears that we are withdrawing from our social groups; and conversing mainly in a virtual sense. However, art and imagination (and sports for that matter) draw people together and in a world of smaller families this lessens the isolation that can often happen when we leave the workplace.

Artistic activities are by their very nature engaging. When working in this area we enter a state of flow that brings to bear all of our mental faculties. Art and creativity means 'doing'. It requires movement, action, attention and focus. Simply put, it leads to a level of fulfilment that few alternative human activities can match.

Your Brain

Your brain is divided into two hemispheres, the left and right brains. The left side is what you bring to bear when using logic, sequential processes, details and analysing. The right side is where your creative abilities reside.

Ideally, you would be using both halves equally well, yet most people have a dominant or preferred side. If your dominant side is the left, you are missing out, but fear not my friend, brain association techniques and exercises will help develop your right brain skills and bring all that lovely stuff that I mentioned earlier into your life

The good news is that even if you don't see yourself as being particularly creative, training can increase your creativity by improving communication between the two sides of your brain.

'There is no doubt that creativity is the most important human resource of all.' Edward de Bono

The Power of Acceptance

'Some people confuse acceptance with apathy, but there's all the difference in the world. Apathy fails to distinguish between what can and what cannot be helped; acceptance makes that distinction. Apathy paralyses the will-to-action; acceptance frees it by relieving it of impossible burdens.' Arthur Gordon

It takes courage to see things as they are and to accept them. Particularly when they are at odds with our view of the world, or how society dictates we should be and behave. It is well known by now that Graeme Obree has 'come out' as gay and his acceptance of this situation has undoubtedly been a factor in his more positive state. When you learn acceptance as a state of mind you accept yourself, people, circumstances and events as they are, knowing that they are exactly as they are meant to be.

Acceptance of this 'fact' for Graeme meant he could move on, act in congruence with his real self, instead of the person he believed others thought he should be. The longer you spend in his company, the more you come to see that he is a man who very much acts in accordance with his convictions, often to his cost. Is it little wonder then that such incongruence could have had such a damaging effect on his psyche?

During our interview he remarked how depression can be common among athletes and not talked about. Clearly, another taboo among sportsmen and women is that of sexuality and a perception of how the gender you prefer to enjoy romantic love with should be the opposite. Anything outside of that causes great mental strain and ill-health.

Accept the moment as it is allows you to see it for what it is.

Then transform it to something better in the future. So this means you don't accept circumstances as permanent. Instead, accept them in the moment, and use the lessons from them to create a better future.

Every obstacle allows you the opportunity for something greater. As Graeme said, adversity is the source of many great things, but if you fight against even the presence of the obstacle, you stay stuck in the negative situation. When you accept it and posit a better outcome for the future, you move one step closer to a healthier situation.

Only when we treat something with respect and accept it rather than rejecting it can we bring about necessary change. Rejecting something that is real in your life brings about more caution and conflict, therefore creating more of what we don't want or like.

Ever get caught up in a form of emotional groundhog day? Keep making the same mistakes with life partners, your children, your work or other areas of your life?

Acceptance works to recognise the issue and puts you in the position to do something that will bring about a necessary change.

Acceptance means dropping the struggle with painful feelings, memories, urges and emotions, giving them breathing space and allowing that they exist. This in turn means we don't become overwhelmed by them. Psychologists say that what we resist, persists.

The mind has a way of reminding you of what you are hiding from and will do so until you allow acceptance. In this process you need to watch out for blind spots, or approaches that have 'worked in the past' even when they have been discredited. Then you might also have a bias, which disposes you to look only for evidence that support our initial beliefs.

Mindfulness is a practice that is becoming more and more useful in the field of therapy. This process teaches us that we are not our thoughts; that we can detach from our thinking, from our harmful self-image and painful memories. This is a term called cognitive defusion. We let our thoughts come and go as if they were traffic passing our front window. We step back and watch our thinking instead of getting caught up in it. We hold our thoughts lightly instead of clutching on to them as if they are the very definition of who we are.

This is a continuous process, so if you decide to practise it, be forgiving, compassionate, and accepting of yourself and your mistakes. As long as you are making an honest effort, you are making inroads.

Consider the process of researching a project for work or a hobby. As you accumulate your information, you judge its provenance. You ensure you have a reliable source. You find its roots, its history and you will probably seek the other side of the story in the interests of balance.

How often do we take time to do that against the tyranny of our own thoughts? Challenge your mind when it gets trapped in a confirmation bias, mental set, or belief perseverance. These are all placing limits to your existence.

Tom Hunter

Sir Tom Hunter

Just like each of the entrepreneurs featured in this book, Sir Tom Hunter's wealth is self-made. For the young Tom there was no cutlery made of precious metal, but where he was blessed was being born into a family where an entrepreneurial spirit was fostered and encouraged.

He counts himself extremely fortunate with his family. He says, 'I was brought up at the kitchen table by a third generation retailer, my dad, so from a very young age entrepreneurialism was, to a degree, in my blood. . . I think I started my first business at the age of 7 running bicycle repairs and I don't think I'll ever stop.'

Home was New Cumnock in Ayrshire, which at first, or even subsequent glances is not the kind of place you would expect to produce one of the wealthiest men in the country. A once thriving community, it was hit particularly hard by the demise of the coal industry.

Even as a youngster he preferred to learn through doing and once he reached school leaving age he applied for a job in a local factory. However, when his family got wind of this they contacted his prospective employer to say that 'our Tom' would not be working for them as he was going to be heading off to university. Dutifully, he did as his family expected and he secured a degree in – somewhat predictably – business from Strathclyde

University. He was initially without work and accepted a placement from Glasgow University for work experience in a local newspaper, the *West End Times*.

Free newspapers were rising in popularity and Tom analysed the *Times* – the column inches, the revenue, the advertising – and comparing it with others in the market at the time, he grew convinced they should turn it into a freebie. This was 1983. He was 22. The owner of the paper, Sir Hugh Fraser was apoplectic and Tom almost got thrown off his course.

It was of course, a sign of things to come from this singularly minded young man. Another opportunity was just around the corner, and this was one that would he would grab with both hands.

His father's business struggled through the miners' strike and he was forced to sell up. An opportunity arose through a fellow businessman and he invested in a market stall in Irvine. Observing events in the market, Tom was quick to realise that training shoes were moving quickly and on leaving university he borrowed £5,000 from his father and £5,000 from the Royal Bank of Scotland.

And the legend was born.

With this money, he bought himself a van, loaded it with boxes of trainers and with the help of his mates sold them in markets the length and breadth of the country.

The profit from this enabled him to take up a concession in the corner of a large clothing shop in Paisley. For a percentage of his profits he was given the space to sell his goods and the next step in his progression was complete.

It wasn't always plain sailing and early on in this venture Tom was faced with an immediate challenge. He recalls, 'Probably one of my worst experiences was loading up the trainers into my van – my entire stock more or less – for a new store opening the following day. I parked up at the B&B, had four hours sleep and then discovered the entire stock had been stolen. Did I think about giving up? I wouldn't give anyone that satisfaction. . .'

He opened his first shop in 1989 selling sports gear and Sports Division was born. Expansion was an immediate and pervasive need. He saw that for his business to succeed long term, he couldn't stand still. He set himself annual targets. He would decide at the start of each year how many new shops he was going to open and in this style he built his business up to be the largest purveyor of sportswear in the country.

Part of this expansion was the purchase of Olympus Sports in 1995, an expansion that wasn't without its challenge. The bank that had been so supportive in his early days refused to fund the purchase. Undeterred, he sought out other methods of funding. He also enlisted the help of a close friend, Sir Philip Green (billionaire owner of Top Shop) for advice.

Never one to stand still, Tom was faced with a game-changing offer in 1998. The smaller sports retailer, JJB Sport offered to buy Sports Division for £290 million. Until this moment, Tom was a prominent success story, responsible for providing 500 men and women in Ayrshire with employment. If he sold a lot of people would lose their jobs.

For the first time he received severe criticism. Employees were interviewed by local newspapers and the MP for the region,

Des Browne was on record saying that he was . . . 'profoundly disappointed the people of Ayrshire have lost out because of the actions of one man.'

It was a time of mixed emotions. The press had usually been kind to him and here he was being roundly criticised. And then there was the opportunity to acquire huge wealth with the few strokes of a pen to paper.

His share of the sale of Sports Division was £250 million.

As his wealth has continued to increase I wanted to know if there was ever moments of doubt or times when success hasn't automatically followed his effort?

'If I can answer that with an example of a bad idea I pursued; the net reason I got it so wrong was I let my heart rule my head . . . I love motorsport and decided to open up a karting venture. One of my all time heroes Jackie Stewart opened it to great fanfare but pretty soon it became obvious the market simply wasn't there at a price point that would sustain the business. So market, price, product and people are what I look at all in the round. . .'

With hindsight, philanthropy looked like an obvious next step in Tom's career, but it wasn't one that happened automatically. Great wealth brought with it a lot of begging letters. In the two years following the Sports Division takeover, he went through a period of anxiety. Previous to this point, a number of years had passed where his company had been a huge part of his life. He now found himself adrift without purpose. Not only did he have no idea what to do with his money – you can, he discovered, only drive one car at a time – he was deluged with heart-breaking letters, with huge numbers of people wanting their cut of his cash. Tom, with the help of his wife Marion would read the letters and send off cheques and never hear from the recipients whether or not the money made a difference to their lives. And still the letters arrived in a steady flow.

His money men were at this point advising Tom on how to avoid paying the tax man great chunks of his money. The main thrust of this was that Tom and Marion should move to a tax haven, like Monaco. However, as a couple they were committed to their local area and keen that their children should grow up grounded and surrounded by family and friends. The next suggestion from the accountants was that they set up a charitable foundation.

They seized upon it. They were already giving away slices of cash. Why not do it in a more measured way? He came across *The Gospel of Wealth* by Andrew Carnegie and found a kindred spirit in the writings of this fascinating individual. In particular, Tom famously agrees with Carnegie's sentiment about 'dying in disgrace' if you die a rich man. He says, 'Once my family are taken care of I've no desire to be the wealthiest man in the graveyard. Investing money for the common good gives me an even bigger buzz than making the money, so why on earth would I leave money to someone else to have that fun?'

Tom says that his best lessons are the ones he learned for himself: by doing, but when stuck he is not too big to ignore those in the world who can help. He talked about picking wise counsel and always hiring people with greater knowledge than he in their particular specialism.

Entirely in keeping with this character, when determining what to do with his millions he sought advice from the best in the business. He approached the head of the Carnegie Foundation, Vartan Gregorian looking for help as to the most effective approach to giving away his millions.

The main lesson Tom Hunter retains from that meeting with Gregorian is that, if you are serious about making a difference with your wealth, you should give the begging letters a miss. He had to choose what he wanted to spend his money on, and then devise a methodology to ensure its efficacy.

The Hunter Foundation has piloted schemes that are designed to augment the learning experience of his children's generation. There has been a push to get those teens not in education, employment or training back into education. He has opened a centre for entrepreneurship at his alma mater and he has moved capital into developing six of the worst secondary schools in Scotland.

It is notable that education has become a mainstay in Tom's drive to be a force for change. He describes himself as being 'just ok' at school and is on record as saying that his own education was not much of a help to the life he went on to forge for himself.

Nonetheless, in numerous interviews he has given over the years, he is passionate about the difference that a strong grounding in education can give a young person.

A new element in this is his decision to get back into the classroom at Strathclyde University as a lecturer. During his own education he frequently found himself questioning the credentials of the person passing on the lesson. Surely a thought process that no-one in the room will entertain while this serial entrepreneur is at the lectern. Typically, for this man who insists on learning from the best, before he put himself through the stresses of a lecture hall, he has undergone a teaching qualification course at the University of California's prestigious Berkeley campus.

He argues, without really needing to, that he has the necessary knowledge of his subject, but he is determined that he should be in the best place to pass that knowledge on to his students.

While he is determined to give hands-on practical help to his own mission, his huge pockets will continue to fund good causes. Cleverly, when contributing to the greater good, Hunter's money forms only part of the equation. When the Hunter Foundation gives money, it is 'an investment' rather than an out-and-out donation. This Tom describes as 'catalytic funding', meaning, rather than being the sole contributor to a worthy cause the Foundation works in tactical partnerships with fellow funders, governments and agencies and like-minded individuals, with the strong belief that partnerships are an important force for change.

This is apparent both in his work with Scotland's youth alongside the Scottish Government and in his philantrophic efforts with former US president, Bill Clinton and his Global initiative. Their efforts are concentrated for the meantime in Rwanda and Malawi, with the view that the change they encourage can then be spread through the continent with care and precision.

In an interview with the BBC's Andrew Marr, Tom said, '. . . what struck us was that there's fantastic work happening in different spheres, but no one had really joined it up together.

So we're going to take a kind of holistic and integrated approach of agriculture, of healthcare, of education, of economic self-sustainability and try to prove the model into different communities, and then hopefully the governments of these countries will then take it on.' The Hunter Foundation kicked this venture off with £100 million.

The subject of our discussion moved on to that of 'success' What did this man who has succeeded beyond most of our wildest dreams view as the definition of the word?

'Success can be measured in so many different ways,' he says, 'and we often confuse success with wealth and that's not right. You can be a successful nurse, teacher or civil servant.' In similar vein, he often argues that an entrepreneurial mindset is not only important in our business people, but in all of us. Anyone doing any job, if they have that kind of attitude can achieve much, much more in their career.

Since banking his huge cheque at the end of Sports Division, Sir Tom has continued to do what he does best, make money. It is reported that through his private equity vehicle, West Coast Capital, he has converted his original stake of £250 million into smidgeon over £1 billion – although the recent economic downturn may have temporarily diluted this. Just like his hero, Andrew Carnegie, making money for his foundation in order to give it all away, has become his *raison d'être*.

Mentoring with Sir Tom Hunter

Contribution

'There are certain things that are fundamental to human fulfilment. The essence of these needs is captured in the phrase "to live, to love, to learn, to leave a legacy". The need to live is our physical need for such things as food, clothing, shelter, economical well-being, health. The need to love is our social need to relate to other people, to belong, to love and to be loved. The need to learn is our mental need to develop and to grow. And the need to leave a legacy is our spiritual need to have a sense of meaning, purpose, personal congruence, and contribution.'

Stephen R. Covey

Sir Tom Hunter freely admits that his own sense of self is enhanced by his good deeds. It brings a significant feel-good factor into his life.

One of the human needs as evidenced by Tom is a need to go beyond ourselves and to serve the greater good. The moments when we can do so are when we experience joy and fulfilment. Unselfish contribution provides an experience of pure joy and love that many of us wish to have in our lives.

Are you like me when you say to yourself: one of these days I'll get round to that? How good would it feel to do this, that or the next thing? But then you shift your position on the sofa and go back to watching brain poison on the telly?

When the UK government first pushed their Big Society plan on us, I was immediately cynical. Wrong, or right, the impression I formed was that the government was desperate to save money and were pushing aside responsibility for certain civil services and expecting big-hearted Brits to take up the slack.

These plans are supported by a Big Society Network, which says 'it exists to generate, develop and showcase new ideas to help people to come together in their neighbourhoods to do good things.'

Labour leader, Ed Milliband said that the Conservatives were 'cynically attempting to dignify its cuts agenda, by dressing up the withdrawal of support with the language of reinvigorating civic society'.

On the other hand, Ben Brogan in the *Telegraph* stated: 'We demand vision from our would-be leaders, and here is one who offers a big one, of a society rebuilt from the ground up.'

If I had a report card and 'contribution' was there to be scored, mine would say 'D minus: could do better', so I'm not in a position to lecture anyone. But whatever your view on this initiative is, what can't be denied is that there is always room for people to take a more active part in their community.

A quick trawl through the Volunteer Scotland website http://www.volunteerscotland.org.uk/ shows that there are a huge variety of opportunities to give something back. Fancy working a till/sorting stock for a charity shop? Driving a bus for stroke victims? Keeping books for a couple counselling charity? Or even occasional work as a ward volunteer in a local hospital?

If you have a shareable skill or excess energy or some free time, why not give it a go? If Tom Hunter is any guide to how this will impact on your life, the effect will be both life-changing and life-enhancing.

Taking that first step

Shawn Achor, the author of The Happiness Advantage says 'common sense is not common action.' He goes on to say that 'without action, knowledge is wasted'.

Individuals like Sir Tom Hunter became hard-wired to take action. Through long habit he instantly saw the worth in an opportunity and took the necessary steps to carry it through. How many of us can put our hands up to such a mindset?

I've lost track of the conversations I've had with friends and colleagues over the years who have said, 'I had this great idea for blah, but someone else out there is bound to have thought of it first.'

Do you recognise yourself in this scenario?

A friend told me about something she experienced before she met me. A talented children's writer, she was on a transatlantic flight on her way to holiday in New York. The passenger beside her was reading from a fist of paper that she could see was a manuscript. She engaged him in conversation, managed to bring the chat around to books and he admitted that he was the head of children's publishing at XY Publishing in New York and he was catching up on some reading while he had the time.

My friend was delighted to report that she wrote for children and she went on to detail her UK successes, which were mainly shorter works and that she was on the second draft of a full-length novel. She pitched the novel to him there and then and he told her that he liked the sound of her work.

As they got off the plane, Man from XY Publishing gave her his business card and asked her to submit the novel when she returned to Scotland after her holiday.

Unfortunately, for most of the two weeks that my friend was in the States she spent the entire time telling herself that she wasn't what he was looking for. Her book wasn't good enough, she knew it, everybody knew it and there was no point in wasting postage just to be told the same thing by Mr XY. When she returned home she managed to 'lose' the business card and didn't send anything off.

Wasted opportunity? Absolutely. She paid way too much attention to the negative voices in her head and passed on the opportunity that writers' dreams are made of.

If you have read any other inspirational books before this one I would be surprised if you hadn't read the following quote.

> 'Until one is committed, there is hesitancy, the chance to draw back. Concerning all acts of initiative (and creation), there is one elementary truth, the ignorance of which kills countless ideas and splendid plans: that the moment one definitely commits oneself, then Providence moves too. All sorts of things occur to help one that would never otherwise have occurred. A whole stream of events issues from the decision, raising in one's favour all manner of unforeseen

incidents and meetings and material assistance, which no man could have dreamed would have come his way. Whatever you can do, or dream you can do, begin it. Boldness has genius, power, and magic in it. Begin it now.'

(This quote has been credited to the German philosopher, Johan Wolfgang von Goethe. However, the Goethe Society of North America researched the source of this for two years to discover it was actually written by a Scottish mountaineer, W. H. Murray in his 1951 book *The Scottish Himalayan Expedition*. Murray's book is sadly out of print.)

Provenance of the words aside, there is a truth in them that is staggering. I can't tell you the number of times people have come into my life at just the right moment, just after I have committed to a positive action.

The cynical among you might interject with the word coincidence.

Carl Gustav Jung coined the term 'synchronicity' which is often used to describe the same experience. It was a principle that Jung felt gave conclusive evidence for his concepts of archetypes and the collective unconscious, in that it described a dynamic that underlies the whole of human experience including social, emotional, psychological, and spiritual elements.

He also believed that synchronicity served a similar role in someone's life to dreams with the purpose of moving a person's egocentric conscious thinking to a greater wholeness, or collective consciousness.

Whatever your view, it happens and all it takes is a decision to take that first step. Then when the opportunity arises, like Tom Hunter does, grab it with both hands.

Gratitude causes positive outcomes

Like my friend who neglected her own ambitions, many of us need to be tuned in to spot the possibilities that are out there.

Scientists believe that there is no such thing as luck. They say that what is happening here is that people expect good or bad things to happen and that expectation is what drives their focus. You see yourself as 'lucky', you will spot the good thing and vice versa.

Chance encounters, synchronicity, coincidence, whatever you want to call it, if you have a positive mindset you will see the opportunity and act.

If this was a TV advert about now would be where the patronising voice pops in and warns that the science bit is coming: listen carefully. So, anyway, here's the science. . .

Cognitive science is an interdisciplinary study that brings together biology, neuroscience, AI research, psychology, linguistics and philosophy. The aim here is to explain how the human brain, as an information processing system can produce truthful representations of your environment.

These clever peeps talk about 'predictive coding' which is the idea that as your mind processes all of the information assailing your various senses, your brain actively predicts what its sensory input will be, rather than just passively registering it.

Let me repeat that: actively predicts.

And what dictates the information you use to 'actively predict'? Your mindset and your focus. Consider for a moment what happens when you buy a new car. Let's say it's a yellow jeep. Suddenly, everywhere you look you see yellow jeeps. They've always been around in the same numbers, but now your focus has changed and your mind picks up on it. With alarming regularity. That's the last time I buy a yellow jeep.

Let's change your focus from looking at all those yellow jeeps to priming yourself to expect a favourable outcome. Doing so actually encodes your brain to recognise the signs when they arrive. Similarly, if you have gotten into the habit of lazy, negative thinking, you are going to pick up on the information that presents a less than favourable outcome.

If at present you are in the latter bracket, you need to train your brain to spot the good stuff. This is where I channel my inner Oprah. Make a daily list of the good things in your life. No, seriously. Every night before you go to sleep either make a mental list, or get a journal and write them down. Not only will this put you in a strong frame of mind to fall asleep quickly, it will have a marked effect on how your brain is wired. The more you do this, the better you will become and your brain will become more skilled at noticing. You will open your mind to ideas and opportunities that will help make you more productive, effective and successful.

Andrew Carnegie, man of achievement

Andrew Carnegie

I have had the good fortune to meet all of the people detailed in this book, Andrew Carnegie being the obvious exception. Given that the long deceased Mr Carnegie was the jumping off point for the book it seemed incumbent upon me to detail his life and achievements in these pages.

When writing and talking about such a person it is too easy to fall into the trap of quasi-deification. After all, that is what we have a wont to do when someone dies, isn't it? We talk about them in all their glory. They are no longer with us to remind us of their biggest fault of all: they are 'only human'. We don't have the skin and bone and teeth before us to demonstrate their frailties, or their ability to make mistakes.

Having said that, it is fair to say that by any standards, Andrew Carnegie was a remarkable man. Towards the end of his life, he was chased around by a media who had titled him the wealthiest man on the planet, but his origins were very modest indeed.

He was born in Dunfermline to a weaver, William Carnegie and his wife, Mag in 1835. His hometown was effectively a one industry town and arguably bang in the centre of the Industrial Revolution and therefore fell victim to all the whims of industrial and economic change. Will, being skilled in only the one area was ill-placed to adapt. It was then left to his mother, Mag to provide for the family from her meagre earnings.

Carnegie's Call

It is clear from Carnegie's writings that his mother was his heroine. She held the family together in times of extreme poverty, refusing to give in to circumstance. With someone as hugely successful as Andrew was, it is fascinating to look at those people, events and circumstances that might have influenced the behaviours that led to him amassing his huge wealth. And it is clear from his writings that his mother was foremost among these.

One could also be forgiven the impression that his hometown of Dunfermline also had power over his growing mind. In his autobiography he refers to a Dunfermline that was historically a seat of kings, where a ruined Abbey and the tomb of Robert the Bruce loom large. He goes on to say that 'the child privileged to develop amid such surroundings absorbs poetry and romance with the air he breathes, assimilates history and tradition as he gazes around.' Did the impressions given by such places set the young boy dreaming and give him a feeling of value; did it allow him to dream, despite his early reality?

When he was five or six the work and welfare of his extended family and other linen workers was at severe risk. The area was losing work due to automation and Scottish citizens were not eligible for British Poor Relief. Unrest was widespread and meetings were held all over the area to voice discontent. His uncles were happy to join in and argue with others about how a change was needed. Open air meetings were held where the London newspapers were read out and commentated on by the assembled crowds. It is a simple task to take this influence and draw a straight line to his fondness for debate as a young man in North America.

At the age of 10, while his father was struggling to put food on the table, his mother took up the mantle of breadwinner and Andrew was tasked with running errands, keeping accounts and helping behind the counter of his mother's fledgling business. At this young age, people remember him as a boy with a sunny disposition, a willing smile and full of chatter and as such, must have been an asset to Mag.

Time marched on and in July 1848, the strain of finding work and placing food on the table became too much and like many other Scots of the time the Mag decided the family should emigrate to the New World. Apart from a brief trip to Edinburgh to view a royal visit from Queen Victoria, Andrew had never been outside of the town. The voyage across an ocean on the deck of a retired whaler must have been a wonderful adventure.

Again, like many Scots, the Carnegies had a strong education and were therefore fortunate among emigrants, but his father was perhaps not the best example to the young Carnegie. He lost heart after all of his financial troubles in Dunfermline and now in the New World at the age of 44, once again found himself unwilling or unable to adapt to the requirements of a changing market. He made tablecloths but struggled to find customers. Carnegie described him in his writings as 'not much a man of the world, but a man all over heaven.' This suggests he loved his father but didn't see much in him that would help form his own character.

Small for his age, he won a job as a Bobbin boy. His willingness to work and quick mind quickly led to promotion and double wages, but he struggled with the nausea caused by working with vats of crude oil. He therefore set his sights on becoming a book-keeper and was offered a change when a position arose for a messenger working with the local telegraph company.

Early colleagues remarked that even from such a young age he was intent on self-improvement and in a letter to his uncle he mentioned that he was attending night school to learn more. He took his self-education seriously and early works he devoured were by Shakespeare, Burns, James Hogg and Sir Walter Scott. And given that he was living and working on the other side of the Altantic, American pioneers of literature also attracted his enquiring intellect.

In the telegraph office, his work ethic and intelligence brought him to the attention of a man who was to prove pivotal in his career progression. Tom Scott was a divisional superintendant for Pennsylvania Railroad and was himself destined for greater things and in the young Andrew Carnegie he clearly identified a like-minded individual. Now, still only 17, he was employed as Scott's personal assistant.

This was a golden age for the railroad and Tom with his young protégé at his side was well positioned to take full advantage. An investment opportunity arose in 1855 in which Scott invited Andrew to invest $500. Adams Express was a company who transported packages along the railway from Philadelphia to Pittsburgh. In a burgeoning market place they were looking to expand and were actively seeking investors.

Carnegie didn't have the money but he borrowed it and this led to a salutary lesson that informed much of his acquisition of wealth. This investment led to a dividend. He had earned money without raising a sweat. This was 'the first revenue from capital' he wrote in his autobiography.

His self-education continued with the focus that could be associated with all of his future endeavours. He was convinced that being able to read, write and 'argue' would make him a better man and earner. He was, if you pardon the cliché, like a sponge. He had an excellent memory, indeed he could recite whole tracts from Burns and Shakespeare and frequently did. He also had a head for figures and a determination to learn from everyone he met, never discounting anyone, never assuming that appearances meant the individual had nothing worthy of his attention.

During this next period of his life, he worked tirelessly. Scott was promoted and in turn left Andrew to mind his previous charges. Carnegie was determined that the business he was working in would succeed and having boundless energy, he expected the men working under him to be the same. Unfortunately, this meant pushing his men beyond the limits of their endurance.

To his credit, he recognised this failing and although he went on to employ thousands of men he never again placed himself in a position where he had to be involved in man management.

Around this time, the rattle of swords and drum roll of conflict was on the horizon with the American Civil War and Carnegie was enlisted to supervise the transport of arms and army volunteers along the railway line. He himself never drew arms, arguing initially that his role was vital to the success of the war effort. The effectiveness of this argument faded as the war machine used up young men of the required age group and in common with many successful men of the time, when Carnegie was officially called up to serve, he paid for another man to take his place.

In spring 1861, Carnegie was appointed by Scott, who was now Assistant Secretary of War in charge of military transport, as Superintendent of the Military Railways and the Union Government's telegraph lines in the East. Carnegie opened the rail lines into Washington D.C. that the rebels had cut; he rode the locomotive pulling the first troop of Union soldiers to reach Washington D.C. After the defeat of Union forces at Bull Run, he himself supervised the transport of the defeated army.

War eventually drew to a close and Andrew Carnegie continued to build up a portfolio of businesses. With skill that many modern media agents would envy he used his facility with the written word to foment a positive image. Being small of stature – no more than five feet tall – he began the task of further polishing the image he presented to the world. He learned to dress, walk and talk like a businessman.

Friends and associates wrote that he was a consummate optimist, charming, brimming with excitement, loyal, sociable, intellectually curious and one acquaintance of the time went to say that he was 'the most consistently happy man I ever knew'.

This improved image was an aid to his business expansion and along with his friends, like Tom Scott he developed an approach to being a capitalist that drove him on to previously unimaginable wealth.

His focus was on investing in companies he had personally investigated, only investing in those that sold goods and services where he could determine a growing demand, only choosing companies where he had insider knowledge and finally, only investing in companies with trusted men who owned a controlling interest.

Yes, you read correctly: insider dealing. It is worth noting that this approach was very common among capitalists of the time and wasn't in fact deemed to be illegal until 1934.

It now appeared that the young Carnegie had the golden touch and his investments began to pay off handsomely. He invested in oil and his interests there grew so much he was able to expand into ever more areas of potential wealth.

On a trip between railway stations he recognised that many of the original wooden bridges the railroad used were beginning to fail. Iron was the way forward, he was certain, and he invited trusted engineers and investment cronies to set up a company which would build bridges of this hardy material. Around 1864 government contracts for this metal made it almost as valuable as the shiny, yellow stuff and Union Iron Mills was born with Andrew Carnegie as president.

Just a year later his wealth was calculated to be in the region of $39,000, which would be roughly, in today's terms, $5 million. Despite all of this, at the grand old age of 30 he was beginning to question his direction in life and wondered if devoting so much time to business meant he was missing out on other areas.

He therefore decided to leave his business interests to take care of themselves and set out on a grand tour for a year which took in places such as Paris, Amsterdam, Venice, Johannesburg and of course, Scotland.

The tour was not just an opportunity to get away from the virtual 24 hours a day focus on business, but it allowed him to indulge in his passion for improving himself. It is reported that he took in every museum, concert, opera and theatrical event in his path, painting an image of a vibrant, worldly young man who threw himself into everything that life presented.

You would be mistaken however, if you thought that business never intruded on this cultural feast. While he travelled the world for artistic experience, he took time out to inspect iron mills, factories and forges wherever and whenever he could.

Once his year of travels was over and he was back at work, his expanding interests and railroad connections continued to accumulate and aged 33 he sat down with paper and pencil and once again took stock of his life and his finances. He pencilled a figure of £400,000 ($75,000,000 in today's values) and then considered his next step.

His decision was one that library visitors over the world still celebrate today. Continuing to work to increase his fortune was deemed by him to be no longer necessary. However he determined that any future funds earned in excess of the then current value should be spent on 'good works'. He worried that if he continued on a path where the growth of wealth was his only purpose it 'must degrade me beyond hope of permanent recovery'.

The next two years, he continued, would have a split focus: in the mornings business would be his purpose and in the afternoons, his mind would be set on continued self-improvement. It was as well that as his career progressed he found that he actually worked less and earned more. He began to value the spirit of delegation and continually looked for trustworthy and effective men who could do the heavy lifting, so to speak, and his directions for much of this time rarely went beyond suggestions.

Philanthropy began to exercise his mind more and more

and his first formal gift was to his hometown of Dunfermline. He donated £5,000 for a recreation and health club.

More time on his hands also meant more time devoted to one of his favourite pastimes: reading and this led in turn to his vocation as a writer. As a thrusting young capitalist his opinions were much sought after and he was more than happy to provide. In tune with this his first words in print were letters to the *New York Tribune* and these were followed by a travelogue which detailed his journeys around the world.

It is worth noting that in contrast to many of his peers of the time, his writing showed him to be a man who was respectful of established civilizations and ancient religions and he was equally concerned about the status of women in these same societies.

His writing continued and his reputation as a man of letters and a man of success found him an audience on both sides of the Atlantic. Among the issues that attracted his attention were the 'Irish Question', British political reform and he also turned out lectures on trade unions and labour disputes. He stated in these that his interests were in rising above the disputes, showing himself as the 'wise man' and promulgating the idea of man and management working together to find a solution.

This undoubtedly raised a storm among his peers. Surely it was unthinkable for a millionaire capitalist to be pushing such radical ideas. This stance initially won him many friends in the trade unions movement, but these friendships shattered under his own truculence when he 'broke' several union actions at his own ironwork plants.

The most well-known of these was at Homestead in 1892.

His workers were demanding shorter hours than the 12 hours per day, 7 days per week they were forced to work for less than $1.50 per day. Carnegie reportedly lacked any guilt over his employees' work situation and in fact saw this as being in full accord with the requirements of the marketplace. To do otherwise, he argued, would endanger the very viability of the steelworks.

The Homestead Strike was a labour confrontation lasting 143 days in 1892, one of the most infamous in US history. The conflict grew out of a dispute between the National Amalgamated Association of Iron and Steel Workers of the United States and the Carnegie Steel Company.

Carnegie left on one of his habitual trips to Scotland before the conflict reached a head. He was confident that events would calm down and he left mediation of the dispute in the hands of his associate and partner Henry Clay Frick, who was well-known in industrial circles for holding strong anti-union views.

After a recent spike in profits of 60%, the company refused to raise worker's pay by more than 30%. When some of the workers demanded the full 60%, management locked the union out. Workers saw the stoppage as a 'lockout' by management and not a 'strike' by workers. Frick then arranged for thousands of strike-breakers to work the steel mills and Pinkerton agents to safeguard them.

On 6 July, a force of 300 Pinkerton agents arrived from New York City and Chicago. This culminated in a fight in which 10 men were killed and hundreds were injured. Pennsylvania Governor Robert Pattison then ordered two brigades of state militia to the strike site. Afterwards, the company resumed operations with non-union immigrant employees in place of the Homestead plant workers, and Carnegie returned to the United States to protect his interests.

He was by this time fully committed to his programme of philanthropy and perhaps he also worried that a failing business would impact on his need to provide for humanity. He stated that adding small amounts to the earnings of his workers would be a waste of funds. Much better to invest, he argued, that same sum in a great educational institution. It is with a strong sense of irony that one notes his urge to give all of his money away may have made him a more ruthless businessman. He pushed his associates and employees hard in the chase for more and more profit, in order that he would have more and more to donate to the betterment of humanity.

This commitment was also highlighted in the pre-nuptial agreement he asked his wife, Louise to sign on the occasion of their wedding. This agreement granted her an annual income of $20,000 ($1.3M) as recompense for relinquishing her rights to her husband's estate.

Happily, this was a situation the new Mrs Carnegie was more than happy to comply with for she shared her husband's desire to make good use of his wealth for the benefit of others.

He continued to use his writing to promote his ideas and in his *Gospel of Wealth* in 1891 he insisted that the wealthy were merely trustees for their communities. He went on to make his famous quote where he said that a man who dies wealthy 'dies disgraced'.

His biggest pay-day came in March 1901 when he sold Carnegie Steel to United States Steel Corporation, in what become the world's first billion dollar corporation. His share of the deal netted him $226 million ($120 billion) and he set about giving it all away with the same passion, energy and commitment that helped him to accumulate it.

By the time he died he had given away $350,000,000. This included the building of around 3,000 public libraries (380 in Britain), the Carnegie Institute of Pittsburgh, the Carnegie Institute of Technology and the Carnegie Institution of Washington for research into the natural and physical sciences. Carnegie also set up the Endowment for International Peace in an effort to prevent future wars and he also established the Carnegie Corporation to 'do real and permanent good in this world.'

This organisation is still going strong today and in their report of 2010 they show that they own assets of $2.5 billion and they detail bequests that have gone to such diverse groups as The International Women's Forum, The Journal Donation Project in New York, the Universities of Pretoria and Johannesburg, a centre for advanced study and education in Belarus, the Carnegie Endowment for International Peace, the Peace Research Institute in Sweden, Haiti Earthquake Relief and much more.

The word philanthropy is derived from Greek: meaning 'love of mankind' and as such has come to describe a generosity that helps promote human progress. In over one hundred years of such promotion it would be impossible to quantify the good work that Andrew Carnegie's life work has achieved. One can only take in the details and allow a moment of awe.

To achieve his goal, Andrew Carnegie had a vision allied to action. He did not simply dream; he studied and acted upon his conviction. He had a vision of America and the British Commonwealth as a vibrant population that needed education to become stronger and one that would thrive in a global community where international peace was of common value.

Mentoring with Andrew Carnegie

There are a number of areas in which I feel I can learn from this great man, and I'm certain you have highlighted several hotspots for yourself as you read his story.

Foremost in my mind is Andrew Carnegie's quest for intellectual fulfilment, his need to study and read: his constant desire to improve himself.

Education was not so much of a basic human right when he was working and living and he grew certain of its value in terms of human potential and therefore devoted much of his money to assisting in its promotion. He built and opened libraries throughout the world at a time when there were few of them and those that were present invariably charged the borrower for the service. As I was growing up one of my favourite buildings was my local library in Ayr. Guess whose money generated the establishment? The clue is in the library's name: The Carnegie.

It's worth noting that if you fast forward 100 years or so from Andrew Carnegie's vision of an educated and well-read world that the library service throughout the UK is in serious danger. It seems that in a world of austerity the offering of free reading is one of the first things to go. Short-sighted much?

I accept that fewer of us access this service as the years progress and this has much to do with the fact that the purchase of books is within the budget of most of us and the fact that books have fierce competition against the likes of television, the internet and computergames.

Neuroscience proves that the brain benefits from a good workout. And reading is more neurobiologically demanding than processing images or speech. As you're reading this book parts of your brain that have evolved to meet other functions, like vision and language connect in a neural circuit that is specific to reading and is much more challenging for your gray matter. Your intelligence is called to action: concentration is also enhanced.

Reading as a means of taking in information gives you more time to think, thereby offering you precious moments to understand and gain insight. Compare this process to your actions when you watch television. How often do you press the pause button while you mentally chew on something? Nah, didn't think so.

(Scientists measured brain activity through a number of activities and apparently our brains are more active when we sleep than when we are watching television. 'Nuff said.)

The benefits of all this brain work includes keeping your memory sharp, your ability to learn topped up and your mind basically more resilient as you age. Also, a literate mind is a more complex one. Reading gives you a depth and quality of experience that is missing from most other mediums.

On the 'The Reading Project' website Carolyn Martin of Cornell University refers to an NEA survey and explains, 'People who read for pleasure are many times more likely than those who do not, to visit museums and attend concerts, and almost three times as likely to perform volunteer and charity work. Readers are active participants in the world around them, and that engagement is critical to individual and social well-being.'

Alan Schlein said, 'Two trucks loaded with a thousand copies of *Roget's Thesaurus* collided as they left a New York publishing house last week, according to the Associated Press. Witnesses were stunned, startled, aghast, taken aback, stupefied, appalled, surprised, shocked and rattled.'

Sorry. Couldn't resist that one.

Bill Gates, multi-billionaire Founder and Chief Executive Officer of Microsoft, said, 'It is pretty unlikely that people will become knowledgeable without being excellent readers. . . I try to make sure I get in an hour or more of reading each weeknight and a few hours each weekend. I read at least one newspaper every day and several magazines each week. I make it a point to read at least one news-weekly from cover to cover because it broadens my interests. If I read only what intrigues me, such as the science section and a subset of the business section, then I finish the magazine the same person I was before I started. So I read it all.'

Groucho Marx said, 'Outside of a dog, a book is a man's best friend. Inside of a dog, it's too dark to read.'

Liverpool University published a paper in November 2010 about the benefits of reading for people suffering from depression. In their conclusion they report 'Get into Reading helped patients suffering from depression in terms of their social well-being, by increasing personal confidence and reducing social isolation; their mental well-being, by improving powers of concentration and fostering an interest in new learning or new ways of understanding; their emotional and psychological well-being, by increasing self-awareness and enhancing the ability to articulate profound issues of self and being. The study also established what types of literature work, why they work and how they work in the specific context of depressive illness.'

Would it be too much of a stretch of the imagination to suggest that people with good mental health would appreciate the same benefits?

Epilogue

It was autumn. I was walking the dog along a tree-less stretch of the south bank of the river near my home. My shoulders were slumped, brow shaped in tight lines and my mind heavy with worries.

Something fell into my field of vision from the right. Snagged my attention. Instinctively, I held my hand out and a tiny, white feather floated down to rest in the nest of my upturned palm. I looked up at the sky around me. No birds overhead. Where did this come from? There were no trees nearby.

I looked down at my hand and the sky's bequest. It was a tiny thing, curled at either end like a plumed smile.

My sister would have said it was a gift from my guardian angel. I snorted and had a wee laugh at the very idea. It was just one of those things, right? A bird preens, a feather loosens, a gust of wind catches it and before you know it, my hand provides a resting place.

I thought about a friend of mine. An astute and intuitive man who, whenever I recount an accident, say a small trip, to him, asks me, what were you thinking about just before your foot caught?

The feather.

If it *was* a gift (another wee snort). What should my attention be brought back to? I looked around. Bob, my Labrador pup, was a blur of gold and a happy wag as he dipped in and out of the water. The trees on the other side of the river were being burnished into season. The breeze was soft on the back of my neck. The river itself was a lazy gurgle. I was missing all of this because my mind was distracted.

The feather.

Was its purpose to bring me back into the moment? I often tell my clients to live in 'the now'. Mindfulness is its own reward I tell people, and here I was being worn and harried by my own dark thoughts.

The dog trotted over, tongue hanging like a damp, pink rag from his mouth, attracted by the fact I had stopped walking. As he got closer he started to do that windmill thing he does with his tail. Never fails to plant a smile on my face.

I recalled an interview with the Dalai Lama. He was asked what surprised him most about humanity? He answered,

'Man. Because he sacrifices his health in order to make money. Then he sacrifices money to recuperate his health. And then he is so anxious about the future that he does not enjoy the present; the result being that he does not live in the present or the future; he lives as if he is never going to die, and then dies having never really lived.'

I pocketed the feather and started walking. My tread was lighter and faster than before. I began to think about the lift in my mood and my hopes for this book you are holding in your hands. Writing it has helped me and I hope it helps you, but how else can I help?

Jack Black talks about the wheel of life – and having a balance so that every area of your life is attended to. I consider 'community'. There's work I could do there. How could I combine that with the writing and publication of this book?

Charity. I could donate a percentage of my proceeds from this book to charity. Which charity? There are so many deserving causes.

Soldiers returning from conflict have been on my mind of late. In particular, the reported lack of care they receive from the MoD. Whatever I think about the rights and (mostly) wrongs of our 'assistance' in far-flung corners of the world I can't help but be disgusted by the shoddy treatment I read about. The decision makers should be ashamed of themselves.

There's a place only a few miles from where I live. Hollybush House is run by Combat Stress and helps in the treatment of Post Traumatic Stress Disorder. That fits, given the fact that a lot of the work I have put into this book has been as a result of my own reach for a positive outcome from the stress I was suffering from.

I walked on, my hand in my pocket, slowly rubbing the feather between thumb and forefinger. Then the chatterbox kicked off in my mind.

'Who do you think you're kidding? Nobody wants to read your stuff. And they'll think you're only doing the charity thing to get more attention for the book.'

Maybe it wasn't such a good idea after all. My intentions were honest, but I didn't want people to question my motives. I decided I would sleep on it.

The next morning found me in the gym getting hot n' sweaty over an hour's cardio workout. In the cafe afterwards I picked up a newspaper to read while sipping my black coffee. The first page I opened at was a two-page spread about injured soldiers who were about to be medically discharged from service before their treatment was finished. This meant they will be thrown on the mercy of the NHS who simply don't have the expertise, funds or facilities to offer the care these guys and girls need.

A chime went off in my head.

Coffee finished, I drove home and decided to stop off in the local supermarket for some groceries. There was a group of people standing just inside the door, collecting for good causes. The charity? Do I need to spell it out?

www.soldierscharity.org.

Another wee chime.

At home, I read the local weekly. I opened at the page with the horoscopes. What harm can it do, right? It tries to argue that a huge swathe of the world's population has the same stuff coming to them, but it's a little bit of fun, yeah?

My horoscope read: 'your communication skills can help you, not least because you understand it's not just about getting along with people, you want to do something solid and genuine to help'.

The chiming became a great pealing bell.

Ok, ok, ok. I get it. Just do it. (I borrowed that from a well-known sports company if you're interested.)

And in case I wasn't paying attention the universe arranged

a further prompt the very next day. Back at the gym, this time for some weight-work, I got chatting to a guy I see there regularly. He told me he has just started a new course at college and he and his mates have decided to do a charity swimathon. Their charity? Help for Heroes.

So thank you for shelling out your hard-earned. As well as (hopefully) learning from what you read here, you are contributing to a very good cause.

Let me leave you with a poem I wrote when my son was still very young. The phrase 'from the mouth of babes' was never more apt.

Within Reach

In the passenger seat beside me
a pile of unopened brown envelopes
steam in the early evening's crisp, winter dark.

My life in a work-day squats on my shoulders
heavy as a rock troll, made flesh from a child's nightmare.

Sam sits in the baby seat behind me and his chatter bleeds
into the space between us. Words hop out of his mouth and
spring towards me, but crash against the bleak imaginings
of my grown-up world.

At the traffic lights he stops speaking as if the red light
was meant for him. Then . . .

'Whassat, Daddy?' he points. Wonder in his voice
forces me to look up at the silver plate
that brightens the black wall of the sky.

'That's the moon, wee pal.'
He reaches up, as if
easily within our grasp

'Daddy, gettit.'

MONSTER IN THE WOODS

DAVE SHELTON

David Fickling Books

Monster in the Woods
is a
DAVID FICKLING BOOK

First published in Great Britain in 2023 by
David Fickling Books,
31 Beaumont Street,
Oxford, OX1 2NP

978-1-78845-221-2

1 3 5 7 9 10 8 6 4 2

Papers used by David Fickling Books are from well-
managed forests and other responsible sources.

DAVID FICKLING BOOKS Reg. No. 8340307

A CIP catalogue record for this book is available from the British Library.

Printed and bound in Great Britain by Clays, Ltd., Elcograf S.p.A.

To the memory of Chocolate Phil

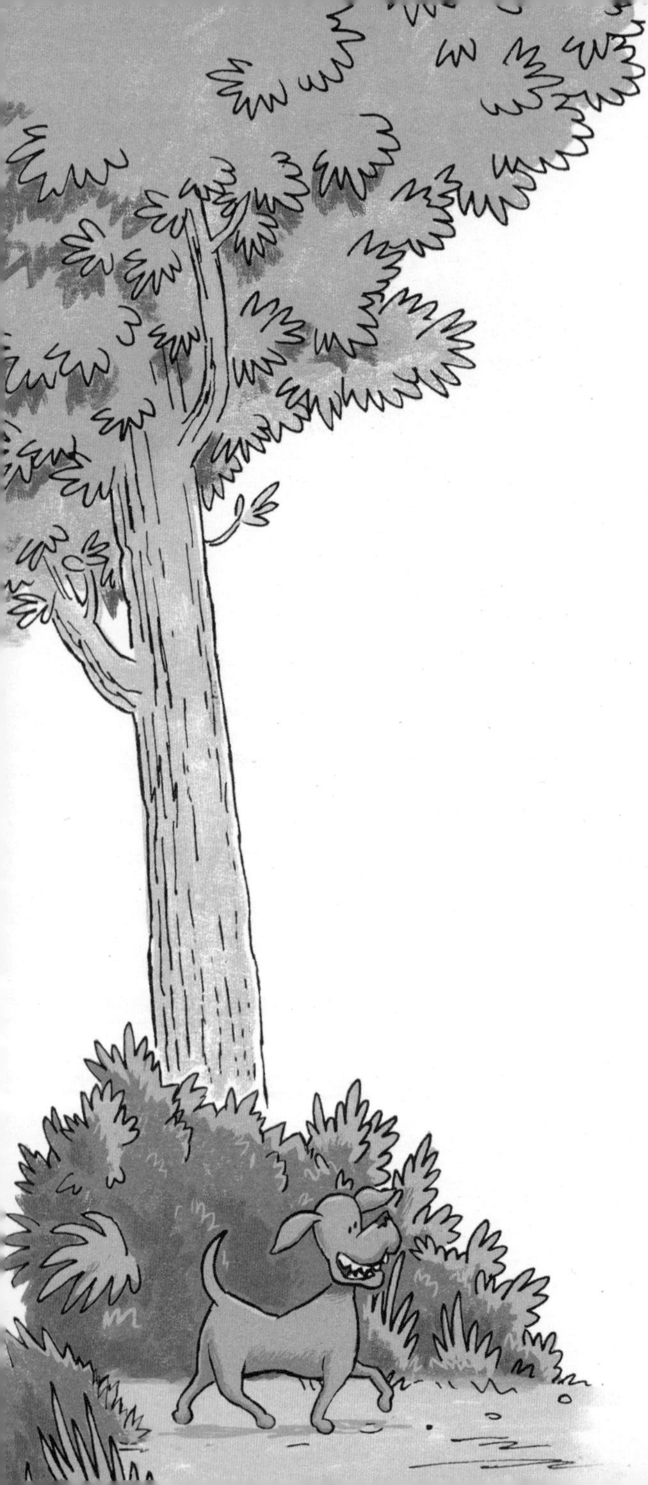

CHAPTER 1

FRITH TURNED FOR HOME, empty-handed. She hadn't caught a thing in any of the snares, and every shot from her sling had missed its target. So, she had nothing to add to the cooking pot. Again. She frowned down at Cabbage, dancing round her legs.

'And you were no help,' she said. 'It's no wonder all the rabbits and squirrels get away when you scare them off before I can even take aim.'

Cabbage looked up at her with bright, adoring eyes, and gave a joyous bark.

'I'm telling you off!' said Frith. 'Don't wag your tail.'

Cabbage yapped, wagged his tail some more, then rampaged off through the undergrowth ahead of them. It was a beautiful afternoon to be out in the woods. Butterflies and bugs were dancing in the slanting beams of afternoon sunlight that cut between the trees. Birds

gossiped and sang, unseen in the canopy of branches high above. The air was crisp, clear and fragrant. But Frith trudged through it all as if her own personal dark cloud hung over her, blocking it all out. She kicked a stone in frustration. It hurt her toe.

'Ow!'

The stone came to a stop a few paces in front of her. Frith scowled at it, stepped forward, and scooped it up.

'And as for you . . .' She hurled the stone off into the distance. 'That'll teach you!'

There was a distant yelp. A flurry of movement and a rustling noise drew her eyes to an agitated bush regaining its composure.

'Cabbage?'

Something brushed against the back of her ankles. Frith leaped in surprise.

'Nyah!'

Cabbage looked up at

her with a big stick in his mouth.

'Bad dog!' hissed Frith. 'Here, give me that!'

Cabbage released the precious stick into Frith's care, and cocked his head to one side, tail wagging.

'I am *not* throwing it for you.'

Frith turned her attention back to the bush. If Cabbage had come up behind her, then what had disturbed it?

Frith weighed the stick in her hand. It would make a good club. Cabbage turned a tight circle at her feet.

Frith pushed aside some foliage and stepped towards where the noise had come from. The undergrowth was thick, but Frith moved through it with silent, practised ease, her eyes fixed ahead of her, her ears straining for any new sound of movement. If the birds were still singing, she didn't hear them.

Two paces from the bush now, and Frith could hear a low snuffling noise coming from behind it. She gripped the stick tighter, took another step, and stretched to peer over the top of the leaves.

'YAAAAH!'

A strange, grotty figure sprang up, arms flailing, yelling into Frith's face.

Frith fell over backwards in shock, dropping the stick.

'Spuggy!' she snarled.

The grubby face of her younger brother grinned down at her. 'Ha! Got you!'

'You stupid . . . I thought you were a boar or something. I was going to bash you on the head and take you home for dinner!' Frith rubbed her bottom as she rose to her feet.

'Serves you right. You nearly hit me with that stone!'

'Maybe I should hit you anyway. Where's that stick?'

But Cabbage had it, so Frith had to settle for punching Spuggy on the shoulder. Spuggy's face curdled in pain for a second, but then his grin returned.

'What did you get us for dinner, then?' he said.

'Nothing.'

'Oh.' Spuggy's face fell. 'That's a shame.'

'Well, it's not as if *you're* doing anything to help. You've probably been crashing about playing with your imaginary friend as usual, and scaring away all the dinners. So stupid and childish!'

Frith took a breath. She hadn't meant to sound so angry, but Spuggy was just *so* annoying sometimes that she couldn't help herself. Deep down she knew that, really, she was disappointed with herself. But knowing that only made her even more annoyed.

So, she hit Spuggy again, but not so hard this time.

'Ow!' said Spuggy, louder than the pain really deserved. 'And Edward is *not* imaginary! He's my *real* friend. And he's much nicer than you!'

'Of course he is. But it's odd that no one else has ever seen him. If he's real, and nice, then you'd think he might have said hello to the rest of us in the village.'

Spuggy scrunched his face up in thought.

'He's just shy,' he said, stooping down to take the stick from Cabbage, then hurling it into the woods ahead of them. Cabbage sprang after it, disappearing into a mass of ferns. Spuggy quickened his pace to follow. 'And he's probably especially avoiding *you* because I've told him how horrible you are.'

'So, now I'm being avoided by an imaginary friend,' Frith said to herself. 'That's a new low, even for me.'

5

She broke into a trot, following the sounds of her irritating brother and her idiot dog crashing through the underbrush ahead of her, back towards the village and home. The cloud of her disappointment was still with her, but she noticed it less now she was running. And she would be glad to get home. Mum and Dad were irritating too, of course. They were grown-ups after all. But she would be pleased to see them even so.

The trees began to thin out as Frith neared the edge of the wood, and she saw Spuggy ahead of her, standing still in the dappled sunlight that filtered through the leaves, Cabbage at his feet jumping and barking in agitation. As Frith drew nearer, she could see that Spuggy's shoulders were slumped, his head hung low, and the first whiff of trouble hit her nostrils.

Smoke!

She sprinted the last few paces, and arrived panting by Spuggy's side. Spuggy raised his arm and pointed down the grassy slope to a hut on the near side of the village. The one with smoke pouring out of it. Their hut. Their home.

'Oh no!' said Frith.

'Disaster!' said Spuggy.

'Mum's cooking!' they both said together.

CHAPTER 2

AT THAT TIME OF a summer's day, the grassy slope down from the woods to the village was a beautiful sight. The golden light of early evening highlighted bright patches of wildflowers on a rich background of shrubs and ferns. The grass rippled like the surface of a lake as a gentle breeze played across it. It was an enchanting, peaceful scene, noiseless except for the songs of unseen birds.

At least until two children and a dog trampled noisily through the middle of it, yelling 'Mum!' and 'Dad!' and 'Woof!'.

Mum emerged from the doorway of the smoking hut, recoiling from the light, just as Frith and Spuggy came to a breathless halt outside.

'Oof!' said Mum. 'It's a bit swearing bright out here, isn't it? Oh, hello you two. What's got you so hot and bothered then?'

7

'Oh, I don't know,' said Frith. 'We just thought we'd better try to keep the hut from burning down.'

'Again,' said Spuggy.

Mum turned, and gave a jump of surprise at the sight of the grey cloud of smoke billowing from the doorway.

'Oh, swear!' she said, and dashed back inside.

Frith shouted after her: 'Don't forget to use a cloth when you—'

There was a brief scream of pain from within.

'Never mind,' said Frith.

'Swearing swear!' yelled Mum, emerging in a swirl of smoke, carrying a large iron cooking pot. 'Burned my swearing hand!' She threw the pot to the ground.

The three of them watched it for a moment as it spat flame and ashes into the air like a grumbling volcano.

'I was cooking,' said Mum.

'We worked that out,' said Frith.

'It went a bit wrong,' said Mum.

'We worked that out too,' said Spuggy.

'Unless we were having fire for supper,' said Frith.

'In which case,' said Spuggy, 'it's perfect!'

'Less of your swearing cheek! Now go and get some swearing water so we can put it out, will you?'

Spuggy grabbed the bucket from beside the doorway and ran off to the stream. He returned a minute later with Dad walking alongside him carrying the sloshing bucket.

With a sigh, Dad poured some of the water into the cooking pot, unleashing a cloud of steam, then some more over Mum's hands.

'I'm all right,' she said. 'There's no need to swearing fuss.'

A puddle formed at Mum's feet. Cabbage arrived to drink from it.

'Didn't I say I was going to cook?' said Dad.

'Yes. But I was getting hungry, so I thought I'd make a start.' Cabbage gave the cooking pot a sniff, yelped in alarm, and ran away. 'Thought I'd have it ready for you when you all got home from farming and hunting and . . .' Mum's gaze passed from Dad and Frith to Spuggy. She looked puzzled for a moment. 'And . . . whatever it is that Spuggy does all day. I thought it'd be a nice surprise.'

'Well,' said Frith. 'You were half right, at least.'

After Dad had cooked, they sat around the fire in the hearth at the centre of the hut, and ate together. Outside, the sun was sinking behind the trees of the

woodland. Inside, the fire spread its own ruddy glow.

'So, Dad,' said Frith, 'what kind of soup is this, exactly? Because, for once, it doesn't taste like cabbage *or* turnip.'

'Ah!' said Dad. 'I'm glad you noticed. That's because it's my new experimental recipe. Due to unforeseen events, I didn't have enough cabbage or turnip to make a soup on its own. So, this is – ta dah! – cabbage *and* turnip. What do you think?'

'I'm sure it's very . . . good for us?' said Spuggy.

'It tastes like it must be,' said Frith.

Dad took a mouthful himself.

'It does, doesn't it?' he said, with a sad nod.

'But at least it doesn't taste of cabbage or turnip,' said Mum, trying to sound much more enthusiastic than she looked.

'No,' said Dad. He set his bowl down and laid his spoon inside it. 'No, somehow I've made it taste worse than either cabbage *or* turnip. It's awful, isn't it?'

'It *is* probably the worst meal anyone has ever cooked,' said Mum. 'But at least it's not on fire.'

'That's true,' said Spuggy.

'Although fire probably *would* taste better,' said Frith.

'Ooh! That's cruel,' said Mum, patting Dad's hand. 'Absolutely true, of course' – she gave Dad a massive grin – 'but also, cruel. As punishment, Frith: you can't have any seconds.'

'Oh,' said Spuggy. 'In that case, can I be punished too, please?'

'Not until you've earned it,' said Mum. 'Say something rude about your dad.'

'Hey!' Dad tried to look insulted but his smile ruined it. 'How come he has to be rude about me?'

'Because I'll clout him if he gives *me* any cheek.'

'Good point. Off you go, son.'

Spuggy gave the matter

some thought, his brow furrowed.

'You smell . . .'

'Yes?' said Dad.

'. . . worse than dog poo . . .'

'Oh,' said Dad.

'. . . from a dog that has eaten nothing but . . . rotten eggs and cabbage . . .'

Dad gave an approving nod.

'. . . for three years, fifteen months and seventy-seven days!' said Spuggy.

Dad thought about this.

'That really *would* be quite smelly. Well done. Ahem . . .' Dad pulled his saddest sad face. 'I am very hurt and offended. You may not have any seconds of my disgusting dinner!'

'Hurray!' said Spuggy.

Then they all laughed, for as long as their hunger would allow.

Later that evening, Frith heard Mum and Dad talking in their serious voices. Their serious voices were the same as their normal ones but quieter, and more serious. Mum and Dad had been using them more and more in the last few weeks, mostly when they talked about work, or food, or money.

'What about the other farms?' Mum was saying.

'I can probably get a few days' work here and there, but they're all the same. Something's got into the fields and made an awful mess, digging the crops up in the night. The best of the harvest is ruined already.'

'What do they think it was?'

'No idea. Something big, though. Maybe a boar? Whatever it was, it's done a lot of damage to four farms at least. And this dry spell isn't helping the crops that are left, either. There won't be much work even at harvest time.'

Mum kept on quietly working her loom, and even by the dim light of the fire Frith could see her frown.

'That's terrible,' she said at last, though Frith couldn't tell if she meant for the farmers or for Dad.

'Old Robert said that Bill had lost some cattle too.'

'Just *lost*?' Mum looked up. 'Or does he mean . . . ?'

'Well, Robert thinks Bill left a gate open, but of course Bill says it must have been' – Dad gave Mum a dramatic look, his face full of mock terror, and dropped his voice to a sinister whisper – 'the Monster in the Woods!'

'Monster?!' said Spuggy. 'What monster?'

'Now you've done it!' said Mum.

'Is there a monster in the woods?' Spuggy's eyes were wide with fright. 'Will he eat me?' He paced a knotted path of worry on the floor. 'He won't eat Edward, will he?'

'No, of course not,' said Dad. 'No one's going to eat Edward.'

'Well, *that's* true,' said Frith.

'But there *is* a monster though?'

Dad shook his head. 'No. Absolutely not.'

'How do you know?'

'Well,' said Mum. 'You play in the woods a lot, don't you? Hours and hours you spend in there. And have you ever seen a monster?'

'No, but . . .'

'And your friend, Edward, he's in the woods a lot too, isn't he?'

'Yes. All the time. He lives there.'

'And has he ever seen a monster?'

'No.'

'Well, there you are, then. Bill Simpson is a nice man, but he's also a silly old fool with too much imagination, and he has never seen a monster in the woods. OK?'

'OK, Mum.' Spuggy rubbed his eyes, smiled, and yawned.

'Now, off to swearing bed with you!'

Spuggy gave Mum a hug, and stumbled back to his straw-filled mattress in the corner of the hut.

'Did you,' whispered Dad, leaning in close, 'just use the imaginary evidence of an imaginary boy to prove that an imaginary monster doesn't exist?'

'Why, yes,' said Mum, 'I believe I did.'

'And that,' said Dad, 'is why I love you.'

'You had swearing well better,' grinned Mum.

Frith turned her head away as Dad gave Mum a kiss, and that meant that she was looking out of the doorway when she heard the noise outside. Only it wasn't just one noise. There was a low, rasping, gasping sound, and a creepy grunting sound, and a scratching, scraping sound, like claws dragging along the ground.

Frith stared out of the doorway through the smoky air, out into the fading twilight, as the noises grew nearer.

Rasp, gasp, grunt, scratch, scrape . . .

A huge, dark figure came into view, framed in the doorway, drawing closer . . .

'Eek!' said Frith.

Mum and Dad's faces snapped round, taking in the giant presence hunching over to squeeze through the doorway into the hut. Frith scooted backwards across the floor towards her parents, squinting through the smoke at the intruder.

'Hello,' it said. 'I wonder if you could do me a favour.'

CHAPTER 3

'HELLO, JAMES!' SAID DAD. 'What brings you here at this time of night?'

Now that she could see him more clearly in the light from the fire, Frith recognized the figure in the doorway as James the blacksmith, and not, after all, a scary monster who had come to eat them.

'Good evening, Arthur Carter,' James said, with a

small wave, then shyly nodded at Mum and Frith in turn. 'Martha Carter. Little 'un.'

'Come in, come in,' said Dad.

'Can we offer you some . . . water?' said Mum. 'I'm afraid we've no ale just at the moment.'

'No. Thank you. I won't stop. But I wondered if Arthur might do a job for me?'

'Yes!' said Mum and Dad together.

Then Dad said: 'That is, I can . . . *probably* help you out. What did you have in mind?'

'Well, I've been making swords and armour and what-not for the king's army. A lot of the smiths from the other villages have too. You know, because of the war with the armies of the north lands.'

Mum and Dad nodded seriously. The war with the armies of the north lands had been going on for as long as anyone could remember.

'I was meant to be delivering a new batch tomorrow, but my horse is sick. She can't pull a cart full of swords and armour and whatnot all that way. But yours is healthy and strong, and you have the best cart in the village. So, could you go for me? To the city?'

'The city!' said Frith.

'Hmm . . .' Dad gave his head a scratch. 'That's each way . . .'

'I'll pay you three gold pieces for your trouble,' said James.

'Done!' said Mum and Dad.

'Now, don't you go trying to drive the price up,' said James the smith. 'I won't pay more.'

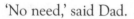

'No need,' said Dad.

'I can't be doing with haggling.' James seemed not to notice Dad's outstretched hand waiting to shake on the deal.

'Nor me!' said Dad, waving his hand about a bit in an effort to gain the smith's attention.

'All that silly business where I say two gold pieces, and you say four, and then we argue back and forth . . .'

'Just ridiculous,' said Dad. 'I quite agree.'

'It's a waste of time, and I won't do it. I know what's a fair price, and you can take it or leave it.'

'I'll take it!' said Dad, though James still did not take his hand. Frith got to her feet and stepped towards them.

'Because if you . . .'

James Smith stopped talking and looked down at his right hand as Frith lifted it from his side and held it out in front of him. Dad grabbed it and shook it vigorously.

'It's a deal!' said Dad.

James looked bemused, then gave a small smile.

'Good. Now let me show you the load you'll be taking.'

Dad, Frith and Mum followed him out.

'Can you manage that lot?' James cast out an arm the size of a small tree trunk to draw their attention to the unmissable mountain of swords, armour and whatnot teetering outside the hut.

'Um, yes,' said Dad. 'Did . . . did you just carry all that here?'

'Yes. Of course.'

'Because . . . we could have brought the cart round to you and loaded up there, you know.'

James Smith placed a massive hand over the hairy rockface of his mighty chin as he considered this.

'Oh. Yes. I suppose so.' He gave a shrug.

'Are you selling that too?' said Frith. She pointed to an anvil just to one side of the pile.

'Oh, no.' James shook his head. 'But there's been thefts from some of the farms lately, so I didn't want to leave it at home. Shall we load up now, then?'

Dad disappeared round the back of the hut, and returned a moment later leading their horse, Geraldine, pulling the strongest and best cart in the whole village, that he and Mum had built the previous year. He was met by the sight of Frith struggling to lift a broadsword, and James holding aloft everything else, except the anvil, in a gigantic tangle of metal.

'I'm . . . helping,' gasped Frith.

James lowered the pile of weapons onto the back of the cart, which gave a creak of dismay at the weight. Frith heaved the sword on too, with only a little assistance.

'I've drawn you a map of how to get there.' James pulled out a folded piece of paper that had been tucked into his belt.

Dad took the paper and began to unfold it as he led them all back inside.

'Oh, I think I remember the way,' he said. 'I went there a couple of times years ago. Let's see . . . Down to Maisden, then west to Greater Fickling, up through Anstey Green, then—' He came to a grinding halt as he saw the map now entirely unfolded before him. 'Oh!' he said. 'Oh. I see.'

'Can't go through all those villages,' said James. 'Not with valuable cargo. And especially not on the way back once you've been paid.'

'But, maybe if I went through the woods, then—'

'No. Haven't you heard? There's a monster in the woods!'

'Not you as well! I really don't—'

'Not through the villages. Not through the woods. You go the way I always go.' James pointed at the map. 'Just follow the dotted line.'

'So, er . . . I go . . .' Dad pointed at the map with a twitching finger.

The smith nodded.

'If it's a problem, then I can always ask Henry—'

'No! No, no. It's not a problem. You're the boss.'

Frith met Dad at the doorway as he came back in from seeing James off.

'Can I go with you, Dad? To the city? Can I? It's dead boring staying here all the time. And Spuggy is *so* annoying. And it'll be dead boring for you on your own all that way. So, can I keep you company?'

'No. I don't think . . . And I'm sure your mother might want—'

'I don't want her getting in the way here. She'll be a right swearing nuisance grumping about the place. Go on, take her with you. Do you both good.'

'Do *you* good, more like,' said Dad. 'And you're not worried about . . . ?' He showed Mum James's map.

'Oh, swearing swear!' Mum looked shocked, then thought for a moment. 'Still, if you *have* to go that way, it's probably best if you're not alone.'

'I'll be *very* good, Daddy.' Frith only ever called him Daddy when she really wanted something. 'You won't even know I'm there.'

Chapter 4

'ARE WE NEARLY THERE yet?' said Frith. Yet again.

'No,' said Dad, his face tense, his hands gripping the reins so tightly that his knuckles were white. 'Do you remember I told you how long it would take to get to the city?'

'Yes,' said Frith. 'About a day. If we're very lucky, and we don't get lost, and the cart doesn't break.'

'That's right,' said Dad. 'About a day. And how long have we been going so far?'

'I don't know . . . Six hours? Maybe seven?'

'Twenty minutes.'

'Twenty minutes? What? That's not possible!'

'And yet, nevertheless, it is.'

Frith was astonished, and dejected, and very bored. She thought for a moment.

'So, *are* we nearly there yet?'

'NO!' yelled Dad. 'No. No. No.'

'Oh,' said Frith. 'That's a shame.'

It was at least five minutes before she asked again. And after only another hour or so, Frith yawned and stretched, then curled up on the bench seat of the cart and fell asleep.

Frith jolted awake as the cart jumped beneath her, and threw her upright, hard against Dad's side.

'Hello, daughter of mine. How did you sleep?'

Frith rubbed her eyes as she bounced about on the juddering seat.

'What happened? Did you swap the wheels for square ones?'

'No,' said Dad. 'But we're not on a road any more. Look.'

Frith looked.

'Oh!' she said.

'Welcome to the Barren Wasteland!'

Frith stared ahead at the miles and miles of emptiness that lay before them, and felt her stomach churn. She had spent virtually her whole life in the village surrounded by people and animals and trees. She had never seen, or even imagined there could ever be so much . . . nothing in one place. It was disturbing and dizzying, and she had to look away.

Looking back the way they had come, Frith saw a low grassy rise beyond which she could just glimpse a handful of distant treetops. A rough track reached partway down the slope, then turned into wheel tracks in the grass. Then the grass became patchier and scrubbier until, where the ground levelled out, there was only bare earth. And before and beside them lay more, much more, of exactly the same.

'So, this is what you were worried about on the map last night?'

'Was I worried? I'm not sure I'd say *worried*, exactly . . .'

'I would. We're crossing the Barren Wasteland! Why didn't you tell me?'

'You didn't ask. Besides, in the end I realized it's not really scary. It's an adventure. And adventures are good, aren't they?'

Frith gazed into the vast expanse of nothingness

that lay ahead.

'It's . . .' she said.

'Sort of magnificent, isn't it?'

'. . . really *boring!*' said Frith.

'Better get used to it, kiddo.'

Frith scanned their surroundings again. On closer inspection the emptiness wasn't entirely empty. Far in the distance in one direction she could see a small dead shrub. The other way, there was a quite big stone. Much further ahead there were some bleached tree branches sticking out of the ground. Or possibly they were bones. So that was something to look forward to. She knelt on the seat facing backwards, leaning her head out sideways to look past the piled-up cargo on the back of the cart. She watched the last thin strip of green drift away from her, growing smaller and fainter with each jolt of the cart. Soon it was just a hairline crack. Then a dotted line. Then nothing.

Frith felt very small, and the world felt suddenly far too big, and far too empty, and she wondered for the first time where she belonged in it all.

CHAPTER 5

'YOU KNOW,' SAID DAD, 'I was a bit worried about this.' He had unfolded the map that James the smith had given him, and was comparing a section of it with the view ahead. 'But, actually, it's very good.'

'How, exactly?' Frith asked. 'Does it say "village" at the bottom, and "city" at the top, and have nothing at all in between? Because that would be pretty accurate.'

'Actually, no,' said Dad. 'Apart from anything else, James's spelling is really bad, so I don't think he'd even attempt to write "village". But actually, it has loads of things drawn on it between the village and the city.'

Frith gestured to the featureless landscape ahead of them.

'But there's nothing there. Or virtually nothing . . .'

'Aha! Virtually nothing! But not *absolutely* nothing! Look ahead, and what do you see?'

'Nothing,' said Frith, glancing lazily into the distance. Then, squinting hard, she could just make out a distant speck of difference, blurred by heat, but definitely something. 'Except . . .' She stared and stared. 'There's some kind of pointy rock over there.' She pointed at the pointy rock.

'Correct!' Dad jabbed at the map. 'And that's exactly what it says here: "pointy rock". Well, not *exactly* exactly, because of James's spelling, but that's definitely what it's meant to say. And then once we reach the pointy rock, we should just be able to see . . .' He consulted the map again. 'Oh.' He dropped his voice to a whisper. 'Then we head for the skeleton of a horse. But we might steer quite wide of that. But the point is, we always have something to head for, so we never get lost.'

'Brilliant,' said Frith. 'Always good to have a dead horse to look forward to.'

It took ages to reach the pointy rock, and it wasn't very interesting when they got there.

'And after the horse skeleton?' said Frith, spotting the tell-tale sun-bleached ribs rising from the earth in the far distance. 'What next?'

Dad looked at the map.

'Oh, well, this is very exciting. There are actually two things close together here. Let's see, what's he written? There's some kind of a tree. And next to it is . . . what's that say? Ah! Well . . . I think we'll mainly concentrate on the tree.' Frith took the map from Dad, and looked for herself.

'Does that say – I mean, is that *meant* to say – "squirrel"?'

'I think so,' said Dad. 'Yes.'

'I don't know much about maps,' said Frith, 'but a squirrel doesn't seem like the best landmark ever.'

'No,' said Dad.

'Because they're kind of small. And they . . . well, they move, don't they?'

'They do. Yes.'

'Which is not ideal for a landmark.'

'As I say,' said Dad, 'we'll concentrate on the tree.'

Frith folded the sheet untidily, and thrust it back at her father.

'Excellent map,' she said. 'Really excellent.' After they steered well clear of the horse skeleton, Dad checked the map and scanned the horizon.

'Do you see a tree?' he said.

Frith looked up, wearily.

'No. Nor a squirrel for that matter.'

Geraldine plodded onwards. Dad stared into the distance, Frith stared at her feet, the cart rattled and creaked and jumped beneath them. The tree continued to not appear.

'How could a squirrel even be out here, anyway?' said Dad.

'It would need to be very lost,' said Frith. 'Oh! *We're* not lost, are we?'

'Don't worry, kiddo.' Dad gave her a smile that didn't last long enough to convince her.

Frith stood on the bench, wobbling unsteadily as the cart bounced and jostled and lurched. The horizon was still a flat line of hopelessness. No tree.

All of a sudden, Frith felt a fizz of worry inside her

head, buzzing like an angry bee.

There was always meant to be something to head towards.

'You all right, love?' said Dad.

'Mm,' she squeaked.

There was still no sign of the tree. So, at the moment, there was nothing to head towards. And the horse skeleton had disappeared from view behind them long ago. So, surely that meant they *were* lost. In the Barren Wasteland. And Dad was worried enough about it to lie to her. Which made the fizzing and buzzing and worrying much worse.

If she looked at Dad, Frith thought she would cry, or scream. So, instead, she stared straight ahead.

And then she screamed anyway.

AAAAAAAAAAA!

One of the wheels hit a rock, the cart tilted, Frith fell over, and landed on Dad.

'AAAAAAH!' said Dad.

'AAAAAAAAAAAH!' said Frith.

'WHY ARE YOU SCREAMING?' screamed Dad.

'I SAW THE TREE!' screamed Frith.

Dad pulled on the reins and brought Geraldine to a halt.

'You saw the tree?'

Frith stood back up, and stared out into the vast blank canvas of the landscape before them. When she again found the tiny, dark speck on the horizon, she pointed at it. Dad stood up beside her, and looked until he saw it too.

'Yes,' he said. 'There it is.' He placed a palm gently to Frith's cheek, then when he realized that she could feel his hand trembling he pulled it away again and sat down. 'Didn't doubt it for a moment.'

Frith sat down next to him, and they set off again. She thought she should say something, but could not work out what. So, she just hit Dad quite hard on the shoulder instead, which seemed to sum up quite a lot of it.

CHAPTER 6

THE SPECK ON THE horizon grew and changed as they drew closer. It was definitely a tree, but there was something odd about it.

'What's wrong with it?' said Frith as they finally reached it. 'It looks like it's been hit with a giant axe, and set on fire.'

'Struck by lightning,' said Dad. 'Quite recently, I think. Look, there's charred bits of wood everywhere.'

'Looks spooky,' said Frith.

'I suppose. And shorter than it was. Which is why we couldn't spot it at first.'

Dad brought

Geraldine to a stop, and climbed down from the cart.

'Are we having a rest?' said Frith, jumping down on her side.

'Little one, yes. And we can gather up some of this wood while we're here. We can build a fire later.'

Frith emerged from behind Geraldine, with her eyebrows askew.

'Why will we need a fire when we're going to be tucked up in lovely cosy beds in the city?'

'Oh, we won't reach the city today. We'll carry on a bit, then set up camp for the night, and head on to the city in the morning.'

'Camp?' said Frith. 'In the Barren Wasteland?'

'Yes.'

'Where who-knows-what ravenous creatures roam in the darkness?'

'Have you seen any creatures here, ravenous or otherwise?'

'Well, no. Not yet. But it's daytime. Maybe there are no daytime creatures because they all got eaten by the night-time ones!'

Dad considered this as he added another charred branch to the bundle in the crook of his arm.

'All the more reason to get a fire going then,' he said. 'Then they can cook us before they . . .'

Dad trailed off as he saw the look on Frith's face.

'Hey!' he said, wrapping his free arm round her shoulder. 'I thought you didn't believe in monsters.'

'I said there wasn't a monster in the woods. I know about the woods.' Frith rubbed her wrist under her nose, which was suddenly sniffly, probably because of all the dust or something. 'But I don't know about out here. And nor do you.'

'No,' said Dad. 'But James does. He's been here lots of times, and he's never had any trouble.'

'But he's about twenty feet tall, and nine feet wide, and strong enough to juggle anvils. If I was a ravenous creature I'd keep well away from him because *he* looks like trouble. Whereas we look like . . . dinner.'

There was a noise behind them.

They both screamed, and spun round so fast to see what it was that they lost their balance and fell in a heap together. Something small and furry cocked its head to one side considering them, then turned and sped away in a cloud of dust.

'Was that . . . ?' gasped Frith.

'Yes,' said Dad. 'That was a *very* lost squirrel.'

Frith stared after it. 'OK,' she said. 'It's official: that map is amazing.'

Chapter 7

'So, are we camping for the night at the duck stone?' said Frith.

'The duck stone?' said Dad.

'The stone that's shaped like a duck.' She pointed at the map. Then she pointed at the vaguely duck-shaped boulder that lay ahead of them. 'Though it actually says "buck" here. And "stone" has a W in it.'

'Oh, *that* duck stone.' Dad looked up. The sun was reddening and easing itself down towards the horizon, but it wasn't yet dark. 'No, we'll press on to the next stop. It's not too much further, and

I'm . . . eager to see it.'

Frith consulted the map again. Next up along the dotted line of their route there were two things close together, but James's writing next to each of them overlapped in a swirly scrawl of letters. And the drawings didn't really help.

'Does that say "Wall"?' asked Frith. 'What's so good about a wall?'

'Not a wall,' said Dad. 'A *well*. At least I hope it is, because we've only got half a cup of water left.'

'Then I hope so too,' said Frith. 'But what's this other thing? Does it say . . . "d.w.h."?'

'No idea.' Dad rubbed the back of his hand across his dry lips, then rolled his head round first one way then the other. 'I'm hoping for "delightfully welcoming hostelry".'

'More likely "dead whiffy horse".'

'Well, whatever it is, it's over that way.' Dad nodded at the latest dot on the horizon, and steered towards it.

They rode on as the sun sank, and the shadows of their stopping place reached out towards them in welcome. The dot on the horizon grew, and split, and took shape bit by bit, and soon there were two distinct silhouettes against the bloody sky.

'I'm *pretty* sure that's a well on the right,' said Frith.

'Of course,' said Dad, as casually as he could manage.

'And it looks like the "d.w.h." is just another rock.' She tilted her head, and squinted a bit. 'Or maybe some kind of statue?'

'Funny place for a statue,' said Dad. He gave it a squint himself. 'It looks like it's just a great big . . . Oh! No. It can't be.'

'What can't it be?'

'The map says "d.w.h.", you said?'

'Yes. I think so.'

'But the map also said "buck" stone instead of "duck" stone?'

'Ye-es . . .'

'So "d.w.h." might actually be "b.w.h."?'

'I suppose so. What is it? You are being extra annoying about this, you know.'

But Dad just stared ahead.

They were nearly at the well now. It looked very old. Dad brought Geraldine to a halt alongside it and dropped stiffly to the ground. He leaned over the circular stone wall and peered down.

'It's deep,' he said. 'And it's dark.'

He took a small stone from the ground and dropped it in. There was a tiny distant splash.

'Good,' said Dad. 'That's good.'

Then he looked over at the other thing. Frith did too.

'Not only is it a funny place for a statue,' she said, 'but it's also a funny sort of a statue. Just a great big head.'

'Yes,' said Dad. 'Just a great big . . .' He wandered off towards it in a daze. 'I'm just going to . . .'

Frith shook her head. 'Go ahead,' she said. 'I'll just get us some water then, shall I?'

She reached up to take hold of the handle, and began to wind up the rope to raise the bucket from the bottom of the well. It took some persuading, and the handle squeaked in protest at each turn, and the rickety wooden frame swayed from side to side and creaked and groaned. But the handle turned, and the rope wound up, and a reassuring weight made it hard work.

'If you wanted to take over,' she shouted to Dad, 'I really wouldn't mind. And I could . . . take a turn at the important task of statue appreciation. You know, if it was getting too much for you and . . . you wanted a break.'

Dad was over by the head now. He leaned in close, examining it, his own head roughly at its eye level. It was grey and dusty, and looked a bit battered by time and weather, but it was remarkably lifelike. Dad paced around it, looking at it from every angle, as Frith continued to wrestle with the handle of the well, which grew stiffer with every turn.

'Come and see,' called Dad.

'In a . . . minute. Kind of . . . busy here!' Frith grunted back.

'It's fascinating,' shouted Dad.

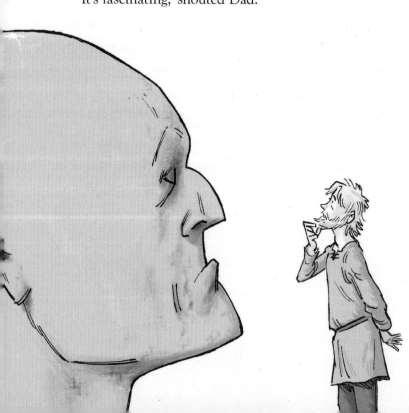

'I'm sure it is. To you. But I don't want to let the bucket fall back—'

'It won't fall. There'll be a ratchet to stop it.'

'I don't think—'

'Trust me. Ratchets are great, actually. Simple device, but so useful. Go on, let go, and the ratchet will—'

Frith let go.

The handle spun violently back the other way. The rope snaked down into the well. There was a distant splash.

'Although,' said Dad, 'of course this particular well is so old that maybe . . .'

Frith's skull filled with fury. She glared over at Dad.

'You're unbelievable.'

'That's very kind but—'

'Not in a good way!' Frith stomped towards him. 'You're meant to be the grown-up. The sensible one.' Her tightly balled fists felt hotter than her head. 'But you bring us out here, into the nowherest bit of nowhere, to a well that may or may not exist. And you lie to me about how long it will take. And I'm very bored, and very tired.' She reached his side and whacked him on the arm. 'But it's me that thinks it might be more important for us to get some water than it is to closely examine a big, ugly stone head.'

Frith stabbed a finger in the head's direction and connected lightly with the tip of its nose.

There was a small dry sound.

'Who are you calling ugly?' said the head.

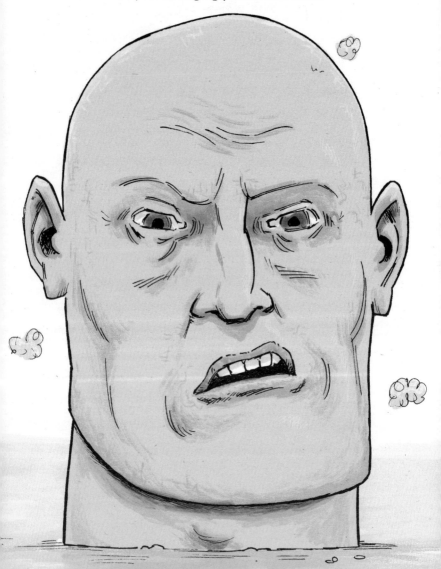

CHAPTER 8

'Aaaargh!' shrieked Frith.

'Nyeurgh!' yelled Dad.

'I thought . . . I thought you were just a myth,' he gasped.

'I get . . .' said the head in a croaky voice. Then stopped, coughed several times, and pulled some odd faces, limbering up his jaw. 'Excuse me,' he said. 'It's been a while . . . Now, what was I saying? Ah, yes. "Just a myth." I hear that a lot. But, as you see . . .'

'I thought you said it was a statue,' whispered Frith.

'No,' said Dad. 'You said that.'

'A statue?' said the head. 'Is your daughter . . . I take it this *is* your daughter?'

Dad nodded.

'Is she a little bit slow?'

'No,' said Dad. 'Well, hardly at all.'

'Hey!' said Frith.

'And you *were* perfectly still,' said Dad, 'and the colour of stone, so . . .'

The head's eyes bulged and swivelled as if he was trying to look at his own face. Then he shook his head, which is to say all of him, and watched as the sunset lit up the resulting cloud of dust.

'Ah! I see,' he said. 'A little dust must have settled on me while I was having a nap. Still, no one with any sense would have mistaken me for stone.' He gave Frith a disdainful look. 'And no one with any manners, or good taste, would call me ugly. Idiot child.'

Frith, with fresh rage boiling inside her, took an angry step towards him. Dad grabbed her arm.

'Hang on,' he said, softly. 'Before you do anything I might regret, let me introduce you: Frith, this is, I assume, the Great Sage of the Barren Wasteland, the Brain of Brains: the Big Wise Head!'

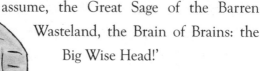

'Wotcha,' said the Big Wise Head.

Frith glared at him. 'I don't care who you are!

You stupid—'

'No time for that,' said Dad, dragging Frith away. 'Excuse us, Big Wise Head, we'd better get a fire going before the light fades.' He steered Frith over to the cart.

'Dad! What are you—?'

'Shh! Don't you realize how amazing this is?'

Frith gave him a look. 'I think you'll find,' she said, 'that I am fully aware of *exactly* how amazing it is to be out in the middle of nowhere, tired, hungry, and being insulted by a *freak* before spending a freezing night sleeping – if I can even get to sleep – on the cold, hard ground, having nightmares about ravenous creatures.'

'But it's the Big Wise Head!' said Dad, passing Frith some firewood.

'And why is this Big Head such a big deal, exactly?'

'They say he's the wisest being in the world!'

'And by "they", you mean . . . ?'

'Well, it was Old Bill Simpson who first—'

'You mean that "silly old fool" Bill Simpson.'

'Ye-es. But not just him. And to be honest I never really believed *anyone* who told me about him. I always thought it was just a story. But here he is! The real-life Big Wise Head!'

'Lucky us,' said Frith. 'But, look . . . I can see he's big. And he's definitely a head. But what makes him so wise?'

Dad had gathered up a pile of branches into his own arms now. With a nod he led Frith away from the cart.

'Supposedly, the Big Wise Head can answer any question – any question at all – and he's always right.'

Frith considered this.

'OK, let's test him. We can ask him—'

'Obviously, you have to pay him.'

'Oh. How much?'

'One gold piece.'

'What?! What kind of question is worth that much for an answer?'

'It'd have to be pretty important, wouldn't it?' Dad stopped walking. 'Anyway, I think about here for the fire. We're far enough away from—'

'Oh, don't be ridiculous!' shouted the Big Wise Head. 'The wind from the west will blow it out if you have it there. You need some shelter.'

'We could go over by the well, I suppose.'

'No, no! Much too small!'

'But there's not really . . .'

'I am the *Big* Wise Head! The clue is in the name.'

'Oh. I see.'

They got the fire going easily enough, once they found the exact spot that the Big Wise Head said would give it the best shelter from the wind. This also seemed to be the exact spot where it would keep him nice and warm without getting him too hot or getting smoke in his eyes, but he assured them that that was just a coincidence. By the time the fire was ablaze, the sun had slipped below the horizon and night had fallen. Dad and Frith lay down beside the fire, and pulled their blankets around themselves.

'Night, Frith,' said Dad. 'Sweet dreams.'

'Goodnight, Dad,' said Frith, and closed her eyes. The ground was hard beneath her, and her back, turned to the infinite night, was cold. And her front, facing the fire, was hot. She was uncomfortable, angry, tired, and afraid. And a second later, she was fast asleep.

CHAPTER 9

THE FIRST TIME THAT Frith woke up it was because of a bad dream. The second time it was because of Geraldine farting. The third time it was Dad's snoring.

Frith let out a frustrated groan, and stared over at Dad, his firelit face puffing and blowing with each rasping snore. Her mouth was dry, so she stood, wrapped her blanket round her shoulders, and shuffled over to the water bucket. She dipped in a cupped hand, drank down two scoops of water, and looked out into the night.

There was a lot of it.

She looked over at the Big Wise Head, and thought she saw the tiniest flicker of movement about his eyes. But she didn't care if he was really asleep or just pretending. It wasn't as if she wanted to talk to him. She shivered, and walked back towards the fire, but after two paces she heard a cough. Again, the Head's eyes were just flickering shut as she looked his way.

This was stupid.

Frith fixed her gaze on the Head and walked on. When he opened his eyes, she was looking straight at him. But he wasn't looking at her. Instead he was glancing over to the side somewhere.

'What's the matter?' said Frith. 'That busy brain of yours won't let you sleep?'

'I only . . .' croaked the Head, then gave another cough. 'I can only answer questions if you pay me. One gold piece each.'

'A bargain! You must have people queuing up for miles! I bet that's why your voice is so croaky, because you spend all day every day answering questions.'

'Don't be sarcastic,' said the Head. 'It's tiresome.'

His voice really was very dry and cracked. Frith glanced over in the same direction the Head had been looking a moment ago, and her eyes settled on the water bucket. A pang of remorse stabbed her conscience.

'Do you want a drink?'

'Question! One gold coin!'

'Oh, for . . .' Frith stamped her foot in frustration. 'I *imagine* that you might like drink.'

'I'm fine,' croaked the Head. Then he coughed again.

She looked at him for a moment, and thought she saw, behind his defiant stare, a deep and ancient sadness.

'I'll get the bucket,' she said.

The bucket was like a thimble to the Big Wise Head. And it was not even half full. Frith felt foolish as she lifted it to his lips.

'Slowly,' he said. 'Please.'

As Frith poured, the Head closed his eyes. The water trickled onto his lower lip. He shifted a little to one side, then the other, then opened his mouth just enough to let the water in. It was gone in a second. But even that little had washed away enough dust to reveal the skin of his lips, blistered and cracked by days of blazing sun.

A breeze of a sigh blew against Frith's face.

'Thank you,' muttered the Head, his eyes open now, but not looking at her.

Frith looked down at the bucket in her hands, then over at the well.

'Do you want some more?'

'Question. One gold coin,' said the Head, automatically.

'Really?' said Frith.

'Question. One gold coin,' said the Head, with an apologetic look.

Frith frowned.

'Can't you just give it a rest?' said Frith.

'Question,' said the Head.

'One gold coin,' said Frith along with him. She looked at the Head. He was staring up at the stars again. Or at least he was looking away from her.

'Can you even . . . ?' She stopped herself and thought for a moment. 'I think,' she said, 'that you really *can't* answer a question without being paid. So, I think I'll just go to the well now and get you some more water, just in case.'

'No!' said the Head, sharply. Then more gently: 'No. Thank you. Perhaps in the morning. But now the squeaking of that stupid handle would wake your father. Though how he manages to sleep through his own snoring even *I*

57

can't explain. And I know almost everything. He sounds like an exhausted warthog.'

Frith sat down beside the Head, facing the fire. 'So how long—?'

The Head coughed, deliberately this time.

'Oh.' Frith rearranged the question in her head so it wasn't a question any more. 'Um . . . Dad told me he thought you were just a myth. And myths are normally really old. So, I imagine you've been here a long while.'

'Yes.' The Head thought for a moment. 'Two thousand and sixty-three years.'

'No!'

'In fact, two thousand and sixty-*four* years next Tuesday.'

'And how . . . ?' Frith winced. 'That is . . . I don't know how you came to be here.'

'I was cursed by a wizard.'

'There's no such thing as wizards!' said Frith.

'No! And don't I know it! Not any more. If there were, then I could try to get one to lift the wretched curse. But there used to be wizards, two thousand and sixty-three years ago. At least a few. And do you know the thing about wizards?'

'No.'

'The thing about wizards is: you should never tell them that they have a face like a shrivelled turnip.'

'That sounds like good advice,' said Frith.

'I am the Big Wise Head. Good advice is what I do. Now, at least. Obviously, back then I was . . .'

'Not so wise,' said Frith.

'No.' The flames of the fire bowed as the Big Wise Head let out a sigh. 'No, back then I was an idiot.'

'But you know *everything* now.'

The Head gave a sharp, bitter laugh.

'Not everything. Not really. But a lot. That's the thing about being stuck alone in the middle of a wasteland for two thousand and sixty-three years: it really gives you time to think. Ha! The things I could tell you!' He stared into the fire. 'If only you could afford to ask.'

'Obviously. But why . . . ? That is: I'm surprised that there aren't people queuing up for miles to ask you stuff. I mean, we could never afford to pay a gold coin just for the answer to a question, but I suppose, you know, rich people in the city might.'

'Yes. They used to come from the city. But not for a while. Not since the king came.'

'The king! Wow! What . . . ? Ahem . . . It would be interesting to hear about the king's visits to you.'

'Visit,' said the Head. 'He only came once.'

'Why only . . . ? I mean: I wonder why he didn't come back.'

The Head turned to look at Frith.

'He didn't like the answer I gave him. Or he didn't like *me*. That happens sometimes.'

'You amaze me.'

'Anyway, the king never came back, and after that, nor did anyone else. I can't say that I miss them, really. They just wanted their answers, and then they'd be straight off again. None of them ever bothered to ask what *I* might want.'

'They probably couldn't afford to.'

Frith grinned. The Head ignored her.

'Nobody ever thought: "Ooh, poor Big Wise Head, out in the Barren Wasteland in all weathers. That must be awful! Let's get him a hat to keep the sun off." No! Didn't occur to them. Selfish blockheads! Good riddance to them! Now I never see *anyone*, except your friend James the smith once in a while.'

'How do you know he's our friend?'

'Question! One gold coin!'

'Fiddlesticks! I mean: I had no idea that you knew he

60

was a friend of ours.'

'The noise of a cartful of arms and armour is very distinctive, and James usually passes through around this time of the month. But on this occasion he asked your father to make his delivery for him, because his horse is ill. Though she'll be better the day after tomorrow.'

'How do—?' said Frith, but stopped herself in time.

'I really am quite clever, you know,' said the Head.

Frith gave a yawn and stretched her arms out. 'So I've heard.'

'The last person I saw other than James was months ago. And I think he'd caught a bit too much sun. You know, gone a bit doolally. He thought he'd seen a squirrel! Out here! Imagine!'

Frith wondered how doolally two thousand and sixty-three years of too much sun would make someone, but she didn't have the energy to talk about it. It seemed to her now that the fire was unnecessarily bright. But perhaps if she half closed her eyes then it wouldn't be so bad. And if she scooched over next to the Head, and leaned against the side of his neck, then she would be warmer too.

'Don't mind me,' muttered the Head. 'Make yourself comfortable why don't you?'

Frith replied with a fluting, high-pitched snuffling snore.

'Oh,' said the Head. 'You already have.'

Frith's snores settled into a rhythm that fitted perfectly in the gaps between Dad's. The Head raised his eyes to the stars in exasperation, but was careful not to move so much that it might disturb Frith.

'*Such* a treat to have company,' he said.

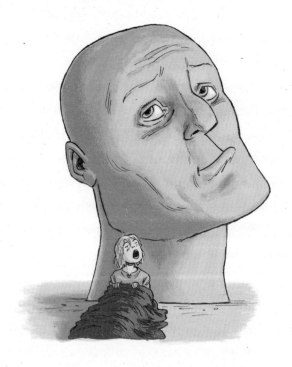

CHAPTER 10

'COME ON, SLEEPYHEAD!' SAID Dad, shouting to be heard over the creaking of the well's handle.

Frith wrenched her eyelids apart, and blinked in the timid light of dawn.

'Who are you calling sleepy?' said the Head.

Frith, slumped awkwardly against his neck, pushed herself upright.

'No,' said Dad. 'I meant sleepyhead . . .' he pointed at Frith, 'not sleepy Head.'

The Big Wise Head frowned at him.

'Never mind,' said Dad. 'Come on, Frith. We need to push off and let the Big Wise Head get on with his thinking.'

Frith stood up and rubbed at the crick in her neck. She ached in seven different places, her left arm had gone to sleep, and her head was stuck leaning over to one side.

'The Big Wise Head,' moaned the Big Wise Head, 'would have been perfectly happy to sleep for several more hours before he started thinking, actually.'

With a great effort Frith pulled her head upright. Her neck gave an alarming cracking noise. 'Ow!' she cried, as her head settled at roughly the same angle the other way.

'Must you *both* make so much noise?'

'Don't worry,' said Dad, gathering up his bedding, 'we'll soon leave you in peace. Come *on* Frith!'

Still rubbing her neck, Frith followed him to the cart. Dad climbed aboard, and Frith was about to join him when she glanced back at the Big Wise Head.

'Hang on,' she said.

'Hey! I just filled that!' said Dad, as Frith lugged the sloshing bucket over to the Head.

'And I'll do it again in a minute! Oi, grumpy!'

'What now?' said the Big Wise Head.

'Open wide.'

The Head sighed, as if this was the most unreasonable request he had ever heard. But he parted his lips. And Frith slowly trickled water onto them, and into his mouth, and he drank it down. Then he was silent for a moment.

'If you've quite finished, can I get back to sleep now?'

'I shouldn't think so. I need to refill the bucket, and that handle on the well makes an awful racket.'

Frith stomped over to the well, and drew up another bucketful of water. The handle made an awful racket. When she was done, she loaded the bucket back on to the cart.

'Right, we're off then.'

The Head grunted and looked away.

'Suit yourself,' said Frith.

By mid-morning, the desolate landscape of the Barren Wasteland had given way first to scrappy patches of grass, then a rough track through flowery meadows, then around noon, to a proper road passing through woodland. It was pretty and charming at first, then dense and dark further in.

'You know how there are no monsters in the woods back home?' said Frith.

'Yes,' said Dad.

'Is that the same here, do you think?'

'Definitely.'

'How about bandits? Are there bandits, lying in wait to rob us?'

'I wouldn't think so, not this close to the city. And even if there are, we have a cart full of weapons.'

'Yes. Weapons we can barely lift. Or at least that I can barely lift and, no offence, you'd be useless . . . Hang on. Did you say: "so close to the city"?'

'Yes.'

'Oh! So . . .'

'Yes?' said Dad.

'Da-ad . . . ?' Frith grinned.

'Yes, beloved child?' Dad smiled back.

'Are we nearly there yet?' Frith shouted gleefully.

Dad pulled the map from his pocket.

'Let me see,' he said.

Dad unfolded the map, one-handed and with deliberate slowness, as Geraldine pulled them on through the woods. Ahead of them the trees began to thin, and the road lightened into a slender ribbon of sunlit earth, winding up a gentle rise.

Dad perused the map, nodding slowly, and muttering to himself.

'So, if we're *here* . . .' he mumbled as his face lit up in mottled, leaf-strained sunshine. 'And the edge of the wood is *there* . . .' he muttered, as the light grew brighter and clearer. 'And then the road bends like that . . .' They passed the last of the trees and started up the gentle incline. 'Then, um, I'm reasonably sure that . . .' He looked ahead, he looked at the map again, he looked at Frith, he looked ahead. They reached the crest of the rise. 'Yes,' said Dad. 'We are. We are very nearly there.'

Before them the road ran downhill, then over a bridge across a stream, and then on towards the huge wooden gates in the gigantic stone walls around the impossibly, unimaginably enormous and unknowable city.

'Coo!' said Frith.

CHAPTER 11

DAD GAVE A GENTLE tug on the reins and Geraldine came to a stop outside the city gates. The two soldiers standing guard eyed him suspiciously. The one on the left took a step towards the cart and lowered a long, pointy spear-type thing in Frith's direction. The one on the right drew his sword with one hand, and raised the other at Dad.

'Halt!' he said.

Dad looked at him, then turned to Frith.

'Didn't we do that already?' he whispered.

'I think so,' said Frith.

Dad turned to the sword-wielding guard. 'I think we're as halted as we can

70

be already,' he said. 'Is that all right?'

The soldier's raised hand wobbled in the air a bit as he considered this.

'Very good,' he said. 'Now please remain seated on your vehicle, and continue in your halted state until instructed to do otherwise.'

'Does he mean "don't move"?' whispered Frith.

'I think so,' said Dad.

'No whispering!' yelled the left-hand guard, waggling his pointy spear-type thing for emphasis.

'Please don't wave that . . .' Dad looked puzzled. 'What is that anyway? Is it a very long-handled axe? Or a spear? Or can't it make its mind up?'

'It's a *halberd*, actually! And I'll have you know that this is very much at the

forefront of
modern security
technologies. It is literally the cutting edge.'

'Just the same, I'd rather you
didn't wave it at my daughter. Now
can we—?'

'Is this your vehicle, sir?' interrupted the right-hand guard.

'Yes,' said Dad. 'Of course.'

'"Of course," he says. You hear that, Stan?'

'I did, Charlie.'

'There's no "of course" about it. Have you seen this cart, Stan?'

'I have, Charlie.'

'A top-of-the-range model, combining the best elements of traditional design with a modern take, resulting in a vehicle that is sturdy, roomy and reliable, without sacrificing good looks or panache.'

'You took the words right out of my mouth, Charlie. It's sensible, but without being boring.'

'Indeed, Stan. It's trustworthy, but still sporty. I'd go so far as to say that – and bear with me on this, Stan, because you'd think this wasn't even possible – it's safe, but daring.'

Stan nodded, and his halberd wobbled in sympathy. 'It's a modern classic!'

'Thank you very much,' said Dad. 'Actually, my wife and I–'

'But does this' – Charlie pointed suddenly at Dad with his sword – 'look like the sort of man who would own a modern classic of cart design?'

'It does not, Charlie. Doesn't smell like it, either, if I'm honest.'

'Hey!' Dad raised a hand to protest, and at the same time caught a whiff of his armpit that proved Stan's point.

'I told you to keep still!' yelled Charlie, addressing his sword tip to Dad's belly button. 'Are you disobeying the instructions of one of His Majesty's Royal Guardsmen?'

'No. But–'

'Name!'

'Arthur. Arthur Carter.'

'Arthur Carter? What sort of a name is that?'

'Um, the sort of a name that someone who carts things around in his cart might have. Especially if his parents liked the name Arthur.'

'A likely story. And what business do you have in the city, so-called Arthur Carter?'

'I've got a delivery to take to . . .' Dad reached for his pocket.

'Easy there, tiger!' Stan jerked the business end of his halberd up in front of Dad's face. 'Nice and slow.'

Dad eased the papers from his pocket. There were three sheets: the map, that he set down on the seat; the

instructions that James Smith's wife had written; and a neatly folded sheet of parchment, sealed with red wax, that Frith had not seen before. Dad held out the last sheet, also extremely slowly, for examination. Charlie lowered his sword and moved closer, pressing his face up close to the important-looking document.

'He's got *papers*, Stan!' he said. 'Papers with *words* on!'

Then his eyes went wide with surprise. 'And the king's seal!'

Stan said nothing, but the tip of his halberd dipped noticeably.

'Yes,' said Dad. With his free hand he held up Mrs Smith's instructions. 'I need to find this place to take my load to. If you could let us in and tell me where it is . . . ?'

'Of course, sir,' said Charlie, returning his sword to its sheath at only the third attempt. 'If you would care to display your documentation to my colleague, who is the more expert of the two of us in matters of reading and so forth.'

Dad shrugged, and passed the paper to Frith who held it out towards Stan. Stan planted his halberd upright on the ground for support, and leaned in to scrutinize Mrs Smith's neatly written words. His brow furrowed like a ploughed field, his lips twitched noiselessly, his eyes alternately bulged and squinted.

'The!' he said, at last.

Charlie nodded in admiration.

Stan wiped the back of his wrist across his brow and took a deep breath, then returned to the matter in hand. He gritted his teeth and emitted a low hum as he once more examined the address.

'Ah,' he said, frowning. Then, 'Ruh,' he said, with a puzzled look. Then, 'Muh!' with a note of surprise.

'Ah, ruh, muh?' said Charlie.

Stan checked the paper. 'Ah . . . ruh . . . muh,' he confirmed. He nodded, confidently. 'Ah, ruh, muh!' he exclaimed, then thought for a long, painful moment. A blazing light turned on behind his eyes, and a look of revelation flooded his face. 'Arm!' he cried, ecstatically. 'The Arm!'

Charlie had to restrain himself from applauding.

'The Arm!' he said. 'Well I never! You are quite something, Stan, my boy! And you were like lightning reading that. It took you no time at all. I take my hat off to you,

I really do. Only I can't, obviously, with it actually being a helmet and regulations not allowing it, but, just the same . . .'

Stan shrugged. 'That's not even the whole word, Charlie! Not even halfway through!'

Charlie shook his head. 'They do not pay you enough, Stan. Not nearly enough.' He gave a low whistle of amazement that there should be such things in the world as words that were more than three letters long.

Frith could stand no more of it. Her patience, and the arm holding the paper, had both been strained beyond endurance. She pulled back the paper and glanced at it.

'The Armoury,' she read. 'Castle Side, St Edmund's Square, Saxcaster.' She looked at Stan and Charlie in turn. 'Do you know it? Only the sooner we get there and deliver our load, the sooner I get something to eat. And I am *staaarving*!'

Stan gaped at her, and clung to his halberd for support. Charlie took three staggering steps backwards.

'No!' said Charlie. 'I don't believe it!'

'You can *read*!' said Stan.

'Well, yes,' said Frith.

Charlie and Stan looked at Frith, then at each other, then at Frith again.

'Can we go in now, please?' said Dad.

'Yes, sir,' said Charlie, steadying himself. 'We'll just need to examine your cargo – regulations, you know, I'm sorry to even ask – and then you can be on your way.' He half raised a hand to indicate the hessian cloth tied over the huge hump of goods on the back of the cart. 'Sorry if we seemed unwelcoming. It's just that we have to be careful, you understand, in case of spies!'

Dad began to untie one of the ropes holding the covering in place. 'Of course,' he said.

'Those armies from the lands to the north!' said Stan.

'Dangerous times!' said Charlie.

'Do you need me to show you everything?' said Dad. 'Or . . . ?' He pulled up the newly freed corner of the cover.

'No, no.' Charlie dismissed the very idea.

'With a letter from the king? Just a peek and . . .' He stopped dead. 'Oh!' he said. 'Stan, come and look at this!'

'Is there a problem?' said Dad, as Stan joined them, his eyes widening with every step.

'Are these . . . ?' Charlie drew his sword again. 'Are these weapons, sir?'

'Well, yes. And some armour. We *are* delivering to the—'

'Are these,' said Stan, clutching at his halberd with renewed meaning, 'weapons from *James Smith of Thornville?*'

'Yes. You see, his horse is ill, and—'

'Oh!' said Stan.

'Oh, indeed!' said Charlie.

They turned to each other.

'They're here!' they both said at once.

'James Smith is *the best!*' Stan lifted the cover a little more and gazed in wonder at the treasures beneath. 'Oh, look, Charlie! Look at the debossed pommels on those swords! That is a *beautiful* touch!'

'Yes,' said Charlie. 'Yes it is.' He reached for the handle of one of the swords. 'Do you mind?' he said to Dad.

'Er, no,' said Dad. 'Go ahead.'

Charlie lifted the sword, weighing it reverently in his hand.

'Oh!' he gasped. 'That is exquisite! That is just *perfectly* balanced.' He held it in front of his face and looked it up and down. 'That man is an *artist*, Stan! Nothing less.'

'I've always said so,' said Stan. 'No one to match him. Not even Yardley of Sheffield.'

Charlie rolled his eyes. 'Tch! Yardley!? Too fancy by half. Nice to look at, I grant you, but to actually *wield*, give me the classic elegance of a Smith sword any day. Far too fussy, your Yardley.'

'Florid quillons,' said Stan, and they both nodded solemnly.

After a few more moments of sighing and cooing, Charlie regretfully returned the sword to the pile on the cart.

'So,' said Dad, retying the cover, 'can we, um . . . ?'

'Oh, of course, sir. Of course. Sorry to have kept you.' Charlie waved a hand towards the tall wooden gates that even now Stan was heaving open.

'And that address,' said Dad, climbing back onto the cart. 'Whereabouts . . . ?' He set Geraldine slowly walking forward.

Charlie kept pace, and as they passed through the gates he pointed across the cobbled marketplace inside. 'Castleside, sir?' he said. 'It's at the side of the castle.'

The great grey castle at the far side of the marketplace was bigger than the whole of Thornville, and loomed like a sullen giant over the courtyard.

Dad gave a nod. 'I should probably have worked that out,' he said. And with a flick of the reins, he set Geraldine trotting into the colour and noise of the marketplace.

CHAPTER 12

DAD AND FRITH'S HEADS turned this way and that as Geraldine pulled them through the bustling marketplace.

'Oh, look,' said Dad. 'The leather on that stall looks *very* good.'

'There's . . .' said Frith.

'And did you even know there *were* so many spices as that chap is selling? Amazing!'

'So . . .' said Frith.

'And on that fabric stall . . . That shiny stuff . . . I think that must be silk!'

'Much . . .' said Frith.

'And those are some fine-looking baskets. Perhaps we—'

'*FOOD!*' said Frith.

'Oh, yes,' said Dad. 'That too.' A light pull at the reins brought them to a stop. 'Are you hungry?'

Frith stared at him with simmering fury.

'Yes!' she said. 'Obviously! Yes! Starving! Of course!'

'Oh,' said Dad. 'You should have said.' He pulled some coins from his pocket. 'Here, James gave me some travelling expenses. You get something to eat while I take the delivery up to the armoury, and I'll meet you . . . by that tree in about half an hour. Is that . . . ?'

The coins had already left his hand, and Frith was halfway to the nearest stall.

'. . . OK?' said Dad.

It was actually more like an hour later when Dad skipped across the courtyard towards Frith, as she sat slumped against the tree. 'Sorry,' he said, 'that took longer than I thought. So, what did you get us?'

'Us?'

Dad noted the rich pattern of crumbs and stains scattered over Frith's smock, the gentle bulge of her stomach, and the queasy smile on her face.

'Ah! I see. So, what did you get *you*, then?'

'Oh, Dad . . .' Frith's wide eyes glazed over in dreamy remembrance. 'I had bread, and tarts, and meat, and fruit, and cheese, and cake, and sweets. Oh, and they had something called *ice cream*. That was the best! It's like delicious snow. Even though it's summer.' She paused to belch. 'And then I had all of it again.'

'I see,' said Dad. 'And is there anything *at all* left for me?'

Frith looked down at her front. 'Some of these cheese crumbs are quite big,' she said, picking up one of them, and examining it with a jeweller's scrutiny. 'Now, was this the really strong, mouldy, smelly one? Or was it the really smooth, creamy one?' She pondered the matter with due seriousness, then popped the crumb in her mouth. 'Oh! Yes! The strong, smelly one. Oof! That is *so* good!'

'I'm very happy for you,' said Dad. 'All right then, give me what's left of the money and . . .'

Frith gave a shrug of apology.

'Everything is *really* expensive in the city!' she said.

Dad rolled his eyes and tried to look disappointed and cross, but he couldn't really pull it off.

'Just as well I got paid then, isn't it?' He pulled a bulging leather pouch from his pocket, and dropped it into his other hand with a satisfying *chink!*

'We're rich!' said Frith. 'Let's eat everything else!'

'No,' said Dad. 'James Smith is rich.' He opened the pouch, extracted three gold coins, and held them up. 'But we are, temporarily, unusually comfortably off. So, do you want to show me around this market?'

It was so unfair. Dad wouldn't even give Frith *one* of the gold coins to spend. And he managed to make going round the market – which had been the most exciting thing ever for Frith on her own – really slow and boring.

He took forever to choose something to eat. Then he ate it really slowly, stopping between mouthfuls to comment on how delicious it was.

Then he took ages deciding whether or not to buy a basket, and then more ages to decide which size of basket, and then he dithered about whether to get two, and then he haggled with the seller about the price, even though he could easily have bought *all* of the baskets if he had wanted.

Then he almost bought Mum some cloth from the cloth stall, but didn't. And then he talked to the man on the spice stall about all his spices for what seemed like weeks, but only bought tiny amounts of three of them, 'just to try'.

Frith tried to get him to buy Mum some jewellery, and some perfume, and a funny wooden carving of a pig, but Dad said she wouldn't like any of those, so eventually, he bought her a pair of scissors, but just ordinary ones, not the funny ones that Frith liked which looked like a bird with a long beak. And then he filled up the baskets with lots of vegetables that were only a little bit more interesting than turnips and cabbages, and bought some bread and cheese, and spent ages listening to the cheese woman tell him how it was a shame they hadn't come a few days later as the king's fair was just coming up and then there would be stall holders and visitors from all over the country.

And then Dad said it was time to go home.

'Home?' said Frith. 'But what about the rest of the city? We've only seen the market! And I thought we were going to stay the night here. In somewhere with *beds*. Or at least walls and a roof.'

'At city prices?' said Dad. 'Not likely. No, we need to get started soon or we won't get back to the Big Wise Head before dark.'

'You're kidding! We have to spend another night in—'

'Yes,' said Dad. 'But I tell you what: I'll take all this back to the cart.' He placed the overflowing baskets on the ground. 'And meanwhile' – he extracted a small, not gold coin from his pocket and handed it over – 'you can spend this however you like, and meet me over by the gate in ten minutes. Is it a . . .'

Dad, empty-handed, looked at the cloud of dust hanging in the air where his daughter had been only a second before.

'. . . deal?' he said.

Frith left the market and headed for the gates, with a funny wooden carving of a pig clutched in one hand and most of a delicious pie in the other, running fast because she was late. So fast, in fact, that by the time she saw the gigantic soldier in her way she had no time to stop, and the best she could do was to swerve round him – and run straight into the short, bearded man behind him instead.

Glimpses of market, sky, shocked faces and ground swirled before Frith's eyes before she fell face down on the cobbles. She heard gasps, and cries, and the sharp *tink* of something metal landing on the ground nearby. As she lifted her head, something shiny caught her eye, too close to focus on properly. She grabbed at it as she rose to her feet and found herself face to beard with the man she had run into.

'For goodness' sake,' she said, 'can't you look where you're . . .'

Frith glanced down at the shiny metal thing in her hand. Then back up at the man's face.

Frith held up the shiny metal thing, noting its surprising weight.

'Um, sorry,' she said, 'but is this your crown?'

CHAPTER 13

FRITH HELD THE CROWN out to the king.

'Sorry,' she said. 'I think one of the pointy bits got bent. But I'm sure you can fix it. That is, I'm sure someone will fix it for you. I don't suppose you do that kind of thing for yourself. You're probably too busy, um . . . king-ing.'

Frith's hand wavered in the space between them. The crown was heavy, and she wished he would take it from her.

'You, erm . . . You *are* the king aren't you?'

Frith became aware that the soldier she had swerved to avoid was just behind her right shoulder, while another equally tall, broad and looming guard stood uncomfortably close just behind her left. There were two more behind the king, and by his side an elegant man with a tidy beard and wrinkles around his kind brown eyes. They all looked very serious, and quite tense.

'Yes,' said the king, finally taking the crown and turning it in his hand to examine it. 'I am the king.' He rubbed a velvet sleeve across a scuff mark on the gold. 'And who are you?'

'Oh! I'm Frith Carter, from Thornville, your, um . . . Your Royal Majestic . . . Highness?' Frith gave an awkward bow, then a terrible curtsey, and then a little wave. 'Sorry.'

The king kept looking at the crown, one finger rubbing against the bent-over point.

'Shall I kill her, Your Majesty?' said one of the guards. 'Or shall I just chop her legs off to stop her running about?'

The king put the crown on his head, and raised his eyes to meet Frith's. His lips were pursed, as if he was weighing up the options.

Someone in the gathering crowd of onlookers gave a nervous squeak. The elegant man with the tidy beard whispered in the king's ear.

And then, all of a sudden, the king's eyes lit up, his mouth widened into a warm smile, and he shook his head and chuckled.

'You boys!' he said, slapping the back of his hand gently against the chest of one of the soldiers. 'Such jokers! Chop her legs off, indeed! Is that any way to talk about a visitor to our fine city? What must you think of us? Please forgive my guardsmen. They are fine fellows, but they have an odd sense of humour. Now, are *you* all right? That was quite a tumble you took!'

'Oh, I'm . . . yes, I'm fine. I'm . . . yes, sorry, thank you, Your High Royalness.'

'Jolly good, jolly good. Thank goodness. Well, that's the main thing. And don't go worrying about this old thing.' He pointed to the crown. 'Now I've got an excuse not to wear it, while it's being fixed.' He leaned in close to Frith's ear. 'Actually, it's horribly uncomfortable.'

Frith giggled.

'Thornville, you say?' The king scratched his beard. 'That's quite a journey. Are you here long? Where are you staying?'

'Oh, we're not staying. In fact, we should have gone already.' Frith pointed, and the king glanced over at Dad, who was stumbling towards them looking horrified.

'Oh, that is a shame,' said the king. 'But I suppose you had better run along. Oh! Or walk. Quite carefully.'

'Yes, Your Maj-ness-ty,' said Frith, bowing her head and shuffling swiftly sideways, and off towards Dad. 'Thank you very much, Your Royalty.'

Dad's eyes looked like they might pop.

'Was that the—?'

'Yes,' said Frith, marching past him. 'Shall we go? I think we should go.'

*

It was much easier to leave the city than it had been to get in. Charlie and Stan, the guards, were busy inspecting a cart full of beetroot, and barely glanced at Dad and Frith as they passed. Dad kept asking what had happened with the king, and Frith kept saying she didn't want to talk about it, until eventually she just pretended to fall asleep. Then a few minutes later she really did. Dad consulted the map, and aimed for the first landmark.

'Oh no, not you again!' said the Big Wise Head, as Dad brought the cart to a halt.

'Yes, us again,' said Dad, dropping to the ground and wincing at the stiffness of his back.

'If it's any consolation,' said Frith, 'I'm not exactly delighted that we're back here either.' She stomped off towards the well. 'But apparently we couldn't stay in the city and sleep in *an actual bed* because we're in too much a of a hurry.'

'Oh, how *awful* for you, having to spend *two nights* outdoors! I can't imagine how *horrible* that must be! Oh, wait . . . I don't have to imagine. I've been doing that for two thousand and sixty-three *years*!'

'That's the point,' said Frith. 'It's all right for you, you're used to it.'

Dad was building a tiny mound of sticks on top of the

ashes of the previous fire.

'Oi! Child! You can get the blankets from the cart if you want to make yourself useful.'

'All right,' said Frith, extracting the full bucket from the well. 'I'm just watering the Big Dry Head first.'

'Ah, yes,' said Dad, turning to the Head. 'I'd been meaning to ask about that. How do you get the water you need when there's nobody here? Should we–?'

'I don't *need* anything. Because of the curse put on me I can't die. But my lips *are* a little dusty, I suppose. So, it wouldn't hurt to wash them. If it will make the girl feel better.'

'That's very good of you,' said Frith, dripping water onto the Head's lips.

Dad noted without com-ment the Head's sigh of relief. He placed a hand on Frith's shoulder and gave it the gentlest squeeze. 'I'll sort the blankets,' he said.

Dad had bought some venison from the market and he put a few small chunks of it onto a spit over the fire along with some of the vegetables to cook. Frith spotted the Big Wise Head's nostrils twitching as a gentle breeze carried the smell his way.

'Would you like some?' said Frith, when it was ready.

'Question!' said the Big Wise Head. 'One gold coin!'

'Never mind,' said Frith.

The meal, Dad and Frith both agreed, was considerably better than turnip and cabbage surprise. Frith fed a little of the meat to the Big Wise Head whether he liked it or not. Dad had bought himself a bottle of beer, which he declared 'very tasty' on the first sip, 'surprisingly strong' when he was halfway through it, and 'I think I'll have a little lie down' when he had finished.

'Ah,' said the Big Wise Head, as Dad's first snuffling snores sounded out, 'the beautiful stillness of a night in the Barren Wasteland. There really is nothing quite like it.'

Frith took her blanket and sat beside the Head, as she had done the previous night. 'Not quite so loud from over here,' she muttered, leaning against the Head's neck.

'Glad to help,' grumbled the Big Wise Head.

The fire crackled, and sparks swam up into the darkening sky.

'I hear you . . . bumped into the king,' said the Big Wise Head, sounding rather pleased with himself.

'Well, I . . . What? How did you know . . . ?'

'Question!'

'All right, all right!' Frith scowled. 'I wonder to myself how you know that I met the king today.'

'I am the Big Wise Head,' said the Big Wise Head, in a deep, important-sounding voice. 'I know ALL!'

'No, you don't,' said Frith. 'But you do know this . . .'

'A little bird told me,' said the Head.

'But we would have seen if anyone—'

'No,' said the Head. 'I mean literally: *a little bird* told me. A red kite called Keith.'

'I don't believe you!'

'I have to admit,' said the Big Wise Head, 'I thought he looked more like a Brian myself, but I've no reason to doubt him. Anyway, Keith told me . . .' and then the Big Wise Head gave a series of whistles that sounded exactly like a red kite.

Frith gaped. 'That's . . . very impressive.' Her eyes narrowed. 'But that doesn't mean that you can understand—'

'It's a good job it wasn't one of the king's best crowns,' said the Big Wise Head, 'or he'd probably have let one of those four guards do something horrible to you.'

Frith spluttered.

99

The Head looked into the fire for a while. 'I've been here a long while. I've had plenty of time to learn how to speak Bird. Even Red Kite, which is a *particularly* tricky dialect, actually.'

'That *is* amazing,' admitted Frith. 'To be able to talk to birds!'

'It's OK. Most of them are a bit dull, really. But they do have a different view of things. I envy them that. And Keith is brighter than most. Oh, he said to thank you for being such a messy eater, by the way. He enjoyed all your crumbs.'

'I am *not* a messy eater!' Frith removed a stray shred of onion from her sleeve. 'He must have confused me with someone else.'

The Head's chuckle shook the ground beneath Frith's bottom.

'Do you . . . ?' Frith stopped herself, thought, started again. 'That is . . . I suppose birds must visit you from all over the kingdom.'

'Yes,' said the Big Wise Head.

'Including ones from the woods by Thornville.'

'Occasionally. There's a warbler called Fitch who's quite clever.'

'Has he ever . . . ? Ahem. Some people say that there's a monster in those woods.'

'I see,' said the Big Wise Head. 'How interesting.'
Then he paused for a long while just to be annoying.
'But Fitch has never mentioned seeing one. Nor any of
the other birds.'

'I knew it!' said Frith. 'I knew there was no such thing
as monsters.'

'Oh,' said the Head. 'Well, I never said *that*.'

'You mean there really are?' said Frith.

'Ha!' said the Head. 'Question! One gold coin!'

Frith jumped to her feet and faced him, scowling
angrily.

'You are infuriating!'

'Yes, I know.'

Frith kicked at the ground in frustration, throwing a cloud of dust up into the Big Wise Head's face. The Head spluttered, and Frith turned her back on him, arms folded.

'Yes,' said the Big Wise Head, more softly now. 'I know. Which is how I got to be cursed in the first place.'

Frith turned to look at him, her anger simmering gently.

'You would think,' said the Head, 'that a Big Wise Head might have learned better by now, wouldn't you? After two thousand and sixty-three years.'

'Yes,' said Frith, spitting out the last of her rage with the word.

'There is no monster in the woods near Thornville,' said the Big Wise Head. 'But there are monsters elsewhere in the world.'

Frith glanced out into the gathering night.

'Not here, though,' said the Head. 'Not tonight.'

'I wasn't worried!' said Frith, then yawned and settled down again. She leaned back against the Head's neck.

'Of course not.'

'Big *Stupid* Head,' mumbled Frith, wriggling into a more comfortable position, and throwing one arm lazily around the Big Wise Head's neck in an awkward, sleepy

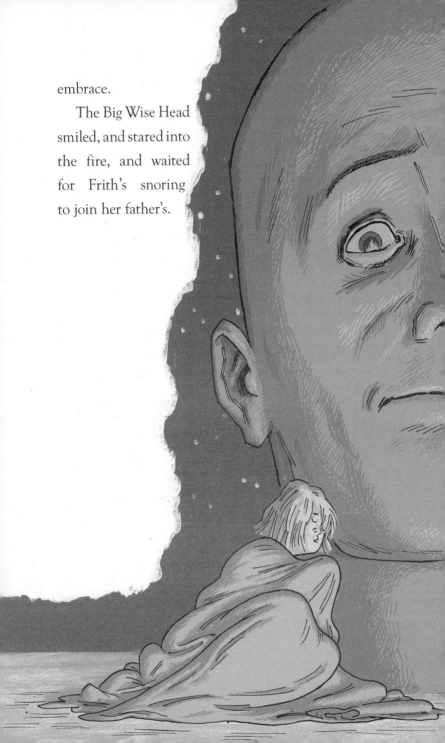

embrace.

The Big Wise Head
smiled, and stared into
the fire, and waited
for Frith's snoring
to join her father's.

CHAPTER 14

FRITH WOKE, MORE OR less.

She lay still, eyelids twitching, piecing together the blurs of sound that drifted to her ears: faint footsteps; the shuffling tread of her father; his voice softly mumbling; Geraldine's answering snort and a brief scuffle of hooves. Frith drank in a fresh cool breath of morning air and opened her eyes, then struggled to focus on whatever was close before them. Skin. A vast expanse of skin, in bright clear detail, tanned and lined and weathered; wisps of hair as long as a finger, pin-sharp in the morning sunlight, bending and bowing like grass in the gentle breeze.

Frith sat up, and rubbed her eyes. The skin rippled as muscle moved beneath it. The Big Wise Head turned to look at her.

'You're awake then?'

Frith shuffled back to get a better view of him, noting the smear of drool on his neck where her face had been resting.

'Almost.'

'I suppose you'll be dashing straight off again.' The Head looked away, off to the horizon.

Frith stood and stretched, wiggling life into all her moving parts.

'Probably.' She looked at the Head, puzzled. 'Is something wrong?'

'Question,' said the Head. 'One gold coin.'

'Oh, suit yourself!' said Frith, pivoting round and walking away.

'I always do,' the Head called after her. 'Try to be quick. I have a *lot* of thinking to do today. The sooner I get started, the better.'

Dad had already loaded up the cart and was strapping Geraldine into her harness.

'Morning, beloved daughter of mine.'

Frith climbed onto the cart. 'Ready when you are,' she said.

Dad, squinting in the morning sun, glanced up at her, then raised a hand in the Head's direction, climbed aboard, and flicked the reins to set Geraldine walking.

'Hey!' shouted the Head. 'You've left your blanket

behind, stupid girl!'

Dad pulled at the reins, and Geraldine and the cart stopped.

'Pop back and get it will you?' said Dad.

Frith slumped off the cart, and trudged back to the Head.

'Typical tourists! Coming here uninvited, and leaving litter everywhere!'

Frith snatched up the blanket.

'There,' she said. 'Satisfied?' Then, as she stomped away, back towards the cart, the low morning sun caught her eye, and she stopped in her tracks, dazzled for a moment.

'Don't hang around on my account,' said the Head. 'Go, if you're going.'

Frith balled her fists in fury, turned, and marched back to face the Big Wise Head. With a low grumble, she held the blanket up in front of her and tied a knot in one corner.

'What are you doing now?'

Frith said nothing, and knotted the next corner.

'Don't you know how to fold a blanket properly?'

Frith knotted the third corner.

'You're just creasing it and—'

'Oh, shut *up*!' said Frith, pulling tight the knot in

the final corner of the blanket. She threw it up onto the Head, then tugged at it to get it even.

'There!' said Frith. 'You wanted a hat to keep the sun off.' The Big Wise Head looked blankly back at her. Frith huffed out a dismissive breath, and stomped back to the cart.

Dad gave her a quizzical look.

'I thought you were fetching—'

'Can we just go?' said Frith.

Dad looked at her, then over at the Big Wise Head.

'Yes. OK.'

And with a light flick of the reins, they went.

The Big Wise Head's voice was barely audible

when he spoke again.

'I was *hoping* for something with a brim . . .'

The air was dry and burning hot, and Dad and Frith sweated and sweltered and simmered the long way home. But Frith's anger burned even hotter inside her. She had never even met the Big Wise Head two days ago, so she couldn't understand why she would be so upset by him now. But she was. And the more she thought about it, the less she understood it. And the less she understood it, the angrier she felt. By late afternoon she was tired, hot and seething.

'Look,' said Dad.

Frith cast a sullen glance the way he was pointing.

Just visible on the horizon was the scantest sliver of green. And beyond it was home.

Frith felt a sharp pang of joy, and turned her head to hide the way that the dusty air was making her eyes water.

'It's still miles away, though, isn't it?' she grumbled. 'Wake me when we get there.' She curled herself up on the bench. 'And no singing!' Then she pretended to fall asleep.

Dad gave a sad smile, and pretended that he was fooled.

CHAPTER 15

FRITH KNEW, EVEN WITH her eyes closed, that they were close to home. She saw the change in colour behind her eyelids as they moved out of the sun into the shade of the woodland. She heard the change in tone of Geraldine's hooves as they passed from track to road. She heard too, the breeze in the leaves, the evening song of the birds, and the soft, terrible singing of her father. And eventually, she heard a voice, then voices. She pulled herself upright.

'Are we—?' she said, fighting a smile.

'We are,' said Dad.

They were even nearer than Frith had thought. It seemed like half the village had come out to meet them, shouting, laughing and welcoming them back, trailing behind a manic Cabbage.

'Well, Arthur Carter,' said Bill Simpson, gesturing

with his pipe. 'I am glad to see you safely home. Though 'tis a wonder, mind, that you were not beset by bandits and murdered. Or eaten by ravenous beasts in the Barren Wasteland, and your bones left to bleach in the sun.'

'Yes,' said Dad. 'Luckily none of that happened.'

'But now that you are back, you'll be wanting to help do something about the monster problem, I'll bet. It's only got worse since you've been away, you know.'

Dad rolled his eyes.

Geraldine pulled them on through the crowd, and

Dad and Frith waved and smiled, and didn't know what to say.

Dad stopped off to give James his money, and sent Frith home ahead of him. She set off wearily up the road. A few steps later she was sprinting, Cabbage yapping happily by her side, racing to keep up.

'Muuuuuum!'

Mum emerged from the far side of the hut, set down the bucket she was carrying, and strode towards her, a warm grin spreading across her face.

'Hello, lovey,' she said, as Frith raced towards her, threw her arms around her middle, and squeezed. Mum wrapped an arm around Frith's back and kissed the top of her head.

'Good to be home, then?'

Frith let go and stepped back, trying to look nonchalant. 'Well, I suppose it's better than being on a rattly old cart, or sleeping on the ground, isn't it?'

'And better than spending three days solid with your dad, I bet. Talking of which, what have you done with him? You haven't left him behind in the city, have you?'

'No. He went to see James. He'll be here in a minute.'

'Oh well,' said Mum. 'Better luck next time.'

'Mum!'

'I'll be very glad to see him, actually.' She ruffled Frith's hair. 'We haven't had a decent meal since you've been gone. And I got us a goose from John Baxter today, so I need your dad to pay for it and cook it for us before we swearing starve to death.'

'And I've missed you very much too, darling,' said Dad, striding towards them with a grinning Spuggy on his shoulders.

112

'Finally, you bother to come and see your poor abandoned wife,' said Mum. 'But only after you stop for a natter with James Smith, I hear.'

'Thought I'd better drop off his money. If I brought it here then Spuggy would probably steal it all.'

'Hey!' said Spuggy.

'Which reminds me,' said Dad, 'have you seen him anywhere?'

'Who did you say? Spuggy?' Mum looked puzzled. 'Well now, it seems to me I do vaguely recall knowing someone by that name.'

'I'm up here!' said Spuggy, tapping on Dad's head.

'Hmm . . . Spuggy . . .' Mum scratched her head. 'Oh, yes! We've got one of those . . . oh, what do you call them? Scruffy little creatures. Always getting in the way. Always making too much noise.'

'I'm right here!' shouted Spuggy.

'Yes,' said Mum. 'That's just the kind of noise they make.'

'Oh,' said Frith. 'You don't mean . . .' She shivered in disgust. 'A *boy*, do you?'

'I'm on your shoulders, silly Daddy,' said Spuggy, pulling hard at one of Dad's ears.

'That's it,' said Mum, ignoring him.

'A boy! I think we've got one of those somewhere, and I've got a feeling *he* might be called—'

Spuggy started slapping at Dad's head like he was playing a drum.

Dad gave a puzzled look, then reached up to lift his son from his shoulders, and lower him to the ground where he examined him closely.

'Spuggy!' he said, at last. 'Where on Earth have you been?'

'You're stupid,' said Spuggy.

'Thank you very much,' said Dad. 'Now I really know I'm home. Right, where's this goose, then?'

As they sat around the fire after eating, Mum gathered up the empty bowls. Dad looked over at Spuggy with a concerned frown.

'Are you OK, son?' said Dad.

Spuggy stared blankly into the fire, a glistening tear trailing down one cheek. 'I didn't know food could be like that!'

Dad gave a sad smile.

'Hopefully we can eat a bit better now. Now that we've a little money.' He dabbed a finger to the corner of his eye. 'Now, time for bed, young Spuggy. Off you go.'

Spuggy snapped out of his trance and raced off.

'I hear you got quite the welcome home when you got back then,' said Mum.

'I think the whole of the village came out to see us. Except my wife, of course.'

'Busy woman, that wife of yours, so I hear. Probably had more important things to do.'

'Or she just wanted to avoid Bill Simpson prattling on about . . .' Dad dropped his voice to a whisper. '. . . monsters.'

'Oh, it's not just Bill any more,' said Mum. 'John Baxter lost half a dozen chickens while you were gone, and Bill convinced him it was the swearing *you know what* as well. And now that John's saying it too, people are starting to take it seriously. And now Bill's trying to organize a hunting party to search the woods, if they can't get the king's men to do it, that is.'

'The king's men?'

'Oh, of course, you don't know! Turns out there's a messenger from the king coming to the village. So Bill's arranged a meeting in the village hall, and he reckons if he can get this messenger along to it and tell him there's a problem, then he'll take word back to the king.'

'And then the king will send soldiers to rid the woods of a non-existent monster?'

'Yes. And then put up our taxes to pay for it, most likely.'

'So, are we going to this meeting, then?'

'What do you think? It's going to be utterly pointless, and Bill Simpson's going to make a right fool of himself. Of course we're swearing going!'

CHAPTER 16

THE VILLAGE HALL WAS the largest hut in Thornville, but even so, on the evening of the meeting, it was packed. Frith and her family got there just before the start, and had to squeeze in at the back. It seemed like the whole of the village was there, and quite a few people who Frith didn't recognize at all.

'Who's that?' said Frith, as Dad lifted her onto his shoulders to see better.

'That beardy string-bean next to Molly Baker? I don't know. Maybe he's over from Hinton. There's definitely one or two from there. And quite a few I don't know at all. Times are hard all over, I guess.'

'Good evening, Arthur Carter, Martha Carter.' Gigantic James Smith squeezed through the doorway.

'Hello, Mr James,' said Spuggy, perched on Mum's shoulders.

'Hello . . . smallest small Carter child,' said James awkwardly. 'Hello, er . . . bigger small Carter child.'

'Right, then . . . shall we get started?' said a voice from the front of the hall. Thornville didn't have a mayor, or any official leader, but for this occasion William Shaw had put himself in charge because he had the biggest beard. 'Thank you all for, um, coming. We're very lucky tonight to have with us the king's messenger.' He

indicated a man with a much smaller, yet somehow more imposing, pointy beard next to him. 'As well as, er, no less than four of the king's soldiers.' William waved a hand to indicate the two pairs of armoured brutes standing to either side. 'We are very honoured, um, to have you all here. So, without further ado, let's give a lovely Thornville welcome to His Majesty's Official Messenger and Herald, John, um . . . Whitehill.'

There was not much applause, except from some of the strangers who clapped and cheered loudly.

'Thank you,' said the messenger, with no enthusiasm. He held up a scroll of parchment, unrolled it, and began to read, quickly and in a dull, bored voice. 'Hear ye, hear ye, citizens of Thornville!' he said, and a few people clapped again. 'Hark well, hold your peace, and listen to tidings and news from His Most Royal Majesty, King Laurence III. Please remain quiet, and attend well.'

'He's a bit boring, isn't he?' said Spuggy, not remaining quiet. 'People of Thornville, the mighty army of our land, under the command of His Most Royal Majesty and his appointed brave generals, continues to defend our borders from the dark forces of the armies of the lands to the north. There have been many victories for our brave battalions, often combating enemy forces that are larger in number, better equipped, and sneakier than themselves. But rest assured that our courageous armies are forever committed to ensuring your continuing safety, now, and going forward. The cost of this hard-won security, however, has been high. Our noble troops desperately need new weapons . . .'

James Smith gave a little hum of interest.

'. . . as well as food, clothing, and medicines. Naturally, these items cost money.'

'Oh, here we swearing go!' said Mum.

'No, it's OK,' said Frith, 'because the king is really rich. He's got gold hats! He can pay—'

'PLEASE REMAIN QUIET AND ATTEND WELL!' screamed one of the soldiers, politely.

'Ahem,' said the messenger, 'as I was saying: these items cost a great deal of money. As such, His Majesty regrets that it is necessary to raise taxes to fund the continued security of our borders, the safety of our country, the safety of your village, your homes and your loved ones. An individually calculated emergency payment will be collected from you all shortly, once we've visited your homes and seen what you've got. In thanks for your loyal support, and your uncomplaining generosity, the king invites you all to the spectacular entertainments on the final day of the king's fair, where there will be music, jousting and diverse other entertainments, all for the bargain price of twenty copper pieces (plus booking fee). Thank you. And long live the king!'

'Long live the king!' shouted the strangers in the crowd, while everyone else began to mutter and grumble.

'Hang on!' shouted Shouty Joe Wheatley, stabbing a finger at the air. 'You can't just–'

'HE SAID: LONG LIVE THE KING!' screamed the loud soldier.

'Long live the king,' mumbled the crowd.

'That's better,' said the messenger. 'And now, the weather: it will be mostly horrible.'

He rolled up his scroll and made to leave.

'Oi!' shouted Shouty Joe. 'Where do you think you're going? We've got questions to ask you, you lackey of an outdated and corrupt monarchy.'

The messenger observed Joe through narrowed eyes, and smiled an empty smile.

'Questions! Why, yes, of course. The king is eager to hear what you have to say. Please . . .' The messenger waved his arm, inviting enquiries, as one of the soldiers moved off into the crowd.

'May I ask . . .' a confident voice cut in before anyone else had a chance. Frith saw that it was one of the out-siders, not anyone she recognized. 'Would you agree that His Most Royal Majesty, King Laurence III, is both wise and noble, and that we are very fortunate indeed to have him?'

'Swearing heck!' muttered Mum. 'What a crawler!'

'Excellent question!' The king's messenger considered the matter. 'I would have to say: yes, he is; he is; and you are. Next question?'

'Why can't the king—' began Shouty Joe, but then stopped short. 'Urf!' he cried, and as all eyes turned his way, he bent over double. If the soldier in the crowd had not happened to be there to catch him he probably would have fallen to the floor.

'Oh dear!' said the king's messenger. 'Are you all right, sir?'

Joe gave a low moan.

'Perhaps he needs some air,' said the messenger. 'Get

him outside, soldier and . . . take care of him, will you?'

The crowd parted to allow the soldier to kindly drag Joe outside for some reviving air.

'Anyone else?' said the messenger.

'I'd like to know,' said a clear voice somewhere near a back corner of the hall, 'is there any way that His Royal Majesty, King Laurence III could be better than he is?'

'Another very good question.' The king's messenger gave a simpering smile. 'I would have to say no. His Majesty is wise, kind, generous, and works tirelessly to—'

'Take all our money in taxes!' shouted someone. There was a mumble of agreement from most of the crowd.

'And then spend it on bloomin' wars,' said someone else. 'We've got little enough as it is, and you want to take more? And what will you do for us in return?'

The mumble of the crowd turned into a rumble.

'That's right,' said another voice, shouting to be heard now. 'What are you going to do about our crops failing?'

'And what are you going to do about our animals going missing?' said someone else.

124

'And there's no fish in the river!'

'And no boars in the wood!'

The messenger looked uneasy and shrank back. The remaining guards put their hands to the hilts of their swords.

'And what are you going to do about the monster in the woods?' shouted Bill Simpson.

There were some groans from some parts of the hall, and at least one cry of 'Shut up, you silly old fool!' But the messenger gave a serious nod.

'Ah!' he raised a finger, and the crowd quietened a little. 'Yes!' he said. 'The monster in the woods! I'm so glad you reminded me. This is, of course, a high priority in His Majesty's plans for the region.'

'Is it?' said Bill.

'Oh, yes,' said the messenger. 'It's quite a common problem now, I'm afraid. The monsters have been deliberately driven over the border from the countries to the north. You say that animals and fish have gone missing?'

The crowd agreed.

'Yes, that sounds very familiar. This has been happening a lot.'

'Is he saying there really is a monster in the woods?' said Spuggy, in a frightened voice.

'Yes, love,' said Mum calmly. 'But he's wrong; take

no notice.' Then she shouted: 'Stop this silly talk about swearing monsters, will you? You're scaring my boy. I've never heard such ridiculous—'

'It's not ridiculous,' said Bill Simpson. 'I seen 'im! I did! Great big 'orrible thing – tall as a tree!'

'That'd be a tree then, wouldn't it,' said Mum, to some laughter.

'No, but I saw it too!' said Fred Thursby. 'With my own eyes. Huge hairy beast with enormous teeth.'

'But you never even go in the woods,' said Mum. 'And you can barely see at all, you blind old fool.'

'I saw it on the way here,' said one of the outsiders. 'Luckily, it was quite a way off and it didn't see me. But it was terrifying!'

'Yes. Me too.' A new voice could barely be heard above the rising hum of worry coming from the crowd.

'And me! And I . . . I saw it breathe fire!'

The crowd gasped. Frith turned her head to try to spot who was talking.

'And it was all slimy!' Frith turned her head again.

Then voices piped up in turn from all around the hall.

'And it had shiny scales!'

'And sharp curly horns!'

'And a long forked tongue!'

Frith's head spun, but she couldn't work out who

had said any of this.

'That don't sound like what I saw,' said Bill Simpson.

'Maybe you saw a different one! There must be two of them! Maybe more!'

'It's an invasion!'

Frith gave up trying to tell who said what. Everyone seemed to be shouting and screaming at once. And even though she believed that there was no monster, there was such an atmosphere of panic and fear in the hall that she couldn't stop some of it from seeping into her. She suddenly felt cold. And now Spuggy was crying.

'Mum!' he wailed. 'What about Edward? If the woods are full of monsters, what will happen to Edward?'

Mum's face was a storm. 'I have had enough of this swearing nonsense!' she seethed, then she hooked the little finger of each hand into the sides of her mouth and took a huge breath.

But the ear-splitting whistle that came next, came from the front of the hall. Everyone shut up and looked round.

His Majesty's Official Messenger and Herald, John Whitehill, took his fingers out of his mouth and smiled.

'I know that these are worrying times. But rest assured, King Laurence and his men are resolute in their mission to keep you safe. We will be searching the woods thoroughly tomorrow as we depart, and will relate our findings directly to the king himself. Appropriate action will then be taken to rid your woodlands of this terrible infestation of monsters.'

'Thank goodness!' someone said.

'Long live the king!' shouted someone else. It wasn't anyone who lived in Thornville, but the next person to shout it was. And the next. And soon more than half the village was chanting 'Long live the king! Long live the king!'

The king's messenger bowed, and smiled, and thanked them all. And when they finally stopped, he informed them that they were welcome to donate extra money for an anti-monster fund to either of the guards on the door on their way out.

CHAPTER 17

'BUT I PAID INTO the bucket at the end of the meeting.'

Dad was talking to someone at the doorway. Frith wiped the sleep from her eyes and looked to see who it was.

'That was very kind of you,' said the king's messenger. 'But that was a voluntary donation. Nothing to do with your tax.'

'But then I paid our *tax* when you came collecting last night.'

'Yes,' said the messenger. 'But now we've found you may have paid the wrong amount.'

'What's going on, Dad?' said Frith, arriving at Dad's side and peering past him at the messenger and two guards.

'Nothing, love,' Dad kept his eyes on the messenger. 'So, are you here to give me a refund?'

The king's messenger shook his head. 'No,' he said. 'We understand that you are the owner and operator of a Grade One commercial goods transportation vehicle, class C (two horsepower and below)?'

'A commercial goods transportation . . . ? You mean my cart?' Dad put his hands in his pockets and leaned against the door frame, blocking Frith's view.

'Yes. Two horsepower or below.'

'With Geraldine,' said Dad. 'Who is one horse.' He took his right hand out of his pocket to scratch his head. 'So, I suppose, one horsepower. Yes.'

'So, you need to pay extra road tax.'

'Oh,' said Dad. He dropped his hand down by his side. 'And how much is that?'

Frith looked at the two gold coins that Dad was holding out behind his back.

'That depends,' said the messenger. 'How much do you have?'

Frith grabbed the coins. Dad slid his hand back inside his pocket.

'Hardly anything.' Dad turned his pockets inside out to reveal a single copper coin.

One of the guards grabbed it from him.

'Shall we search the place, boss?' said the other.

The messenger stared at Dad for a moment. 'No, we'd better get on. Busy day ahead,' he said, tapping Dad's chest with a finger. 'Luckily for you.'

'Oh, yes!' said Frith. 'You're searching the woods for the monster, aren't you?'

The guards looked alarmed.

'Don't worry, little girl,' said the messenger. 'These men are highly trained professionals. We'll be perfectly safe.'

'Will we, though?' said the first guard.

'The woods are crawling with monsters,' said the second. 'That's what I heard.'

The messenger scowled, and hurried them over to mount their horses. Dad and Frith watched them ride off up the slope towards the woods. As they disappeared into the trees, Frith spotted the scrawny figure of Shouty Joe rising from the long grass and following them in. Turning, she found herself facing Dad.

'Well done, daughter of mine,' he said. 'They're all gone. The coast is clear.' He held out a hand. 'I'll have the coins back now, please.'

'No, you won't,' said Frith.

'Oh, come on,' said Dad. 'You know I wasn't giving

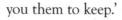

you them to keep.'

'It's not that,' said Frith. 'You can have them back, just . . . not yet.'

'Why? What have you done with them?'

'I thought they might search me, so, um . . . I swallowed them. But don't worry, you can have them back tomorrow.'

'I see those swearing bandits, the king's men, are off, then?' Mum marched towards the hut with Spuggy at her side, almost naked and dripping wet. 'And good swearing riddance! They already robbed everybody blind last night, and still came back for more this morning.' She looked from Dad's face to Frith's, and then back again. 'They've not been here as well, have they?' Spuggy wandered past them into the hut.

'Yes,' said Frith.

'Oh, swearing swears! How much did they take?'

'One copper coin,' said Dad.

'Oh, thank swear for that,' said Mum. 'So, we've still got the gold ones. That's a relief.'

'Oh, yes,' said Dad. 'They're . . . in a safe place.'

'I should swearing well hope so. Now, Frith, your

dad's taking the cart over to Ingleton for a job this morning, and I'm going with him to take some cloth to Lizzie Bramble, so you'll have to look after Spuggy while we're gone, OK? Keep him out of the woods.'

'Why? Are you worried about monsters after all?'

'Don't be daft! But those swearing soldiers are, and they've got bows and arrows, and about as much sense as Cabbage. I don't want your brother getting shot because he's been mistaken for something horrible and disgusting.'

They all thought about this for a moment.

'Something *else* horrible and disgusting, I mean,' said Mum.

'I am not horrible and disgusting!' A drier Spuggy, with more clothes on, re-joined them.

'Only because I've scrubbed you clean in the stream,' said Mum.

'You put him in the stream?' Frith pulled a face. 'No wonder all the fish have disappeared.'

'Hey!'

'Be nice to your brother, Frith,' said Dad. 'You need to get on if you're going to be together all day.'

'Dad!' said Frith. 'Do I really have to? Can't I just tie him to a tree?'

135

'No!' said Mum and Dad together.

'That would be cruel,' said Dad.

'And it doesn't work,' said Mum. 'Even with my best knots.'

Frith looked downcast.

'I tell you what,' said Dad. 'Look after Spuggy properly, and when we get back, I'll teach you' – he reached into his pocket and pulled out a folded paper frog – 'how to make one of these.'

'Wow! That's amazing!' Frith took the frog and examined it closely. 'But why is there writing on it?'

'It's James's map. I thought as we don't need it any more it might as well be a frog now. So, is it a deal?'

'OK then,' said Frith. 'But I get to keep this.'

'All right, if you chop some firewood as well.'

'Deal.' Frith stuffed the frog in her pocket.

'Right,' said Mum, 'if that's all settled, we'll be off.'

'Be careful,' said Dad as they walked away.

'That's right,' Mum said over her shoulder. 'Because if we get back and find you've both been shot through the head with arrows, then I will swearing murder you!'

And with that, they were gone.

Chapter 18

It took Frith about twenty minutes to lose her brother. She'd left Spuggy outside, playing with Cabbage, while she went in to fetch the axe. When she came back out, just a moment later, neither horrible little brother nor dog were anywhere to be seen. She yelled for them, but neither reappeared. Instead, Old Robert lolloped into view.

'Spuggy!' shouted Frith in one direction. 'Cabbage!' she screamed in the other.

''Scuse me, Miss Frith,' said Old Robert.

'Yes?' said Frith. 'Spuggy! Cabbage! You stupid hound!'

'Are you looking for Spuggy? And Cabbage?'

'Yes! Why? Have you seen them?'

'Now, as it happens, I did just see them, yes.'

'Oh, thank goodness! Where are they?'

'Well, I can't say that I know where they are *now*. But

137

I can say where they was when I seen them a minute ago.'

'Yes. Right. Where was that?'

'Well, first I seen old Cabbage, bless him. Tearing along after a squirrel, he was. Going like the clappers. And then I seen young Spuggy, chasing along after Cabbage.' Old Robert chuckled. 'Ha! It were quite a sight, I can tell you, all of 'em in a row like that.'

'And where did they go *then*?'

'Oh, well now, old Mr Squirrel, I s'pose he thought it'd be better for his health, like, if he was up a tree, so—'

'Oh, don't tell me they went into the woods!'

Old Robert looked at her blankly. For a long while.

'For heaven's sake, you silly old man. Where did they go?'

'Don't you go getting all radgy with me, Frith Carter, when I'm just doing what you told me. That's not fair, is it? First you says, *don't tell me they went into the woods*, then you gets all mardy when I don't tell you that they went into the woods, even though that's what they did. I swear I . . .'

But Frith was already halfway to the woods, still carrying the axe, and running as fast as she could.

I need to think about this logically, Frith told herself. It seemed a reasonable conclusion. After all, she'd tried lots of running about and shouting without any thinking, and that had done no good at all. She sat down on a fallen tree trunk. *Now, if I was a stupid young idiot chasing a dog, where would I go?*

That was an easy one: wherever the dog went.

Next question: If I was a daft dog chasing a squirrel, where would I go?

That was easy too: wherever the squirrel went.

OK, so: If I was a squirrel being chased by a daft dog being chased by a stupid Spuggy, where would I go?

Up a tree, obviously.

This logic thing was easy. Frith wondered why she didn't use it all the time.

So, now the crucial bit: What would happen next?

Cabbage would jump about and bark up at the tree. Then Spuggy would catch up with him and . . . they would go home.

Oh.

So, Spuggy and Cabbage were probably home, but Frith was miles away, and she had no idea where she was.

Oh.

Frith made a mental note that maybe logic worked best if you used it before you set your legs going. She was just about to test this theory on the problem of how to get home when she heard something moving nearby.

Frith told herself to be calm. Whatever it was, she was pretty sure it wasn't Spuggy and Cabbage because there was no barking, but it hadn't sounded like a monster either. So that left either someone from the village, or some of the king's men, and either way they could probably tell her which way she should go to get home. As long as they didn't shoot her with an arrow first. In any case, if she was careful and quiet, then it would be safe to investigate. Yes, now that she had properly thought it through, she would make her way over to where the sound had come from and . . .

She realized that she was already on her way.

Stupid legs! What have I told you?

Frith stopped walking. She could hear the low

mumble of voices. Two, she thought. Low, rumbly voices. She moved past a patch of rampant ferns and crept up behind the broad, ivy-covered trunk of a tree. Peeping round, she could see two of the messenger's guards. They looked agitated, out of breath and nervous, and the area around them was devastated. The undergrowth was trampled, tree branches were snapped and something had torn great gouges into the earth. Frith shifted on her heels to get a better view and, as she did so, spotted a long smear of blood trailing across the ground.

Frith gave a little squeak of shock.

'What was that?' The soldiers turned Frith's way.

'Probably just a bird, or a squirrel, or something,' said the other guard.

'Still, we'd better take a look. Come on.'

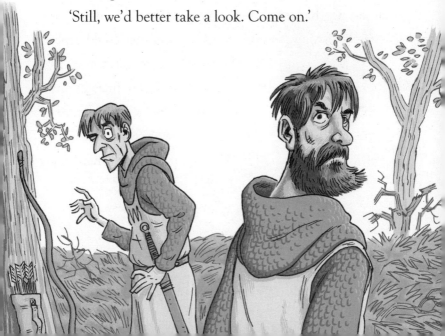

Frith decided she had two choices: she could step into view and explain herself, or she could make a run for it. And if she ran for it, she would probably get even more lost.

'Hello,' she said, waving her hands in the air as she emerged from hiding, and noted with interest that each of the soldiers had now nocked an arrow onto the string of his bow.

And that was when she remembered what was in her hand.

'She's got an axe!'

An arrow thudded into the tree; a second whistled past Frith's ear.

Maybe explaining wasn't the thing after all. Frith gulped and ran.

She didn't look back. She heard the soldiers behind her, their footsteps adding another urgent rhythm to her gasping breath, and the rat-a-tat beat of her heart. The soldiers were shouting too, but she didn't care what. If she could just stay ahead of them a while longer, she thought, then they would tire before she did, because she wasn't wearing heavy chain mail or carrying a sword. She thought about throwing away the axe too, but it was useful to help clear her way through the undergrowth. Though that also made it obvious which way she . . .

Oh! Now there's an idea!

Veering left, the ground ahead sloped up. Frith sprinted up the slope. At the top she took in the terrain before her. There was a sharp dip down through a clearing, before the ground rose up again to dense woodland.

Perfect!

She hurtled down the steep drop, struggling to stay upright, then dashed to the far side of the clearing before the soldiers had reached the top of the rise behind her. With a few wild swings of the axe, she thrashed a way through a thick patch of vines and scrub, then ducked sideways to lean her back against a good,

thick tree trunk and wait.

'That way!' cried a distant voice.

'I can . . . see that . . . I'm not . . . stupid, you know.'

The soldiers' footsteps drummed closer and louder. Frith held her breath. They burst into view through the gap she had cut into the undergrowth, and Frith ducked round the tree trunk and out of sight once more.

Don't stop! Don't stop!

The footsteps and voices faded into the distance. Frith allowed herself one short moment to savour her cleverness and luck, then set off, back the way she had come, across the clearing to the foot of the slope. Halfway up she realized she should have gone a different way. The slope got steeper and steeper, so that Frith progressed from walking, to scrambling, and finally to climbing the last short section, using the axe as a handy climbing tool. She hauled herself up to the top of the ridge, then, on her hands and knees, turned to check the soldiers were still nowhere to be seen. Satisfied that the coast was clear, she spun back round to continue on her way.

But now there was something blocking her path. Something very big.

145

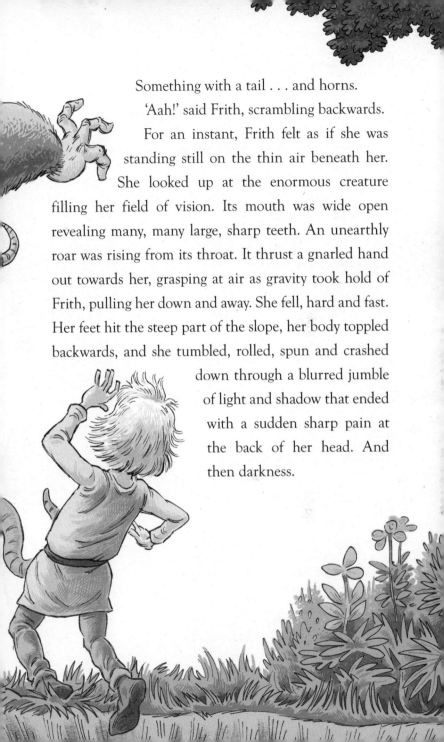

Something with a tail . . . and horns.

'Aah!' said Frith, scrambling backwards.

For an instant, Frith felt as if she was standing still on the thin air beneath her. She looked up at the enormous creature filling her field of vision. Its mouth was wide open revealing many, many large, sharp teeth. An unearthly roar was rising from its throat. It thrust a gnarled hand out towards her, grasping at air as gravity took hold of Frith, pulling her down and away. She fell, hard and fast. Her feet hit the steep part of the slope, her body toppled backwards, and she tumbled, rolled, spun and crashed down through a blurred jumble of light and shadow that ended with a sudden sharp pain at the back of her head. And then darkness.

Chapter 19

Frith's head hurt, and she had no idea where she was, and it was too dark to see anything.

Then she realized her eyes were closed, so she opened them, and she still did not know where she was.

She was about to raise her head and take a look around when she heard a slow shuffling, scuffling noise, accompanied by a low rumbling, mumbling noise, and she decided to have a bit of a think before she did anything rash, like moving.

She closed her eyes again and thought back. She remembered running through the woods, tricking the soldiers, running, climbing, and then . . .

Oh. Yes.

AARGH! THERE WAS A MONSTER!

And then she had fallen, and must have hit her head, and been knocked out, and now she was . . .

Where was she?

She was face down on the ground. The ground was hard. Stone, she thought. And it was dark. Now she listened. There was no birdsong, no breeze, no rustling leaves, so, she was inside somewhere. And there was someone, or something, in here with her. And the last someone or something she had seen had been the monster.

Frith's nose twitched as a first faint scent of smoke reached it. The monster had started a fire. But it wasn't cold, so why . . . ?

The monster was going to cook her!

Frith opened an eye, just a crack, to look over at where the shuffling sound was coming from. Through the curtain of her hair she could just make out the monster, and beyond it the newly started fire.

The monster was facing away from her, and far enough away that Frith could risk a look around. Peering up, there was a rough ceiling of stone. So, they were in a cave. Beyond the monster, in the deep, dark distance, was a thin crack of daylight. Looking the other way there was only darkness.

What if she made a run for it? She wiggled her toes, then her feet, then bent her knees just a tiny bit. Everything felt more or less in working order. The rest of her seemed all right too, and despite the pain, her head seemed to be working OK. Frith cautiously touched a finger to the sore place at the back of her skull. Her finger recoiled at a new pang of pain, and also the shock of sticky wetness. But when she looked, her fingertip wasn't covered in blood, as she had expected, but some kind of yellow goo. She sniffed it, then gave it a nervous lick. Honey.

Frith glanced back at the monster. The fire was building nicely now, as the creature fed bigger sticks into the flames. Soon it could turn its attention to cooking delicious roast girl in a honey sauce.

Frith considered her options: she could fight, or she could run. She still had her sling, and a monster would be an easier target than a rabbit. But she didn't think a pebble would stop it, however well aimed.

So, running away definitely seemed best. But there was a monster in the way. If only it would wander over into the furthest depths of the cave, then at least Frith could have a head start. But how could she make it go there?

Well, maybe . . .

She looked at the monster. The fire was going nicely now. She didn't have long. She felt in her pocket and pulled out her sling and a pebble, looped the cloth, placed the pebble in it, sat up without making a sound, and drew back her arm. Then she hurled the stone as hard as she could into the darkest depths of the cave, and lay down again quickly and silently before it landed.

The monster froze as the pebble hit some unseen distant stone wall with a satisfying ping. It stood up straight, gazing after the noise. Then it turned to stare at Frith for what felt like an eternity. Frith kept perfectly still and quiet as every particle inside of her fizzed with panic. At last, the monster turned away, grabbed a branch from the fire, and held it aloft as a makeshift torch.

Good monster! Clever monster! Off you go! Go and see what the noise was.

But instead of heading into the back of the cave, the monster shambled towards Frith. She closed her eyes. She heard the shuffling footsteps drawing closer, then the monster humming, and its stomach churning. A breath ruffled Frith's hair, and she felt the warmth from the burning branch close by her cheek. And she kept perfectly still. After what seemed like forever, the warmth and the breath went away, and then, the sound of huge shuffling footsteps faded into the distance.

When she could barely hear the footsteps any more, Frith opened one eye a crack, and looked into the cave. She saw a dim flame far away, and the enormous monster bending and peering, looking for whatever had made a pinging noise.

Frith sat up, then rose to a crouch . . .

And then she ran.

CHAPTER 20

FRITH WAS PAST THE fire when a growl emerged from the depths of the cave behind her. The tantalizing crack of daylight lay ahead of her, but she couldn't yet see if it was a way out. A roar echoed through the cave, and distant footsteps. Frith kept running, and she didn't look back.

The stone floor was uneven and damp, and Frith's eyes darted restlessly, seeking a safe route across it. She glanced up. The crack of light was now four bright gashes in the darkness, like gaps between sharp teeth. The monster's moans and footsteps were closer now. Frith dodged round a rocky outcrop, splashed into a shallow puddle of slimy water, slipped, stumbled, regained her balance, and ran on, the laboured breathing of the creature closer behind her than ever.

The cave mouth came properly into view now, vines and creepers hanging down, and jagged stone pointing up. And the daylight between them was wide enough for Frith to get through, but not for her pursuer. Her heart swelled with hope. She was going to get away. She was going to be safe.

So why was she worried?

No time to think. She ran towards the light. And leaped. Over the jagged rocks, out through the curtain of vines and creepers.

The full force of the daylight hit her, blinding after the dark of the cave. The cave mouth was set high in a cliff wall. The ground was a long way down. And then she realized there was nothing beneath her feet.

She gave a sharp cry, then she fell, the world tumbling and turning in chaos around her.

Something brushed against her palm.

The vines!

Frith twisted and flipped in the air. Wind whistled past her ears. She reached up, her starfish hand silhouetted against the light as she thrust it desperately at a snaking vine.

Her hand closed around it, and she held on tight. Then her arm pulled up hard as her body tried to keep falling. Pain tore through her shoulder. She cried out, but she didn't let go, and she swung in towards the cliff face. She buffered herself with her free hand, and her knees scraped against the rock, but the pain seemed distant. She steadied herself. Both hands on the vine, feet braced against the cliff face, she gasped in a huge breath.

She was alive.

She was hanging from a vine, suspended between a monster and a long drop to the ground. But she was alive.

Frith looked up at the monster leaning out from the cave mouth. It was staring at her, and for some reason it had the axe in one of its hands and was waving it about.

Oh!

If it cut the vine with the axe . . .

Frith looked down, searching for her next move. There was a wide ledge below her, but a long way below. The vine didn't reach anywhere near that far down, and it was too long a drop. So, she couldn't go up, and she couldn't go down, but to her left there was a half dead, scraggy excuse for a bush growing out of the cliff face. It wasn't much, but it looked like it might just take Frith's weight. Clinging to the vine she shuffled sideways, reached out a hand, and managed to grab at the base of the bush. It held firm. Better yet, she found footholds for extra support. She was safe, for now at least. She looked up at the monster and gave it a defiant grin. Then, as she scanned the cliff face below, Frith's right hand jerked. Puzzled, she looked up and saw the vine, cut loose, snaking down towards her.

'Ha! Too late! Stupid monst— Ah!'

Frith cried out as the weight of the falling vine tried to pull her free from the footholds. She clung on tight to the bush and to the vine, and steadied herself once more. She glared at the vine in her hand, about to cast it away, but stopped herself just in time.

Frith looked up at the monster, still peering out from the cave.

'Not only are you stupid,' she said, 'but you've helped me out.'

It wasn't easy to tie the vine to the bush, but she managed it eventually. And the free end hung almost down to the wide ledge below. So, now she could climb safely down. So long as the vine didn't snap, and the roots of the bush didn't give way.

Frith took hold of the vine and leaned out, then stepped first one foot, then the other, down from the footholds. The vine made a creaking noise, and the bush gave a woody moan, but neither of them snapped. Step by tiny step, Frith descended until she reached the end of the vine. From there it was a short enough distance to drop to the ledge.

Standing up straight, she caught sight of the cave mouth far above, and the monster's head still poking out from it, watching. Frith stared up at it, triumphant.

'I made it!' she shouted.

The monster's head tilted to one side, then its arm reappeared briefly to waggle the axe about.

'Is that meant to be a threat?' Frith muttered.

She followed the ledge carefully downwards to the upper end of a rocky outcrop. From there it was an easy scramble down to ground level. She glanced up one last time at the cave mouth, saw the monster still there, watching, and waving the axe. Then she turned, and disappeared off into the trees.

Chapter 21

OF COURSE, FRITH WAS still lost. She had no way of knowing which way to go to get home, so she decided just to walk away from where the monster was. Hopefully she would eventually recognize where she was and find her way home. Or she would come across a track through the woods, and then find someone to ask the way. If she kept going straight then she was pretty sure she would be fine, eventually. So she walked in a straight line for an hour or so, at the end of which she did recognize where she was. Which was more or less back where she started.

How did that happen? That's not fair!

Frith took out her sling and fired a stone at a squirrel in frustration. The squirrel didn't even move, except to turn its head when the stone flumfed into a patch of ferns beyond it. Frith was scanning the ground for a suitable pebble for a second shot when she heard voices.

She walked towards them, hopeful but cautious.

'. . . just a bird or something.'

'Whatever it was, we're not stopping to find out. You two have made us late as it is.' Whoever it was, they were close.

'I can't help it if I'm nervous. My mum won't half be mad at me if I get myself eaten by a monster.'

Frith crept forward. There was a lot of foliage in the way but she could see a horse's head now, and a human arm with a bandaged hand at the end of it. She reached up to the hanging greenery, and with easy skill swept it aside in complete silence.

'How many more times: there is—'

It was a shame that Frith hadn't spotted the bird. Rudely disturbed, it took off, squawking loudly. Now Frith had a clear view of the king's messenger and four guards, all on horseback, all now gawping in her direction. Beyond them were another two guards on a covered wagon.

'Oh,' said Frith. 'Hello again.' She gave a little wave, then held up the other hand to show that there was no axe in it, and so there was no need for anyone to fire arrows at her.

The messenger raised a hand, and dropped down from his horse.

'Steady, men,' he said. 'It's just a child. You were in Thornville, weren't you? The carter's daughter?'

'That's right, sir.'

'What are you doing all the way out here? The woods can be a dangerous place, you know.'

'Yuss,' said one of the guards. 'There's a monster!'

'Oh, yes,' said Frith, 'the monster. Have you seen it? Was that what had made such a mess where I saw you two before?' She pointed at the pair of guards she had encountered earlier.

'Oh, er . . . yes,' said the messenger. 'That's right. These brave fellows were lucky to escape with their lives!'

'We were?' said one of them.

'We were!' said the other.

'And while they weren't able to slay or capture the savage beast, they did scare it away. We will send search parties to seek out its lair in due course, and the kindly King Laurence will rid you of this terrible scourge once and for all.' The messenger smiled at Frith, then muttered quickly under his breath: 'Monster-slaying services are supplied as and when resources allow and may incur additional charges. Terms and conditions apply.'

'Oh, there's no need for search parties.' Frith puffed herself up proudly. 'I could show you where its cave is now, if you like.'

The messenger looked puzzled.

'You've seen the monster?'

'Oh, yes,' said Frith, nodding cheerily. 'It was going to eat me, but I got away. It had already coated me in honey, and lit a fire to cook me.' She pointed at the splodge of honey on her head.

A guard leaned in for a closer look, then sniffed at Frith's smock.

'It does look like honey,' he said. 'And she smells smoky.'

'Shall I take you to the cave, then?' said Frith.

The messenger was still considering his reply when he was interrupted by a muffled moan from the back of the wagon.

'Actually, we have to hurry back to the city because . . .
we have an injured . . . man in the wagon.'

'Oh no! Did the monster . . . ?'

The messenger nodded gravely, while behind him a
guard climbed into the wagon.

'I'm afraid so. But nothing that our doctors in the
city won't be able to fix. And Albert will keep him . . .
comfortable on the journey back.'

'But who is it? I've seen all your men. Oh! It's not
Shouty Joe, is it?'

'Shouty Joe?'

'The tall skinny man from the meeting? Who
shouted a bit but then he was ill? I saw

him heading into the woods earlier.'

'Oh! Yes, I'm afraid so. He must have stumbled upon the monster and been attacked. But luckily, my brave men were able to save him from further injury.'

'Thank you.' Frith cast a sorry look at the wagon. 'Well, I'd better head home, I suppose, and tell them the news.' Frith looked around. 'Um, which way *is* home, by the way?'

The messenger stroked his chin for a moment.

'Actually,' he said, 'as you've been in the monster's cave, then really it would be best if you came with us now so you could tell us

– and the king – all about it.'

'But—'

'We'll send word back to the village so they know that you and . . .'

'Joe.'

'Yes, of course. That you and Joe are with us.'

The messenger muttered some instructions up to one of the soldiers, who looked confused. Then the messenger muttered something else, more angrily, and the soldier dug his heels into the flanks of his horse and set off slowly back through the wood.

'Couldn't I just go back with him?' said Frith. 'Only I

was meant to be looking after my brother, and our dog, and I'd really—'

'It's up to you, of course,' said the messenger, leaning down and resting a hand on Frith's shoulder. 'Though it'll be a shame to miss out on the feast.'

'Feast?' said Frith, over a low rumble of interest from her stomach.

'Yes. The king would be sure to throw you a feast for your heroic escape from the monster. He adores that kind of thing.'

'He does?'

'Of course! And he's not known as *King Laurence the Just and Also Very Generous* for nothing, you know.'

Frith hadn't ever heard anyone call the king that, but probably that was because she didn't live in the city and so was poorly informed about such matters.

'Oh, well, I suppose . . .'

'Splendid!' The messenger gently but firmly steered Frith towards the wagon. 'It's probably best,' said the messenger, 'if you sit up front. Just so your friend has plenty of space in the back while he . . . rests.'

'Oh. OK,' said Frith.

The misshapen lump of a soldier sitting at the front of the wagon shifted reluctantly over to one side, and Frith climbed up beside him. The wagon set off, with the messenger and one soldier on horseback ahead of them, and the remaining two soldiers riding behind.

Frith looked up at the wagon driver. He looked the grumpy type, but she felt sure some conversation would cheer him up.

'Excuse me,' she said.

'Yurr?' said the driver.

'Are we nearly there yet?'

Chapter 22

It was nearly dark when they arrived at the city, and Frith was tired from all the talking she had had to do to keep the driver entertained, but the thought of eating, at last, woke her up a bit.

'Do you think the king will want to throw the feast for me tonight?' she asked the wagon driver. 'Or will it have to wait till tomorrow to get it all organized properly?'

'I should think,' he said, 'that the king will give you just what you deserve, as soon as he can.' He pulled wearily on the reins, and brought the horse to a stop. 'Now, get off my wagon so I can have some peace!'

Frith climbed down, taking in for the first time where they were.

On her last visit with Dad, Frith had seen the rear of the castle and thought that it was amazing, and impressive, and very, very big and fancy. But now she was round the front where all the *really* amazing and impressive stuff was. Just the mighty oak door, with two armed guards, would have been enough to make a young girl from Thornville goggle, let alone the gargoyles, and knights, and kings, and who knows what, that were carved into the stone. So much *work*, by so many people, must have gone into building it all. She couldn't really comprehend it.

'Come with me.' The messenger and one of the soldiers appeared either side of her.

'Oh, OK. Are we going to see the king now?'

'We'll see,' said the messenger, as a guard opened the mighty oak door for them. 'He may be dining.'

'I don't mind,' said Frith. 'I could join him, if he'd like.'

The messenger smiled, and led Frith across a paved inner courtyard to another impressive door with another impressive guard outside it. Inside, Frith dumbly trailed behind, through corridors and halls, her eyes bulging at each new sight. In Thornville she had only seen a picture a handful of times, and half of those had been little Geoffrey Baker's drawings of a bottom, scratched into the earth with a stick. Here there were paintings on every wall, of ladies and gentlemen, and dukes and duchesses, and kings and queens, and a very square-looking cow. And there were tapestries, and stained-glass windows.

And every one of them was even more impressive than one of Geoffrey's bottoms. After a while, Frith felt like her eyes were full to bursting, so she closed them. And that's when she heard the music. Music, and voices, laughing and talking and shouting.

'Wait here,' said the messenger, leaving Frith with the soldier and disappearing through a door. 'Aha!' A voice rose above the general hubbub beyond the door. 'John Whitehill! Back from your travels! What news—?'

The door closed, muffling whatever was said next.

There was an awkward silence until the door opened again and John Whitehill, messenger to the king, reappeared.

'His Majesty will see you now,' he said.

Frith blinked up at him just as a wafting scent of deliciousness reached her nose.

'Oh,' she said. 'Thank you. I'm honoured.' She gave the air a long sniff. 'Is that . . . beef?'

'Your Majesty,' said the messenger, raising his voice to be heard above the din as they passed through the door. 'This is Frith Carter of Thornville.'

They were in the great hall of the castle. At the far end of it was a long table running along almost the full width of the room, laden with plates and dishes of all kinds of foods. The king was seated at the centre of the table, and along the sides of it sat about two dozen other men, all of whom now turned their attention to Frith.

'Ah, yes!' bellowed the king. 'The Thornville girl.'

A group of musicians off to one side stopped playing. The king's fellow diners muttered and whispered as Frith approached.

'Yes,' said Frith, wondering why her voice had suddenly gone all squeaky. 'Hello again, Your Majesticness.'

'Again?' said the messenger.

'Oh, yes, didn't I mention? I, um, ran into him last week.' Frith came to a halt at what she hoped was a respectful distance from the king and bowed down low, glancing up at him apologetically. 'Sorry, again, about that, Your Highnesty.'

'It *is* you!' The king stood up. 'When John Whitehill told me he'd a young girl from Thornville here, I did wonder if it might be the same . . . enthusiastic child who knocked me to the ground in the market place.'

There were a few quiet gasps from the crowd of diners.

'And now I hear you have news of a *monster*?'

'Yes, Your Highnessness. In the woods next to the village. I escaped from its cave before it could cook me and eat me!'

'How positively *thrilling*! Well done, you! You can tell John Whitehill all the details. That will be a great help. Then I shall send my champion to seek out your monster and slay it.' The king turned to address the tall, upright fellow sitting at his side, who Frith recognized from the marketplace. 'That all right with you, Dunstable? Bit of monster-slaying?'

'As Your Majesty commands, sire,' said the Duke of Dunstable, in a tired voice.

'Excellent! That's settled then. Just as soon as I can spare him, we'll get that sorted for you. Top priority. Although we are *terribly* busy with the war against the armies of the north lands, so I can't quite say when *exactly* . . . But rest assured it's right at the top of our to-do list.'

'Thank you very much, Your Magicness. That's very kind.'

'It is, isn't it?' The king returned his attention to the well-stocked plate of food in front of him. 'Now toddle along home, will you? And do feel free to tell everyone in your village how marvellous I am.' He waved Frith away with a flick of his hand.

Frith stared at the king, and at all the food, then very slowly turned to leave, only to find John Whitehill, the king's messenger, standing in her way with his hand raised.

'Actually, Your Majesty, I wonder if perhaps it might be better if Miss Carter stayed.'

'Good idea,' said Frith.

'In jail,' said the messenger.

'Bad idea!' said Frith, as she felt herself grabbed by the shoulders by the soldier who had entered with her.

'You see,' John Whitehill continued, 'we had a run-in with someone else from Thornville in the woods, and had to capture him and bring him back with us. This girl saw us shortly afterwards. If she were to return home and talk then they would probably piece it together before long and it would cause unnecessary unrest.'

'I see,' said the king. 'And no one from her village knows she's here?'

'No, sire.'

'So, you're suggesting that this *child*, should be thrown in a cold, smelly dungeon?'

'Yes, sire.'

'I hardly think that would be right,' said the king.

'No,' said Frith.

The king pointed at Frith with the chicken leg he was holding. 'She *humiliated me* in front of dozens of dirty

peasants in the market place.' He looked to left and right, holding his fellow diners' attention. 'I'll need to think up something much worse than just being thrown in a cell.'

The crowd cheered drunkenly.

'Put her in the stocks,' said one of them.

'Feed her to the hounds,' said another, and got a cheer.

'Feed her to a bear.'

'No . . . feed her to her monster!' This got a huge cheer and a lot of laughs, although Frith didn't think it was funny at all.

'So many delicious possibilities!' The king looked away, distracted by the arrival of a procession of servants carrying dozens of ornate

tarts, cakes and pastries on large silver trays. 'Oh, talking of delicious . . .' He glanced back at Frith, squirming in the iron grip of the guards. 'Throw her in the dungeon, and we'll decide what to do with her in the morning. Right now, I have some very important puddings to attend to.'

The crowd gave the loudest cheer yet, and the musicians started up again, as Frith was dragged from the room.

'But I really could show you where the monster—'

'There's no such thing, silly girl! We only made it up to keep you yokels scared and quiet.'

'But—'

The heavy oak door swung closed.

They were back out in the hallway, Frith's feet flapping, barely touching the floor as the guard half dragged and half carried her along.

'Just because you made up a story,' she said, 'it doesn't mean it couldn't be true by accident.'

'But we know it's not,' said the messenger. 'The king asked the wisest being in the land, and he assured His Majesty that there were no monsters in any of the woods.'

'Well, he was *wrong*!'

'The Big Wise Head is never wrong!'

'He's not *wise*. He's just a big head!'

They passed down a short stairway to a dark and smelly corridor.

'You've met him?'

'Yes. He was big, and full of himself, and quite rude.'

'Oh. You really have met him.'

They came to a halt outside a dank stone cell closed at the front with iron bars. The guards dangled Frith in the air, awaiting further instruction. The messenger considered Frith thoughtfully as a jailer unlocked the cell door and pulled it open.

'All the more reason to keep you locked up.' The messenger gave a tiny nod to the guard, and Frith, after a brief and unpleasant flight, found herself flat on her back on a cold stone straw-covered floor. The cell door clanged shut behind her.

Frith got to her feet and shouted through the bars after the departing messenger.

'So, does this mean I don't get a feast *at all*?'

CHAPTER 23

FRITH SAT ON THE floor of her cell and wondered two things: what was that awful smell? And was it anything to do with the pile of straw in the corner that seemed to be breathing?

'Euuurrgh!' said the pile of straw, rolling and shifting. 'What is that awful smell?' Then Spuggy sat up out of it, scanning his surroundings with bleary eyes.

'Ah!' yelled Frith.

'Eep!' squealed Spuggy.

Then they both pointed at each other and said, 'What are you doing here?'

Spuggy went first.

'It's not my fault!' he said. 'Cabbage chased after a squirrel. Then I chased after Cabbage. And then I got a bit lost in the woods. But then I heard barking, so I ran over to where Cabbage was, and there were two soldiers, and they were messing up the woods, and breaking branches, and digging up the earth, and one of them had a bucket of some kind of blood that he was splashing about on the ground and everywhere. And then I was going to ask them what they were doing, but Cabbage was barking at them, and one of them went to hit him with a shovel, and I said: "Don't you hurt my dog! He's done nothing to you." And then Cabbage bit him.'

'Oh,' said Frith. She thought back to the bandage that one of the soldiers had had. 'On the hand?'

'No, the leg,' said Spuggy. 'Then he tried to hit Cabbage. So, I bit his hand. Then they caught me, and tied me up, and gagged me, and put me in the back of their wagon. Then a guard sat on me while we travelled here, which took *ages*, and then they threw me in this place. What about you? How did they manage to catch you?'

Frith thought that *they told me I'd get a feast* didn't sound all that heroic, so she said: 'By being devious and rotten.' Which was sort of true.

'Where are we, exactly?'

'In the city,' said Frith.

'Brilliant!' said Spuggy.

'In the castle,' said Frith.

'Ooh!' said Spuggy.

'In the dungeon,' said Frith.

'Oh,' said Spuggy. 'Because I bit that soldier?'

'No, I think because you saw them faking evidence of a monster in the woods.'

'Oh, *that's* what they were doing!'

'Yes! They want us to believe that there's a monster that's been ruining our crops and stealing our cattle when it's actually been the king's men all along.'

Spuggy looked horrified. 'They'll be in trouble once the king finds out!'

'No, they won't, you idiot! The king knows all about it! It was probably his idea.'

'No!' said Spuggy. 'The king is naughty? Surely that's not right.'

'And the thing is, those soldiers thought they were making it up but, actually, there really is a monster! I saw it myself. It was going to eat me, but I was too clever and fast for it so I got away.'

'A real monster! In the woods! That's scary! I hope Edward will be all right.'

'Never mind your imaginary friend! I nearly got eaten! Me! Your sister!'

'I suppose that would have been a *bit* annoying,' said Spuggy. 'But I'd have got over it in a day or two. And you didn't actually get eaten, so it's fine.'

'Oh, yes! It's absolutely fine!' snorted Frith. 'Now that I'm stuck in a smelly dungeon! Which is all your fault!'

Spuggy stood up, and stepped towards Frith ready to argue. But then, instead, he sniffed the air and looked around.

'It is *really* smelly, isn't it?' he said.

Frith took a proper look round too. There wasn't much to see. The walls were stone, with no window. The floor was stone, with an uneven covering of straw. Neither floor nor straw was especially clean, but it wasn't possible to tell quite how dirty either was because the light, from a burning torch on the wall opposite the cell, was so dim. Even so, it didn't look filthy enough to explain the horrific stench in the air.

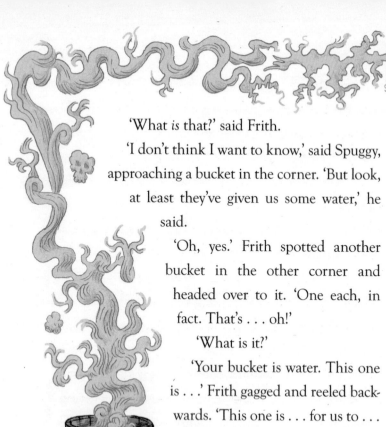

'What *is* that?' said Frith.

'I don't think I want to know,' said Spuggy, approaching a bucket in the corner. 'But look, at least they've given us some water,' he said.

'Oh, yes.' Frith spotted another bucket in the other corner and headed over to it. 'One each, in fact. That's . . . oh!'

'What is it?'

'Your bucket is water. This one is . . .' Frith gagged and reeled backwards. 'This one is . . . for us to . . . erm . . . This one is where the smell is coming from.' She stepped away from it and resumed breathing. 'And it looks like it hasn't been emptied in a long while.'

'Eurgh!' said Spuggy. 'Well, that settles it. We can't stay here. Let's escape.'

'Oh, yes, brilliant idea. How are we going to do that, then, genius?'

186

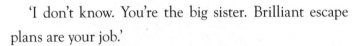

'I don't know. You're the big sister. Brilliant escape plans are your job.'

'Thanks a lot.'

Frith looked round the cell again. 'So, your job is to get us locked up in a dungeon, and my job is to get us out, is it? I'm sure that won't take long. Let's see, what do we have to work with? Straw, mostly. Maybe we can make a key out of straw and unlock the door. Or how about we weave some straw into spades and dig a tunnel? Or maybe we can make a lovely bouquet of straw and use it to bribe the guard to let us go.'

'Sorry, Frith, but I don't think that any of those ideas will work. In fact, they're a bit silly.'

'Yes!' yelled Frith. 'And do you know why?' She jabbed a finger into her little brother's chest. 'Because I don't have any sensible plans to escape using only straw.' She jabbed him again. 'Because there are . . . no . . . sensible . . . plans.' Jab, jab, jab. 'Because we're stuck here, Spuggy!' Her voice cracked. 'Until the king thinks of something even worse to do to us.'

And then she crumpled to the floor and started crying.

'Frith!' said Spuggy, sharply. 'Stop it!'

Frith looked up at Spuggy's big, round, stupid face, with its big, round, stupid, wide-open eyes.

187

'I know this looks bad,' he said. 'Well, it *is* bad. And there might be no way out. But if we give up, there is *definitely* no way out. But if we think, and we try . . . it might not make a difference, but *maybe* we'll think of something that gives us at least a teeny bit of a chance. And that's better than none at all. Isn't it?'

Frith sniffed.

'OK.'

'OK, good. So, is there anything we've missed? Have you got anything else that might help?' He pushed his hands into his pockets and felt about for a while. 'Because I haven't.'

Frith rummaged in her own pockets.

'I've got my sling,' she said, holding it up. 'But nothing to throw with it except a paper frog.' They both frowned, and thought a bit. Then Frith brightened a little. 'Oh, but if we could get the guard in here, and overpower him . . . somehow, then we could tie his hands with it. Or gag him. Or something.'

'I suppose,' said Spuggy. 'Maybe if he brings us some food . . . Do you think he'll bring food? I haven't eaten a thing since breakfast.'

'That does seem a long time ago,' said Frith. She thought back. It really did seem very distant. Spuggy and Cabbage running off. And before that, the king's men coming to the hut, and Dad talking to them, and handing Frith . . .

'Oh!' she cried out suddenly.

'What is it?' Spuggy looked alarmed.

'I just remembered,' said Frith, 'I do have something else that might be useful.'

'What?'

'Turn your back, and I'll tell you in a minute.'

Frith braced herself and headed over to the bad bucket. Spuggy turned his back. There were some noises.

He didn't look round. Then he heard her go over to the good bucket, and then there were some splashing sounds.

'OK,' said Frith, a while later. Her face, when Spuggy turned to see, looked as if she wouldn't want him to ask what she'd just been through. 'Maybe these will help,' she

said, and held up a palm, with two gold coins on it.

'Coo!' said Spuggy, amazed. 'But how—?'

'Long story. Don't ask.' Frith shook her head grimly. 'But . . . don't drink the water.'

Chapter 24

NORMAN HATED GUARD DUTY. And he especially hated guard duty in the dungeon. And he most especially hated guard duty in the dungeon on the early shift. So, arriving at the castle dungeon shortly after dawn, Norman was in a rotten mood. But at least he could take it out on the prisoners. Apparently, there were two new ones, and they were only children. So that would be fun.

Norman stood still and quiet at the cell door, sizing them up. The girl was lying curled up by the bars, probably to keep as far as possible from the stinky bucket. The boy was flat on his back at the rear of the cell, snoring softly.

As they were both happily asleep, the first thing to do was obviously to wake them up with some good old-fashioned shouting. Norman enjoyed shouting, and he liked to think that he was rather good at it.

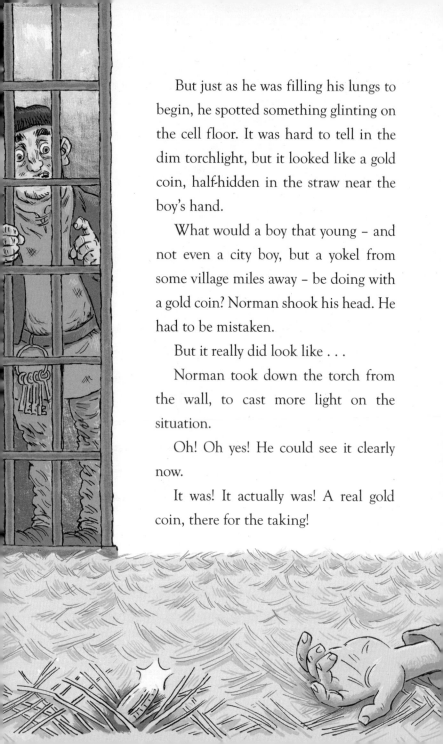

But just as he was filling his lungs to begin, he spotted something glinting on the cell floor. It was hard to tell in the dim torchlight, but it looked like a gold coin, half-hidden in the straw near the boy's hand.

What would a boy that young – and not even a city boy, but a yokel from some village miles away – be doing with a gold coin? Norman shook his head. He had to be mistaken.

But it really did look like . . .

Norman took down the torch from the wall, to cast more light on the situation.

Oh! Oh yes! He could see it clearly now.

It was! It actually was! A real gold coin, there for the taking!

With great care he took the huge ring of keys from his belt, and placed the right one, with barely a jingle, in the keyhole of the cell door. Slowly, carefully, silently, he unlocked the door, and pulled it open. Leaving the keys in the door, he pulled a cudgel from his belt, the torch held aloft before him in his other hand. He fixed his gaze on the boy's face, and stepped into the cell, watching for the slightest sign that he might wake. So he didn't look at Frith at all. He didn't see her eyes open. Didn't see her pull tight her sling, tied across the doorway. He felt his ankle catch, and tipped forward, dropping the torch and the cudgel as he fell. Spuggy sprang up, snatched up the coin, and stepped over him. Norman lifted his head to the sound of the door clanging shut, and the keys being pulled free from the door.

Dazed, he looked round. The escaped prisoners were staring in at him through the bars of the locked door. Oddly, they didn't look very happy about their escape, or eager to run away. Instead, they stood, their mouths hanging open, staring past him. He turned his head to see what they were looking at. He saw the flames at the same time that he smelled the smoke.

'Let me out!' he said, stamping at the patch of straw that the fallen torch had set alight.

'Don't do that,' said Frith. 'You'll only—'

'Ow!' said Norman, as flames licked at his leg.

'Oh!' said Spuggy. 'Now your britches are on fire.'

'Let me out!'

'Don't panic,' said Frith. 'There's a bucket of water.'

Norman grabbed the bucket and emptied it over his leg.

'Oh dear!' Spuggy said, holding his nose.

'The other bucket!' said Frith.

She and Spuggy stepped back and watched as Norman emptied the water bucket onto the flames.

'There, you see. You'll be fine,' said Frith.

'Smelly,' said Spuggy. 'But fine.'

Frith and Spuggy emerged onto the inner courtyard in the early-morning light, and closed the door on the distant shouting of Norman back in the dungeon.

'I've never even heard *Mum* say those words!' said Spuggy. He gave his eyes a rub and scanned their surroundings. 'So, which way is out?'

'I suppose,' said Frith, pointing ahead of them, 'it's

through that door in the outer wall. Have you got the keys?'

Spuggy held up the jailer's heavy bunch of keys, and gave them a jangle as they set off towards the door.

Frith shot a look over her shoulder. 'Uh oh! Company,' she said, as a pair of soldiers emerged from a door on the other side of the courtyard.

'Oo-o-oh!' Spuggy quickened his pace.

He reached the door, tried it, then pushed one of the big iron keys into the keyhole. It wouldn't turn.

'Wrong one.' He took it out and tried another.

'Hurry up!'

The second key didn't turn.

'I am hurrying!'

Key three was no good either.

The soldiers quickened their pace towards them.

'Oi!'

'Come on! Come on!' said Frith as Spuggy tried key number

195

four. 'How long does it take to open a door?'

'There are a *lot* of keys here!'

Spuggy swapped key five for key six. No good.

One of the soldiers drew his sword.

Seven.

'This is all your fault, Spuggy!'

Eight.

'Hang on!'

'But . . .'

'Stop right there!'

The soldiers were only a few paces away.

'Don't . . .'

Key number nine turned. Spuggy yanked the door open. 'Go!'

'Stop, in the name of the king!'

Frith ran out, looked back to watch Spuggy following her.

But he wasn't.

'Run, Frith,' he said, then slammed the door closed. There was a muffled jangle of keys.

'Spuggy!' Frith pushed at the door. It was locked. 'SPUGGY!' She beat her fist against the thick oak. 'SPUGGY!'

Frith collapsed against the door, her ear pressed to the wood. Through it came the faint sounds of her stupid,

stupid brother being chased by soldiers. Frith swallowed
hard and pushed herself upright. Tears streaking her
face, she turned, and ran.

CHAPTER 25

THE PROBLEM WITH CITIES, thought Frith, *is that they're just too big.*

Stupid cities! They made her angry. And she would much rather be angry right now, because it kept the tears at bay. *Stupid, stupid cities!*

Thornville was small enough that she knew every inch of it: every street, every hut and everyone who lived there. But the city was like a gigantic maze, and Frith had run into it and got lost. She stopped running and slowed to a walk. It was still early, and with hardly anyone out and about in the streets, Frith worried she would be easy to spot if any soldiers came by looking for her. She turned a corner and came to a dead end.

Stupid city streets that go nowhere!

Frith turned round and headed back along the street. All the houses were at least twice as high as the huts in Thornville, looming over her like threatening giants. More than ever, she wanted to get out, but two more turns took her down another dead end.

Frith slumped to the ground, and sat with her back against a wall, her head full of panic and confusion. She wanted to escape this rotten city and get home to Mum, Dad and Cabbage. But she couldn't just run off and leave Spuggy.

Frith gave a little sniff.

Mind you, Mum and Dad were probably really angry with her by now. And she didn't even know if Cabbage had got home all right. And Spuggy was . . .

Can't think about Spuggy right now.

Her lip began to tremble. She felt very far from home. She leaned her head back.

The buildings seemed even taller now, reaching up to block out more and more of that little patch of sky, that distant glow of hope.

Then a little bit of it disappeared as a head poked out of a window directly above her. Frith gave a quiet yelp of

surprise. The head heard her and looked down, a halo of untidy blonde hair framing a shadowed face. The girl, younger than Frith, gave her a puzzled look, then a smile, before a muffled voice called from within, and she disappeared again.

But that glimpse of a smile had been enough to set off a spark of hope in Frith's heart.

She stood up and took a breath. Then she took a step. She didn't know where she was going, but she was not going to sit still doing nothing any longer. And the good thing about being in a dead-end street is that it's easy to decide which way to go to get out of it. Once she got to the end of the street she could go left or right, but she'd already come down the road to the right, so she turned left.

It wasn't so hard if she made small decisions one at a time. At the next crossroads she spotted a cart piled high with pots and pans, clanking along the street behind a labouring horse. Most likely it would be heading to the marketplace, Frith reasoned. If she could get to the market, soon there would be a crowd there to lose herself in, and she could think about what to do next. She ran after it.

Frith hurried into the centre of the market to lose herself amidst the traders busy setting up their stalls. From there she could see over to the open gate, and through it, to Stan and Charlie. They were busy checking carts coming in, so anyone wanting to slip out the other way would probably not be noticed at all.

So, if Frith wanted to try to get home, to get help, then she could leave easily enough. And then . . .

Then it was more than a day's journey, and alone this time, across the Barren Wasteland to get back home, even assuming she could find the way. She took the battered paper frog from her pocket. Its legs were all twisted and bent, but the writing and drawing on the paper still looked clear enough. Not that a map was much use without a horse and cart and some provisions.

'Mind out, missy!'

'Sorry.' Frith jumped out of the way of a man wheeling a handcart stacked high with wooden boxes.

As the stallholder swerved past,

the tower of crates leaned alarmingly, as if about to topple over completely. But with a deft hand he returned the stack to perfect balance without spilling more than a single hazelnut. Frith stared after him, amazed at his skill. Then she snatched up the hazelnut, just as a familiar-looking squirrel dashed out from beneath a stall.

'Oh! Hello again,' said Frith, still bent over with her face more or less at squirrel level.

'Are you still lost? Or are you home now?'

The squirrel didn't answer. Instead, it stared hard at the hazelnut in Frith's hand.

'Oh no you don't,' said Frith. 'I haven't eaten for— Aargh!'

A man carrying the two big crates had been doing his best to watch where he was going, but with the top box coming up to his nose, he hadn't been able to see Frith crouching down in his path. The two of them crashed to the ground as fish rained down around them.

'Ow!' said Frith, as she landed on the cobbles. And then 'Eurgh!' as a trout landed on her head.

She looked up to see the squirrel standing over the hazelnut.

'Don't you dare!'

The squirrel shot her a defiant look, but then something distracted it, and it shot off under a stall. Frith staggered to her feet, snatched up the hazelnut, and noted as she did so how angry the fishmonger looked.

Then she spotted the soldiers heading her way to see what all the noise was about.

CHAPTER 26

THE FISHMONGER CHASED AFTER Frith for about three paces then slipped over on an eel and gave up. But when Frith scurried under a stall to escape the two soldiers chasing her, she emerged on the other side right beside another one.

'Grab her!'

Frith ducked, and a pair of burly arms closed around thin air above her head.

'Stop her!'

Frith ran for the gate. There were a few people arriving early for the fair now, and Frith had to dodge between them as she ran. There were more soldiers too. Lots more. The market square suddenly seemed to be full of them, and all rushing her way. Frith's one spark of hope was that Stan and Charlie, outside the gate checking a cartload of goods, still hadn't spotted anything wrong inside. She glanced behind her at the pack of soldiers racing, close, but not yet too close, in her wake. Then she checked ahead again. Charlie and Stan had let the trader in, but still hadn't noticed her. They were staring off the other way. Stan was pointing, while Charlie shaded his eyes from the low morning sun.

Frith ran on. The gates drew closer, the rumble of soldiers' trampling feet grew louder behind her.

'Close the gates!' shouted a soldier.

Stan and Charlie stiffened to attention, as if ready to take action, but didn't turn round.

'Stop that girl!'

'Oi! Stan! Charlie! You useless lumps!'

Stan and Charlie, still staring the other way, edged inside.

'Shut the bloomin' gates!' yelled a voice, close behind Frith now.

Stan and Charlie did not shut the gates, but they turned to face Frith. Still running, Frith fumbled in her pocket and pulled out her sling. Stan and Charlie set off towards her, running hard, their faces determined and urgent. But if Frith could fell one of them with a shot from her sling, and dodge past the other, then she could be out of the gate and free. She reached into her other pocket for anything she might use as ammunition,

and pulled out the hazelnut and the two gold coins. Frowning, she slipped the coins back, loaded the nut into the sling, drew her arm back, and wondered which of them she should aim at. It wasn't easy. She quite liked them, really. Before she could decide, they split up and ran past her on either side, looking terrified. Surprise and relief flooded through her, and the pounding of the soldiers chasing her seemed to fade away. She slowed a little, and glanced back. The whole pack of soldiers had come to a dead halt. Frith stopped running, and turned

to face them, twirling her sling at her side.

'Smart move,' she said. 'I *am* pretty deadly with this thing. I don't blame you for . . .'

Frith trailed off. The soldiers weren't looking *at* her. They were looking *over* her, and they were edging away from whatever was there.

Well, that doesn't seem good, thought Frith.

Still twirling her sling, Frith turned to face the gate.

The good news was that were no soldiers in her way.

The bad news was that there was a monster with an axe.

Frith's sling fell slack at her side. The hazelnut dropped to the ground, and skittered from cobble to cobble. The sharp *tok tok* of it bouncing was the only sound. Once it came to a halt at the monster's feet there was silence.

Frith looked at the nut. The monster did too.

Then the monster looked up, looked about, taking in the soldiers and the terrified bystanders.

'What are you doing here?' muttered Frith, almost to herself, as she backed away unsteadily. 'Why couldn't you just stay at home in your cave?'

The monster lowered its head, and fixed its gaze on Frith. Then it raised the axe high in the air.

And that's when the screaming started.

Chapter 27

Soldiers were screaming, stallholders were screaming, and customers were screaming. Children were screaming, and so were their parents. Even cats and dogs and birds seemed to be screaming. There was plenty of screaming going on already, but Frith still added some more as she turned and fled, back towards the soldiers who she had been running away from only a moment ago. But they were running too, and not paying her any attention. One of the few who stood their ground – some kind of captain, judging by the fancy feather on top of his helmet – drew his sword, and pointed it (hardly trembling at all) in the direction of the monster with the axe.

'All right, now, sonny,' he said. 'Let's not do anything hasty.' He took a step forward as Frith ran past in the opposite direction. 'Put down the axe and no one needs to get hurt.'

The monster grunted.

Frith looked back in time to see a handful of soldiers spread out on either side of the captain, swords and spears shaking in their hands.

'Nice and easy,' said the captain. 'Everyone just stay calm, and—'

With a yelp, a soldier launched his spear at the monster. It flew in a low arc and lodged itself in the creature's side. The monster looked down at it with a puzzled expression, and made a short, low noise.

'I said *calm*, Wilkins!' The captain glared at the spear chucker, then turned an apologetic smile to the monster. 'Sorry about that. You can't get the staff, you know. What with the war with the armies of the north lands and everything. The rest of you men, *do not* throw your spears unless I say so.'

The monster plucked the spear from its side, held it up in front of its face to examine it for a moment, then dropped it to the ground.

'So . . .' said the captain.

And three more soldiers threw spears.

'What are you doing?'

'But you said *so*!'

212

'I didn't mean—'

The monster pulled each spear in turn out of its thick hide, emitting a low grunt of annoyance with each one. Then it dropped the spears to the cobbles, and roared, a mighty, earth-shaking bellow, and stomped through the soldiers, casually sweeping aside with an arm or its tail those few who failed to run.

And it headed straight for Frith.

Frith ran, and the monster chased after her, shaking the ground beneath her feet with each mighty step it took.

Frith dived under a stall, darted this way and that through the now deserted aisles of the market to stay out of sight, and

emerged behind a wagon on the far side of the square. There was no sign of the monster, but the relief she felt was short-lived. If she couldn't see it, then she couldn't be sure where it was. Could she risk dashing across the cobbles and into the streets beyond? Or was it just out of sight on the other side of the wagon?

She heard it then. Its deep rasping breath close by, still out of sight, but not for long. Frith had to hide. She leaped into the back of the wagon.

It was freezing cold inside, and Frith had to hold back a gasp of shock. She sat, hunched and still, in the

darkness of the straw-lined cart, and listened. She heard the shuffling of enormous feet, and the snuffling, sniffling breath of the monster, and the nervous clatter of horse's hooves. Then the footsteps stopped, and very close by the beast gave a long, low moan, then another long sniff. A thin crack of morning light cut through the darkness as a clawed hand pulled at the canvas flap at the back of the wagon. Frith held in a squeak of fear and clutched her knees against her chest. The crack of light widened, and the monster's enormous face peered in at her.

As Frith scrambled away from it in a flurry of limbs, the creature looked away at the sound of a shouting voice.

'Steady, men. We've got him this time. But remember: we want him alive, so—'

There was a dull thud. Then a colossal roar. Then a whinnying cry of fright. Then Frith was tipped over as the cart lurched into violent motion beneath her.

There were more shouts and cries and roars, but they were soon lost in the clatter of hoofbeats on cobbles, the rattling of a creaky old cart going much too fast, and Frith's own cries of alarm, as she was thrown about in the back. As she struggled back to her feet, the cart bucked beneath her and she fell back once more and hit her head on a huge block of something hard.

She briefly wondered what could be so very cold. But the thought quickly dissolved as darkness wrapped round her, and she sank into oblivion.

CHAPTER 28

FRITH WOKE UP FLAT on her back, wet and cold, and wondering why her head hurt. Opening her eyes she found that she was in the back of a cart, with some half-melted blocks of ice amidst a lot of wet straw. Puzzled, she crawled to the front of the wagon, passing three large metal churns as she did so, and emerged blinking into bright sunlight. The horse between the shafts of the cart raised its head to look at her, then returned to munching at a sorry looking scrap of vegetation on the dusty ground. Frith stood on the bench seat to see what else she could see. Mostly, there were large areas of nothing much scattered amongst larger areas of absolutely nothing at all.

So, she was back in the Barren Wasteland. She reached into her pocket for the map, but it wasn't there.

'No!' Frith dug around in her pockets, double and

217

triple checking, but the map was gone. 'No, no, no!' She remembered she'd been looking at it in the marketplace, but then so much had happened so fast. 'Aaargh!' She slumped down onto the seat.

'Oh! It's you again. I might have known.'

Frith rolled her eyes, climbed down from the cart and turned to face the speaker.

'Oh!' she said. 'It's *you* again. *I* might have known! Nice hat.'

'Oh, this old thing?' said the Big Wise Head. 'You couldn't really call it a hat. Just a tatty old blanket with knots in the corners.'

'I can take it off you if you don't like it.'

'I suppose it does keep the worst of the midday sun off. Which I'm . . . quite grateful for.' There was a tiny hint of apology in the Head's voice. His cracked lips pulled themselves into a tight smile.

'Actually,' said Frith. 'I have something else you might like.'

She climbed back into the cart, picked out the largest of the blocks of ice, then stopped and looked again at the metal churns. She realized now that she had seen them before. She pulled the lid from the nearest one and looked inside.

The churn ploughed a groove into the dry earth as Frith dragged it over to the Head. She set it upright in front of him and pointed at him with a large metal ladle.

'Close your eyes and open your mouth.'

'Why?'

'Question,' said Frith. 'One gold coin.'

The Big Wise Head closed his eyes, and opened his mouth.

Frith took the lid off the churn, dipped the ladle in, and dug out a big dollop of sloppy, drippy ice cream and tipped it on to the Head's tongue. The Big Wise Head gave a squeak of surprise, and closed his mouth. For a moment he was entirely still, then tiny ripples of movement passed over his face. His lips trembled, his brow furrowed, and a single tear rolled down his cheek.

'Oh!' His eyes opened wide and he stared at Frith in wonder. 'Oh!' he said again. 'Thank you.'

'You're welcome,' said Frith, smiling and reaching out a hand to gently touch the Head's dry cheek. 'Now, do you want to try the strawberry?'

The Big Wise Head screwed up his face, squeezing a tear out of the other eye.

'Question,' he said, apologetically. 'One gold coin.' He gave a grunt of frustration. 'I'm sorry,' he said. 'I really can't help . . . I'd answer all your questions for free after that, if I could. It's just that the curse—'

'I know,' said Frith. She stuffed her hands in her pockets. 'It's a shame though. I could do with some good advice at the moment.'

'Yes?' The Big Wise Head looked at her with kind, questioning eyes.

'I've just escaped from a dungeon, fled from the city in an accidentally stolen cart full of ice cream, and I only got away at all because my little brother let himself get caught. So, he's probably back in the dungeon. And home is that way somewhere' – Frith waved a hand in one direction – 'but I'd never find it without the map, which I've lost . . .'

'I assume you dropped it when that fish seller bumped into you.'

'But you couldn't possibly...'

'I am *very* wise,' said the Head. 'And you smell of fish.'

'Even so . . .'

'And a crow saw the whole thing and told me all about it. Sorry. Go on.'

'And back that way, somewhere' – Frith waved her other hand at the nothingness in the other direction – 'is the city. Which I could *probably* find again. Where Spuggy – that's—'

'Your brother. I know.'

'Of course you do. Where Spuggy's in a dungeon, and the king's men will be looking for me to put me back in there with him.' Frith's hand closed around the sling in her pocket and she began to bunch up the material in her fist. 'Oh, and there's a monster on the loose.'

'A monster?' The Big Wise Head looked surprised.

'Yes. The one that lives in the woods that *you* said didn't exist.'

'There is no monster in the

woods,' said the Big Wise Head.

'Not any more, no. Because it followed me to the city.'

'There has never been a monster living in the woods near Thornville,' said the Big Wise Head, firmly. 'But there's certainly one in the city. You're right about that.'

Frith frowned. 'I'm right about all of it!' she said. 'I'm . . . I'm . . . righter than you are!'

'I am the Big Wise Head,' said the Big Wise Head. 'And the birds of the woods are my friends. And I have had a lot of time to learn about monsters in the past two thousand and sixty-four years. And I am right about this. And you are wrong.'

'Well, if you're so swearing clever, then why don't you tell me' – Frith took her hands out of her pockets, and threw her arms out wide, pulling the loose end of the sling free – 'what I should do?' Her voice cracked, and tears welled in her eyes. Sunlight glinted off something small and shiny pulled from her pocket by the sling.

'Question,' said the Big Wise Head.

The shiny something fell to the ground.

Ting.

Frith and the Big Wise Head looked down at it.

'One gold coin,' they both said.

Frith picked it up and held it in front

of her face. The Big Wise Head sniffed the air.

'It smells a bit funny,' he said.

'Yes,' said Frith.

'Do you want me to answer your question?' said the Big Wise Head.

Frith looked at the coin, turning it from side to side and watching it glint in the sunlight. Then she looked at the Head.

'Yes,' she said.

'Drop the coin into the well.'

Frith walked over to the well, held the coin out at arm's length, and let go. There was a faint and distant splash. Frith shuffled back over to the Big Wise Head. Shoulders slumped, she stared into his eyes. 'What should I do?' she said.

The Head closed his eyes and thought for a moment.

'You should do what is right,' he said.

223

'Brilliant,' said Frith. 'And what's right?'

'Question,' said the Big Wise Head. 'One gold coin.'

'Really?'

'Sorry.'

Frith felt for the other coin.

'But you know already,' said the Head. 'The only answers worth anything at all are the ones we already know are true. And you do know, Frith Carter, don't you?'

Frith scowled at him. But then the scowl melted away.

'Yes,' she said. 'I suppose.'

'You should go now.' The Big Wise Head smiled.

Frith nodded, walked quickly to the cart, and climbed aboard.

'Worst gold coin I've ever spent,' she shouted.

'Do not request a refund,' yelled the Head, 'as a refusal often offends.'

Frith took up the reins, and with a twitch of her wrists set the cart in motion. If she remembered the details of the map correctly, then she hoped to see three big rocks stacked on top of one another soon. She was *almost* sure. She rode on, staring so hard at the horizon that she didn't even notice the squirrel carrying a tatty map passing her in the opposite direction.

CHAPTER 29

'OH NO!' SAID SPUGGY. 'What are you doing here?'

'I came back to rescue you,' said Frith, as Norman the jailer pulled her past Spuggy's cell.

'Brilliant!' said Spuggy, pressing his face between the bars. 'How's it going?'

'Worse than Mum's cooking.'

Norman hauled Frith to the doorway of the next cell along and gave her a shove. Frith fell on to her face on the straw-covered floor.

Norman chuckled, locked the door, and walked away.

'Frith,' whispered Spuggy.

Frith crawled over to the corner of her cell nearest to Spuggy.

'Yes?'

'Is this all part of the plan? Did you deliberately get caught, and now you've got a really clever way to get us both out?'

'There's no plan, Spuggy. I got out of the city, and into the Barren Wasteland. Then I came back. Then I got caught.'

Frith leaned her head back against the stone wall and closed her eyes tight. She could hear Spuggy's breathing, fast and shallow.

'Well, that was stupid!' he said. 'I had to be quite brave so you could get away. Why didn't you *stay* away?'

'I couldn't just *leave* you!'

'Well, you should have!' said Spuggy. 'It was my stupid fault you ended up here. You said so.'

'I know what I said!' Frith's voice broke from a yell to a croak. 'And I was wrong. I was the stupid one.' She leaned her head down between her knees and gave a sob. 'I'm the big sister. I should have been looking after you. It's *my* fault we're here.'

There was a long pause.

'OK,' said Spuggy. 'I'm glad we've cleared that up.'

'I mean, partly my fault. Obviously it's quite—'

'Anyway,' Spuggy cut in, 'I'm in a nicer cell now. This one's much less smelly. What's yours like?'

'Er . . . it's . . .' Frith took a look round, and gave the air a sniff. 'It's smaller, but the straw is cleaner, and I've got two buckets . . .' She stood and gave them a closer

look. 'One water, one empty. And I've got a window.' She walked over to stand beneath the small, square window set high in the wall, and crisscrossed with iron bars.

'Ooh! Lucky! What's the view like?'

'I can't tell. It's too high up.'

Voices, and the sound of hammering, drifted in from outside.

'Something's going on, though,' said Frith. 'I wonder if . . .'

It took Frith six attempts jumping up from the upturned bucket before she managed to catch hold of the bottom edge of the window. Even then, it was a struggle to pull and scramble herself up far enough to peep out. And even then it took a while to work out what she was looking at. The window was just above ground level looking out on to one of the interior courtyards of the castle, so Frith had a worm's eye view of what was going on. There were at least twenty men bustling about, sawing and hammering, or fetching sturdy wooden posts or metal railings from one of the wagons that were grouped together on the far side.

'They're building something,' grunted Frith

'What?' said Spuggy. 'Oh! Frith—'

'Some kind of big fence, I think. Maybe they—'

'Hey!' A cry came from behind her. Frith jolted in surprise, lost her grip, and fell with a bump to the floor.

'Ow!'

'I wouldn't bother,' said Norman the guard, pointing up at the window. 'Them bars is iron, and that stone is . . . well, it's rock hard. You ain't gonna get out that way.' He gave his forehead a lively scratch. 'Besides, you don't wanna go now, and miss out on your chance to be famous.'

'Famous?' Frith said.

'Oh, yes. You two are the king's favourites. He likes you so much he's making you stars of the fair.'

'That . . . doesn't sound very likely,' said Frith.

'It's true. He's invited everyone in the kingdom to the final day, and you pair are the star attraction.' Norman chuckled to himself. 'Well, you two and . . .' He pointed up at the window.

'Who?' said Frith, only slightly distracted by all the

different bits of her that hurt. 'Who's out there?'

'Well now,' said Norman, 'that is for me to know, and for you to . . . be really annoyed that you don't know.' He gave Frith a contented grin and shuffled away, chuckling to himself.

Frith and Spuggy sat on either side of the wall between their cells, and Frith told her brother about the monster, and escaping the city, and the Big Wise Head. And about coming back and getting immediately caught while staring at a very bad picture of herself on a 'Wanted' poster in the marketplace.

'Oh! What's going on up there now?' she grumbled, glancing up at the window. The hammering had stopped, but something else was going on now that involved a lot of shouting.

Frith repositioned the empty bucket, and jumped, and grabbed, and pulled, and scrambled again to look out of the window.

'Oh! They've finished building and they're clearing out,' she said. 'And it's not just a fence. More like a cage. A big one. I think . . . I think it must be for the monster!'

'What? Why do you think that?'

'Because they're putting the monster in it.'

Straining to hold herself up, Frith watched in fear

and wonder as the monster from the woods, tethered by a dozen ropes, was dragged into the cage by one lot of soldiers, while a second group encouraged it along from behind with spears and halberds. The creature writhed, and strained, and resisted, and stamped, and grunted, and growled, but little by little the soldiers pulled, and pushed, and poked it into the middle of the cage.

'That's a relief,' said Spuggy.

'What?' Frith watched the soldiers hurry out of the cage and lock and bolt the heavy iron door, then she dropped down to the cell floor. 'How is that a relief?'

'Well, if they're keeping the monster here, then it won't go back to the woods,' said Spuggy. 'So, Edward will be safe.'

'Edward?' spluttered Frith, pacing in a tight circle that threw a whirlwind of straw into the air. 'Never mind Edward! What about us? Your imaginary friend was already safe because *he's imaginary*! But we . . . Remember what the jailer said?'

'What?' Spuggy's voice was nervous and small.

'He said the *three* of us were going to put on a show for the king. You, and me . . .' Frith looked back at the window.

'And . . .' said Spuggy.

'And . . .' said Frith, still staring at the small square of light high up in her cell wall.

Neither of them finished the sentence.

After a long while, Spuggy said: 'What *kind* of a show do you think it will be?'

'Well,' said Frith, 'if we're lucky, I should think they'll give us a sword each, and get us to fight it.'

'And . . . if we're unlucky?'

'If we're unlucky we won't have swords.'

CHAPTER 30

'RIGHT,' SAID NORMAN, STANDING outside Frith's cell door holding a wooden tray, 'back against the far wall, sit down and don't move.'

Frith moved with insolent slowness to the rear of the cell, looking deeply hurt that anyone wouldn't trust her to behave herself. Just because they'd made nineteen attempts to escape in the past day and a bit. She turned to face Norman, hands in pockets.

'Come on, come on!' Norman barked. 'Get a move on! You don't want your . . .' he stared, wincing, into the steaming bowl on the tray he was carrying, '. . . whatever this muck is to get cold, do you?'

'I shouldn't think it'll be any worse if it does,' said Frith. She took hold of the sling in her pocket as she leaned back against the wall.

'You'd be surprised.' Norman gave her an ugly grin.

'And you really ought to get a good meal inside you tonight, ready for your big day tomorrow.'

Norman enjoyed teasing them both about their 'big day', though he was careful never to give them more than a hint of what it might involve. Each time he had brought them a meal, or passed by on his rounds, he had let slip another morsel of information, but without ever fully revealing what awaited them. Now it was the last night before they would find out for themselves, and time to put into action their final remaining escape plan.

Frith's hand closed around the gold coin in her other pocket, as she slid, inch by slow inch, down the wall. Norman put the tray down, his eyes still fixed on Frith.

'Come on! All the way down!'

She just needed him to look away for a moment.

'La, la, la!' yelled Spuggy from the next cell. 'The guard smells of poo!'

Norman's eyes flicked sideways.

'Take that back!' he said, as Frith whipped her hands from her pockets, placed the coin in the sling, and in one quick movement propelled it with all her might. 'It's not my fault if—'

Bullseye!

The coin hit Norman straight between the eyes. His body stiffened. He teetered and tottered as his feet

234

flapped about beneath him, stumbling in all directions. His eyes rolled up inside his head, his knees buckled, and he slumped down on to his face, his head pressed up between the bars.

'Did it work?' called Spuggy.

'Yes!' Frith made no effort to hide the surprise in her voice.

'Brilliant! Get the keys and let me out, then.'

Frith raced over to the bars. 'Ah, yes, hang on . . .'

'You *did* wait for him to unlock the door before—?'

Frith reached through the bars, scrabbling at Norman's belt, where the big jangly bunch of keys ought to be.

'You started shouting too soon!'

'Never mind that. Can you reach the keys?'

'I can't *see* the keys! He must have fallen on top of them. Maybe if I turn him over . . .'

Frith grabbed hold of Norman's shoulder, and tried to heave him on to his side.

'NYEUURGH!' said Frith, as Norman failed to roll over.

'How's it going?'

'How does it sound like it's going?'

Footsteps sounded down the corridor, accompanied by a jaunty but unmusical whistle, then a high, fluting voice.

'Norman, you silly sausage! You forgot the . . .'

Frith, with her arms and head stuck through the bars, turned her attention from Norman's immoveable carcass to the second guard who had just come to a standstill outside Spuggy's cell.

'. . . keys,' he said, holding up the big bunch of keys.

He stood, thoughtful for a moment, eyeing the scene before him: Norman unconscious on the floor; Frith's head poking out between the bars; a gold coin glinting on the floor. He picked up the coin, admired it for a moment, and stuffed it in his pocket.

'Naughty!' he said, waggling a finger at Frith. Then he

grabbed hold of Norman's feet and, whistling joyously, dragged him away.

Frith hauled herself up to look out of the window again. Watching the monster lolloping about was no kind of comfort. It seemed just as big and terrifying now as it had before, and as far as she could tell, precisely none of its unnecessarily big and pointy teeth had fallen out in the meantime. If anything, she thought it might have grown a couple of new ones. Frith told herself that it was only sensible to study it, in the hope that, somehow, she might identify a weakness, some small hope to cling to. But really, she'd given that up long ago. Now, she watched only out of morbid fascination. And because there was nothing else to do.

Even when she wasn't watching the monster, Frith was constantly reminded of its existence. She heard it stomping about. She heard its snorting breath. She heard it wailing, and moaning, and howling, and roaring. And perhaps worst of all, she heard the rumbling of its stomach.

'Get down from there before you do yourself a mischief!' The other guard was back again, pushing Frith's cold dinner into the cell with his foot. 'I'll get in so much trouble if you hurt yourself!'

Frith lowered herself from the window as he relocked the door.

'That'll be stone cold now, and serve you right, frankly, after what you did to poor old Norman. Now, eat up. Big day for you tomorrow. And you'll have quite an audience. I've never seen the city so packed.' He wandered away again.

'At least it sounds like we'll have a big crowd watching us tomorrow,' said Spuggy. 'It'd be a shame to be torn limb from limb and eaten by a monster, and have no one turn up to watch. That'd just be embarrassing!'

'I suppose,' said Frith. 'But I still think *not* being torn limb from limb, *or* eaten, at all, would be better.'

'Yes,' said Spuggy. 'I was trying to look on the bright side. But I'm not sure there is one. Not unless we either come up with a brilliant plan that gets us out tonight . . .'

Frith thought back through all the brilliant plans they'd had so far.

'Or?' she said.

'Or we fight the monster, and win. And they let us go because we're just so amazing.'

The walls shook as, outside, the monster took a gentle stroll round its cage.

'I think we should try for a brilliant plan,' said Frith. 'But this one needs to be *actually* brilliant. Not one that seems like it's brilliant when we talk about it, but which turns out to be rubbish. Like the model of the king made out of straw.'

'That *could* have worked,' said Spuggy, 'if you'd done the voice better.'

'I don't think so. Anyway, what we need is . . .'

'A *brilliant* brilliant plan?'

'Yes.'

They both thought about this.

'Anything?' said Frith.

'No,' said Spuggy. 'You?'

'Not a sausage.'

And then they both thought about sausages for a while.

CHAPTER 31

FRITH AND SPUGGY COULDN'T get to sleep. They were scared, exhausted and, because the cold soup had been too disgusting to eat, they were hungry. So they thought, and worried, and their stomachs gurgled, and from outside the monster's stomach rumbled thunderously in reply.

'Maybe we should try to eat the monster before it eats us,' said Spuggy, trying to sound hopeful.

'I don't think monster would taste very good,' said Frith, trying to play along. 'Probably no worse than the soup, though.'

Spuggy gave the smallest, darkest laugh. 'It does smell *disgusting*, doesn't it? And horrible. And bleurgh! And AAARGH!' He thought for a moment. 'Do you think they got the recipe from Dad?'

They both sniffed the air. It really did smell like Dad's

terrible inedible gloop, which reminded them of home, and made them even more miserable.

Frith woke to the sound of distant padding footsteps, a faint jingling sound and Spuggy hissing from the next-door cell.

'Frith, wake up!'

'Whurr?' said Frith, as the fog of sleep began to clear from her head. 'What is it?'

'Have you thought of a plan? The guard's coming! We need a plan now, and I can't think of *anything*. And I'm scared!'

'A plan? Yes . . . No. No, I haven't thought of anything.'

Footsteps, jingle, jingle, stop. Some chat between the jailer and another prisoner, close now.

'But we've got a bit of time yet,' said Frith. 'If we're the main event at the fair, then I think we'll be on last, won't we? Not first thing.'

The guard's footsteps started up again; the jingle jangle of his keys drew closer.

'Now then, Roger,' said the guard. 'I've got some good news, and some bad news.'

'Is that right?' said Roger, the chicken thief in the cell next to Spuggy's.

'Oh, yes! The good news is: we're letting you out.'

'Oh! Great! And . . . ?'

'And the bad news is that you'll be put in the stocks and people will throw things at you.'

'Oh. Nice things?'

'That depends. How much do you like mouldy vegetables and rocks?'

Roger groaned in a way that suggested he wasn't keen on either.

There was a jangling of keys.

'Come on then,' said the guard. 'Oh, and, children?'

'Yes?' said Frith and Spuggy.

'I'll be back for you in a minute or two. Be ready to go, and no messing about.'

They did not reply. They listened to Roger being led away, and the jangle, jingle, tinkle of the keys on the guard's belt fading.

'A minute or two?' said Spuggy.

'I know, I know,' said Frith. 'What can we do?'

She scanned the cell frantically for inspiration, as if somehow there might be something she had missed all the other times she had looked. But just like all the other times, there was straw, and there were buckets, and there was nothing else, except for a bowl full of cold, disgusting, inedible soup.

Unless . . .

'Have you still got your soup?'

'Yes. Why?'

'Because it's so disgusting that no one would ever choose to eat it.'

'What?'

'So maybe no *thing* would choose to eat it!'

'Oh!'

Frith turned her face away and picked up her bowl of soup.

'So, maybe if we're . . . covered in it, the monster . . . won't eat us.'

'That's a terrible idea.'

'Absolutely,' said Frith, raising her bowl above her head. 'But still the best one we have. Come on.'

'On three?' said Spuggy.

'Yes,' said Frith. 'One . . .'

'Two . . .' said Spuggy.

'Three,' they both said together. Then: 'Yeurrgh!' as the horrible, claggy, cold, gloopy soup poured over them.

They coughed, and gagged, and choked, but neither of them died, or even passed out.

The guard returned with four large soldiers.

'What on earth have you done?' he said. 'I said no messing about, and you've covered yourselves in soup! You look *dreadful*! Oh well, I suppose it won't matter, once you're in your costumes.'

'Costumes?' said Frith, stepping out of her cell, and immediately finding herself trapped between two of the towering soldiers.

'Oh, didn't I tell you?' The guard unlocked Spuggy's cell. 'Can't have anybody from your village recognizing you and making a fuss, can we?'

'What sort of costumes?' said Spuggy, stepping out into the tight space between the other two soldiers.

'You can see for yourselves.' The sound of approaching footsteps drifted down the corridor. 'Here they come now.'

CHAPTER 32

'I DON'T THINK,' SAID Frith, as they traipsed past the other cells, 'that this makes our chances of escape any better.' The huge, floppy feet of her costume made it difficult to walk. And it was heavy too. And the head was too big for her, which meant the eyeholes weren't where her eyes were, so she couldn't see out properly. Plus, the smell of the cabbage and turnip soup, trapped inside, made her gag and gasp for breath.

'No,' croaked Spuggy. 'What are we even meant to be?'

'I *think* maybe you're a sheep?' said Frith uncertainly. 'And I'm . . . possibly a chicken?'

'It's very disappointing,' said Spuggy. 'I wanted to be a dragon.'

'I know,' said Frith, sympathetically. 'I'm . . . disappointed too.' Frith awkwardly adjusted her possibly-a-chicken head in an effort to get a clearer view of the steps they were approaching. It wasn't easy getting up them, because of the possibly-a-chicken feet, and eventually one of the soldiers carried her to the top to save time. A short stumble from there, Frith and Spuggy were bundled into the back of a covered cart, packed in tight between the soldiers. The journey was a short one, but it seemed longer to Frith, as the churning fear inside her stomach grew, and outside a distant noise grew alongside it, from a low hum to a loud excited buzz, like ten thousand giant bees.

Frith gulped as she dropped down from the cart. A guard grabbed her roughly by the arm and dragged her, stumbling towards a gate in a tall wooden fence. Beyond it was whatever was making all the noise. Rising above the fence she could see a wooden structure sloping down away from them, held up by crisscrossing posts. As they passed through the gate, and into the shadowy darkness beneath the structure, the noise was above them, louder now, rumbling and thundering like a gigantic storm. Frith wobbled and lurched along, dragged by the guard, towards a small oblong of light amid the shadows. Frith's fear grew with the noise and the light, then she picked out a voice amidst the thunderous roar. And then another, and another, and she realized that the whole tumultuous din was people. Hundreds of people. Hundreds of voices, shouting, and calling out. Hundreds of feet stamping. Hundreds of hands clapping. All of it combining into one immense, ragged, terrifying noise.

Frith recoiled from it, then felt herself lifted clear of the ground, and carried forward, feet flapping uselessly beneath her, out into the light and noise. And once she had blinked away the dazzle she could see that they were at the edge of a muddy field surrounded by vast wooden stands containing . . .

Oh!

Not hundreds of people.

Thousands!

Frith swung her head from side to side, snatching glimpses of the huge wooden arena through the costume's eyeholes. On the muddy ground at the centre of the field were two knights on horseback, charging at each other, as the crowd roared. The riders lowered their lances as the distance closed between them. Then the head of Frith's costume flopped and folded, and she couldn't see. In the momentary darkness, Frith heard the sickening impact of metal on metal, and thousands of voices joined in one gigantic gasp. Throwing her head back she saw the stricken figure of a man lying next to a metal shield folded almost in two.

'Ooooooh!' said the crowd.

Released without warning from the grip of her guards, Frith dropped to the ground, tripped over her chicken feet, and stumbled to her knees. Somewhere nearby a child laughed.

Another harsh tug on her arm jerked Frith's gaze away, up and to the side, past the blurry sight of a man and a woman with a scruffy dog, some rows further back, reluctantly taking their seats. They were so far away, and she only half saw them out of the stupid chicken head, but she knew her own parents.

'In you go!' The guard pushed her, and Frith stumbled down some steps into a small area dug into the ground beneath the stands. The guards lifted her on to a low bench next to a scrawny young man. Spuggy landed heavily into place beside her.

Pushing back the chicken head, Frith reeled from the noise of the crowd, louder than ever now that it was no longer muffled by the rough cloth. Beyond the guard looming over her, she caught a glimpse of the unconscious knight being dragged from the field, as the crowd laughed and cheered.

There was a metallic clunk from near her feet. Frith looked down to find her ankles shackled with a sturdy chain, just as Spuggy was locked into place beside her.

'All set.' A soldier stood behind them. 'They're not going anywhere.' He joined his colleagues at the front of the dugout, and the four of them turned their attention to the brutal delights of the arena.

Frith and Spuggy lifted their feet, pulling the chains tight. They didn't budge.

'Oh,' said Frith. 'We're not going anywhere.'

CHAPTER 33

THE JOUSTING WENT ON for ages, and was, for Frith, both terrifying and boring. When it was finally over, the soldiers left the dugout as a terrible musical performance began.

Spuggy stared at his chains. Frith stared at hers. Then, unable to bear the sight of the floppy chicken feet of her costume any longer, she looked over at the man sitting next to her. He was a scrawny fellow in a scruffy red and yellow costume, and he looked even more afraid than Frith felt. His legs were trembling, his head was twitching, sweat ran down his forehead, and his lips moved, as if muttering a prayer.

Frith reached over and laid a hand on his shoulder.

'Are you OK?'

He flinched at her touch, yelped, and turned to her in alarm.

'Where did . . . ? Who . . . ?' He looked at Frith and Spuggy properly for the first time. 'What on *earth* are you meant to be? Those costumes are a disgrace! I can't believe I have to perform on the same bill as such amateurs!' He shook his head. 'This . . .' he waved his hand at the musicians who now seemed to be playing three different songs at four different speeds, 'and this . . .' he pointed at another knocked-out knight being dragged through the mud, 'are bad enough. But do I really have to go on after a double act of a threadbare goat and a baggy goose?'

'I *think*,' said Frith, 'that we're a sheep and a chicken.'

'It hardly matters!'

'I suppose not. So, are you being fed to the monster after us then?'

The man looked stunned.

'Oh! Oh, no! You're . . . you're being *fed to the monster*? But that's *awful*!'

'Yes, but—'

'That means . . . you're higher up the bill than me!'

'Well . . . sorry? What?'

The man stood up, throwing his arms out wide, and Frith noticed that his feet were not shackled.

'Sixteen years! Sixteen years I've been a professional jester, honing my craft, stealing only the best jokes,

working tirelessly on my delivery. And what's my reward? Warm-up act to a badly dressed lunch in front of these Philistines.' He stared out at the crowd, booing and hurling rotten fruit at the musicians. 'They haven't got a clue! Barbarians, the lot of them! My comedy is the finest in the kingdom. Sophisticated, like a fine wine. Daring as the bravest knight. As finely crafted as a well-made . . . um . . .'

'Cart?' suggested Frith.

'I suppose. The point is, I'm too good for them. It's to be expected, I suppose. I'm so ahead of my time, I can't expect these, these . . . *peasants* to appreciate me, but . . . it's just . . . sometimes, you know, however much I'm paid, and however lavishly they feed me, and however many times I'm told how wonderful I am . . .'

Out on the field, a pair of knights emerged, and set about each other with a mace and an axe.

'It's just so *wearing*! Do you know what I mean?'

The jester collapsed back down on to the bench and began to bite at his nails.

'It must be *awful*,' said Spuggy, flatly.

'Mum and Dad are out there,' said Frith after a while.

'Oh!' said Spuggy. 'So, maybe if they see us, they'll cause a fuss and . . .'

'And they'll get thrown in a dungeon and never let out?' said Frith. 'Or they'll be fed to the monster too. I . . . I don't think we can risk that. We'll just have to go out there and hope . . .'

Frith couldn't think of anything to hope.

'That the monster dies of old age before it eats us?'

'Will you two *please* shut up?'

Frith and Spuggy stared darkly at the jester.

'I'm *trying* to run through my routine, and all your jabbering is ruining my concentration.'

'Well, I'm very sorry, I'm sure,' said Frith. 'I mean, we'll be out there getting *eaten* soon, and we're maybe just a tiny bit upset about it, but we wouldn't want to put you off practising your oh-so-clever jokes. It's *so* much harder for you!'

'Well, it is, actually, if you think about it.'

'How do you work that out?'

'Well, you've got it easy, haven't you? How many lines do *you* need to learn? "AARGH! *Please! No! Oh, the pain!*" That's about it, isn't it? Just thrash about a bit and scream. Piece of cake for you. Those idiots will just lap it up, whatever you say. One word out of place for me and it's disaster. No wonder I'm a slave to nerves!'

'*You're* nervous?'

Frith shut up as one of the soldiers, with a finger pressed to his lips, led a smaller older man carrying a bulging cloth bag down the steps.

'Bit of hush,' said the soldier, pointing at the knight displaying his skills out on the field. 'That's the king's champion, the Duke of Dunstable. Show some respect.'

He turned to the jester.

'And you! Funny man! You're on in two minutes.'

The jester stared back at him in silent terror, and began to breathe very quickly.

'You two.' The soldier pointed at Frith and Spuggy. 'Heads up for George here.'

The older man dropped his bag to the floor and smiled at them apologetically. Frith and Spuggy raised their heads.

'He means your other heads.' The old man rummaged in his bag with one hand and waved the other at Frith's costume head. 'The, uh . . . the bird thing and also the . . . whatever it is. I am to be sewing them closed so the peoples are not to be seeing you, yes?' He produced a spool of thread and a needle from the bag. 'By orders of His Majesty himself, I am being told, because you are being very important.'

Reluctantly, Spuggy pulled his costume head back up, and the old tailor began sewing round the neck, sealing him in. Meanwhile, the Duke of Dunstable, having defeated all comers with his skilful swordplay, departed the field of combat to riotous applause.

'You're on.' The guard pointed at the jester who gulped so hard that Frith heard it even above the sound of stomping feet on the wooden stand above them.

'Listen to them!' The jester, wobbled to his feet. 'Bloodthirsty animals!' He climbed the steps. 'Pearls before swine,' he said. Then he took a breath, stood up straight, and marched to the centre of the field, where he promptly dropped his breeches, stuck out his bare bottom, and wiggled it around.

The crowd went wild.

'Sophisticated,' muttered Frith. 'Like a fine wine.'

Then the tailor pulled her maybe-a-chicken head into place and began to sew.

CHAPTER 34

'GOOD LUCK, YES?' SAID the tailor as he cut the thread. He gave Frith a sad smile, then picked up his bag and paused at the bottom of the steps to allow into the dugout a breathless young woman in a flouncy shirt.

'And you two are, let me see . . .' She consulted a parchment scroll. 'Ah, yes! Enemy of the People number one, and Enemy of the People number two. Which is which?' Her eyes darted between Frith and Spuggy. 'I don't suppose it matters. This whole day is madness, I don't mind telling you. His Majesty commands that there will be a grand event to end the fair, and so there must be a grand event. And who has to organize it?' She looked at

Spuggy and Frith in turn, then pointed a thumb at herself. 'Muggins, here. Me.' She shook her head and sighed. 'Still, it seems to be going down well enough.' A gale of laughter led a rumble of applause through the crowd, as the jester fell on his face repeatedly behind her. 'Anyway, my dears, as I'm sure you know: you're on next! Top billing! Lucky you! So sorry there was no rehearsal, but it's a simple enough routine. I'm sure you'll be fine. Just to run you through the basics, though . . . You'll head out on to the field from here.' She pointed out across the field. 'Now, don't rush. Give the audience a chance to get a good look at you. Then your co-star – the fearsome, ravenous monster – will enter from the other side. Cue gasps of horror and awe from the audience, maybe a scream or two if we're lucky. He'll be led to the middle and released. He's not been fed for days so we're *pretty* confident he'll eat you both just as soon as he can, but if you could try to run away a bit, and act scared, then you'd really be adding to the overall effect. Can you do that for me, darlings?'

'*Act* scared?' said Frith.

'If you wouldn't mind,' said the woman. 'But don't overdo it. Let's be honest, *you're* not the stars. So, nothing *too* theatrical? Just plenty of running about, maybe some terrified shrieking. Then . . .' She consulted her scroll again. 'Ah, yes, of course. And then the king's champion comes on and demonstrates the might and goodness of His Majesty's reign by slaying the fearsome monster. Cue thunderous applause and cheering.'

'He slays the monster?' said Frith.

'Yes, of course. Not much of an act if the monster isn't killed at the end. Don't you know how stories work?'

'So . . . so we *don't* get eaten!'

'Eh? Oh, no, obviously this is *after* you've been eaten. Sorry, did I not mention that? You really must excuse me, it's been a *very* trying few days. So, you get eaten, Dunstable kills the monster, then . . . Oh, but you don't really need to worry about the rest. Not if you're . . .'

'Eaten,' said Frith.

'Quite. So, anything after that is *my* problem. As usual.' She rolled her eyes.

A deafening storm of cheering and applause rolled around the stands. Frith caught sight of the jester, half covered in mud, arms aloft, basking in the adulation of the crowd.

The woman gave Spuggy and Frith each in turn a serious nod. 'Your turn now. Please, do your best, darlings, will you? Thanks ever so.' She stepped aside as the guard unshackled them, and hauled them to their feet.

The jester stepped down into the dugout.

'Did you see me?' he said. 'Wasn't I just *marvellous*? Not that those idiots understood half of it, of course!'

'Julian, darling,' said the woman. 'You did it again!' She ushered the jester away from the steps to let the guard haul Spuggy and Frith out. 'Off you go, my loves. And remember: do *try* to look scared.'

Frith didn't have to try. The guard prodded her from behind with the tip of his sword. Thousands of pairs of eyes watched her every move. The roar of the crowd, all-consuming now, was louder than anything Frith had ever heard before. And archers, posted round the ground, trained their arrows on her and Spuggy in case they tried to run. So, as Frith tripped and stumbled to the middle of the field, knees knocking and her body shaking with fear, it took no effort at all for her to look scared. Ahead of them stood His Majesty's messenger, John Whitehill, who gestured for the crowd to be quiet.

'Ladies and gentlemen,' he said, in a booming voice, 'we come now to our final event. Allow me to introduce to you the Dark Enemies of Our Glorious Nation' – he raised a hand to indicate Frith and Spuggy – 'whose dreadful villainy is so apparent in their hideous appearance that we had to hide their faces to spare you the horror.'

There were shouts of alarm from the crowd, a lot of

booing, and at least one cry of: '*But what are they meant to be?*'

'Their crimes,' John Whitehill went on, 'are so dark, so cowardly and so treasonous, that no usual form of punishment would be sufficient. And so, with deep regret, even our most merciful king has agreed to allow that these two most odious criminals should face, in unarmed combat . . .' He paused dramatically.

On the other side of the arena a pair of drummers, standing either side of a gap in the stands, filled the charged silence with a drumroll. Six soldiers entered the arena, straining at the ropes they pulled behind them, dragging the monster into view. The crowd gasped. The drummers stopped drumming and scarpered.

'This foul beast was captured by our brave soldiers after it had terrorized the villages around the Thornville woods. For many miserable months it has stolen cattle . . .'

'Ooh!' said the crowd.

'. . . ruined crops . . .'

'Boo!' said the crowd.

'. . . terrified children . . .'

'Shame!' said the crowd.

'. . . and peed in the river, killing all the fish.'

'Eurgh!' said the crowd.

'But now, its dreadful reign of terror is over, and once

it has dispatched the vile and loathsome enemies of our land, it will itself be slain by the king's champion, the heroic and noble Duke of Dunstable.'

'Hurrah!' roared the crowd.

Frith felt dizzy and hot.

'Can you see it?' said Spuggy, facing sideways, his small, scared voice barely audible from inside his costume. 'I can't . . . I can't see . . . anything in this thing.'

Frith had a clear view of the monster, twisting and writhing, and straining against its ropes as the soldiers struggled to hold it in place. Her legs buckled beneath her and her vision blurred. The messenger's words sounded as if she was listening to them from underwater. And the inside of her costume was dank and stale, as if she had used up all the air. She felt herself begin to fall, but then jerked back to her senses as the guard yanked her upright. Frantically she looked back at the stand behind her, searching the crowd for her parents. She caught a glimpse of Cabbage running down the steps, and Mum and Dad rising from their seats to chase after him.

A rough pull on her arm made her face forward again. The messenger hurried off, as the monster was dragged to the middle of the field. Spuggy and Frith's guards released them and backed away.

'Frith . . .' whimpered Spuggy.

'Now, don't panic,' Frith said. 'We'll just have to . . . Um . . .' She looked up at the monster, glanced at the soldiers still clinging to the ropes holding the beast in place, then back at her little brother, stumbling blindly towards her. 'Oh swear!' She stepped in front of the monster, with her arms out wide, and called back: 'Little brother, do as your big sister says, and turn to your right.'

She looked at the monster, found that it was, for the moment, eyeing her curiously, then looked back at Spuggy who had turned to face the end the field.

'That's fine,' said Frith, quickly glancing between her brother and the beast looming over her. 'Now run!'

'But what about you?'

The monster sniffed the air, and looked at Frith.

'Never mind me! Do as you're told, for once!'

The creature craned its head towards Frith, the ropes around its neck pulled tight, and brought its face up close, staring straight into the chicken head's eye holes.

'RUN!'

A hush fell over the crowd. Frith felt the creature's breath cold against her eyeballs. She heard Spuggy stumbling away from her. She heard the low rumble of the monster's breathing, the creak of straining ropes, and the grunts of the soldiers fighting to keep hold of them.

The monster tilted its head by the tiniest degree and

narrowed its eyes. Frith held her breath.

Everything was still. Everything was quiet.

A bead of sweat dropped from Frith's forehead into her eye.

And she blinked.

'Ah!' she said.

The sleeping world awoke with a start. The monster rose to its full height, roaring, and twisting, sending soldiers flying from the ends of the ropes in all directions. Frith staggered back an awkward chicken-footed step. The monster dropped back down and turned a circle, bellowing as the soldiers scrambled to their feet and fled. Then it rose up again, unbowed by the ropes now, towering above Frith.

Frith gasped, shot a look at Spuggy stumbling away from her, then, filled with fierce resolve, turned to face the monster.

And in a voice that wasn't hers, she said: 'Come on, then!'

She had no idea what she intended to do. She had no way to stop this fearsome beast. But it wasn't going to get to her brother without a fight.

'Run, little brother,' she said, under her breath, her eyes still fixed on the monster's. 'Run, Spuggy!'

The monster's eyes narrowed. It considered Frith for a silent, aching moment. Then looked up, and past her.

'Oh, no!' said Frith.

The monster gave a rumbling growl.

'No, no, no!' cried Frith. 'Look at me!'

But the monster did not look at Frith. Instead, it brushed Frith effortlessly aside, throwing her to the ground, and lurched after Spuggy.

'No, no, no!' Frith scrambled to her knees, caught a blow from the monster's tail as it passed, and was knocked back down into the mud.

Frith climbed unsteadily to her feet, dazed, and dimly aware of the rising noise of the crowd. She heard the bark of a dog too, and faintly registered a glimpse of Cabbage running past guards at the edge of the arena. Light was leaking into her costume where the stitching had torn at the neck. She ripped the head back, and blinked in the sunlight. Then she locked her eyes on the monster, chasing after the ridiculous, hopeless figure of Spuggy, and with fear, and an awful, beautiful rage coursing through her, she set off after it.

The costume head shook and bobbed and bounced, then tore away completely and fell behind her into the mud. Frith ran on. Even the stupid flapping feet of her ridiculous costume could not slow her. She kept on, pounding after the monster, gaining on it.

Somewhere near her heels, Cabbage barked.

And Spuggy heard him, and looked round, and he stumbled. And he fell. He tumbled, and he rolled, and came to a halt in the mud, and the monster caught up with him, with Frith still paces behind.

'No! Spuggy!'

The crowd gasped as the monster came to a stop, and leaned over Spuggy, crying out in panic, gasping for breath and terrified, blind inside his suffocating costume, pulling at its head.

'Leave him alone!'

The monster leaned down and gave Spuggy a curious sniff.

'Don't you—'

Cabbage raced past Frith, yapping excitedly.

The crowd held its breath.

Spuggy went still.

And the monster bit his head off.

Chapter 35

The crowd gasped.

The monster straightened, twisted its body, threw its head back, and spat out something that landed on the ground to Frith's side. She did not turn to look. She felt as if all of her insides had crumpled. She fell to her knees, gasping for breath, then tipped forward on to all fours. The crowd were screaming now. She caught a woozy glimpse of the monster, then the world began to spin. She stared at the ground, concentrating on the few square inches of grass directly before her eyes, trying to fix them in place, and to block out all the things that she could not let herself think about right now. She focused on the grass.

There was an ant climbing to the top of one blade of grass, and in that moment that was her whole world. One ant on a blade of grass, in pin-sharp detail, everything else a distant blur. And by the time the ant got to the top, she could breathe again. And the sound of the crowd came back to her. And the ant stood on the tip of the blade of grass, and seemed to look up. And Frith raised her head, and stared at the monster, with Cabbage, barking and running in circles around its feet.

Distantly behind her were the urgent voices of her parents. And soldiers shouting. And the barking and the cries and the shouting all added to the great soup of noise that was coming from the crowd, but still, somehow, Frith heard a single voice in the midst of it all.

'Oh, that's better!'

A pang of hope stabbed at Frith's chest. Steeling herself, she looked round to where whatever the monster had spat out had landed, and there, next to a broken sword half buried in the mud, she saw the empty head of a stupid maybe-some-kind-of-a-sheep costume.

Now she was running, though she had no memory of standing up, nor of tearing off the rest of her own costume, nor of picking up the broken sword. But all these things had happened. The monster heard her coming and turned to look, revealing Spuggy, wiping sweat from his eyes, and blinking up at the huge creature before him.

'I could barely breathe with . . .'

Spuggy stopped talking. His face froze as he stared up at the beast.

'Oh!' he said.

Frith was nearly with them now, blazing towards them, screaming. The monster turned to face her. Frith gripped the sword handle tight, fire in her veins.

Then she tripped over Cabbage.

'Get off, you stupid—'

The sky above Frith's head disappeared from view as the monster's giant head loomed over her. Panic coursed through her. Cabbage licked her face.

'Frith!' yelled Spuggy, and the monster went still. 'Isn't it wonderful? There's no monster after all!'

Frith brushed Cabbage off her chest, and stared up at the great big enormous scary monster that absolutely definitely was leaning over her.

'But, look,' said Spuggy. 'Edward's here!'

Frith stared up at the monster. The monster stared down at Frith.

Cabbage jumped back onto Frith's chest and licked the monster's face. Edward the monster giggled and pulled his face away. Spuggy, with the head already torn off his costume, was trying to wrestle his way out of the rest of it.

'This is Edward?' said Frith.

'Yes, of course,' said Spuggy, tugging at a sleeve.

'Pleased to meet you,' said Edward, reaching down a hand to help Frith to her feet.

'So, *you're* Edward? Spuggy's imaginary friend?'

'His friend, yes.' Edward poked one of his monstrous fingers into the fleshy folds of his belly. 'But, um, not imaginary. Obviously.'

'And you can talk?'

'Yes,' said Edward, patiently. Then something seemed to occur to him. 'How's your head?'

'Fine. Why . . . ?'

'Oh, good. I thought maybe you were a little . . . confused after that bump when you fell in the woods . . . But you're all better now? The honey did the trick?'

'Honey . . . ? That was to make me better?'

'Yes, of course. It's good for bumps. Why else would you think I'd—?'

'Oh! Er, no reason. Thank you, by the way. Very much. That was . . . very kind.'

Spuggy, still pulling at his costume, stumbled and lurched towards Edward.

'Oh, Edward, I'm so pleased to see you! I was ever so worried. Apparently, there's been a monster in the woods!'

'Really?' said Edward. 'I haven't seen it.'

'I s'pose you've just been lucky.'

'I suppose so,' said Edward, looking round at all the soldiers. 'Up to a point.'

Spuggy and Frith looked too, while Cabbage ran in

excited loops round all of them. A little way off, a group of soldiers had caught up with Mum and Dad and were doing their best to hold them back. Mum strongly believed that this was a bad idea, and had already made this very clear to the soldier with the nosebleed, and the unconscious one at her feet.

The crowd, meanwhile, were growing restless.

'Boo!' shouted someone.

'Get on with it!' bellowed someone else.

Edward the monster looked round, puzzled. 'Oh,' he said. 'Is something the matter?'

'I think,' said Frith, 'they're a bit disappointed.'

'I'm not surprised,' said Edward. 'That jester was *terrible*!'

'No,' said Frith. 'I mean, they're disappointed with *us*.'

Another voice from the crowd shouted: 'Rubbish!'

'Oh dear,' said the monster. 'They do seem very unhappy. What should we do?'

Frith looked at Edward. And she ignored his size, and his teeth, and his horns, and instead she looked at his eyes, which seemed kind, and eager to please. And she thought about what the Big Wise Head had said.

'There are no monsters in the woods,' she muttered to herself.

'Maybe we could do a dance?' said Edward.

Frith looked up at him and gave him a sad smile.

'No,' she said. 'I don't think so.'

'You're probably right. My back's playing up a bit after all that being pulled about by ropes. But what do they expect, then?'

'Well, I, um . . . I think they *expect* you to eat us.'

Edward looked horrified.

'Why on earth . . . ? Are they savages?' He looked at Frith and Spuggy. 'I really don't want to. Especially Spuggy. At least not without giving him a good wash first.'

'Hey!' said Spuggy.

'Spuggy! Frith! Get away from that thing!' shouted Mum, as four soldiers struggled to hold her back.

'It's OK, Mum!' yelled Spuggy.

'Mum?' Edward strode over towards her. 'Hello. You must be Mrs Carter. I'm *so* pleased to meet you. Spuggy's told me so much about you.'

Mum shrieked.

'It's all right, Mum,' said Spuggy. 'Edward wouldn't hurt a fly.'

'Edward?' said Mum. 'Your imaginary friend, Edward?'

'I do wish people would stop saying that,' said Edward.

'Beg your . . . pardon,' said Mum, struggling to resist as the soldiers holding her backed away.

Edward leaned down to address them.

'Gentlemen,' he said, 'Please let this young woman go. I really think . . .'

The soldiers pulled Mum and Dad away with renewed force. Those with a free hand drew their swords as they went.

Edward's face tightened suddenly. He rose to his full height, towering above them, threw his head back and let out an earth-shaking, terrifying roar that echoed around the stands. The soldiers fled, leaving Mum and Dad quaking. The crowd hushed before one voice called out: 'That's more like it!'

Frith tottered backwards, staring up at Edward fearfully.

'Sorry about that,' said Edward. 'My back. It's agony when it goes.'

Mum and Dad cast him a nervous glance, then edged forward and took hold of their children.

Frith gasped as Mum's strong arms squeezed all the air out of her in an enormous hug.

'We thought we'd swearing lost you! What have you been up to, the pair of you? "Enemies of the nation", indeed!' She looked away as a new group of soldiers, led by the captain with the feathery helmet, marched towards them. 'Ah, good. Let's get this all sorted out. Who's in charge out of you lot, then?'

'Mum!' gasped Frith. 'I don't think . . .'

'I suppose,' said the king, emerging from behind the captain, 'that that would be me.'

'Good,' said Mum. 'Now look here, Mr King, this 'un here is my daughter.' Mum pointed a thumb at Frith.

'And she's a pain in the bum at times, I'll grant you, but she's not an enemy of the kingdom. And that daft lad there is my son.' She pointed to Spuggy, who gave a friendly wave. 'And, aside from being a bit smelly, he's no threat to anyone. So, if you don't mind, I'll take them home and give them a talking to, and we'll say no more about it. All right?'

'No,' said the king. 'Far from it.' He turned to the captain. 'See to this, will you?'

'As Your Majesty commands,' said the captain, drawing his sword.

'Just a moment.' The king's champion, the Duke of Dunstable, held on to the captain's arm as he addressed the king. 'Your Majesty, are you sure this is wise? Children?'

'I don't *care!*' spat the king. 'If they're old enough to be enemies of the kingdom, they're old enough to face the consequences. So, be a good fellow and get out of the way, will you?'

The captain shrugged off Dunstable's hand.

'And the creature, Majesty?' said the captain.

'Yes, what a disappointment he was. The children, the monster, these two . . .' The king waved a hand at Mum and Dad. 'Kill them all!'

CHAPTER 36

SWORD IN HAND, THE captain stepped forward.

'Don't even swearing think about it!' growled Mum.

'That's . . . right,' said Dad, crouching to pick up the broken sword.

The crowd buzzed with fresh excitement.

The captain raised his own sword, and pointed it at Dad. His eyes darted between Dad, with half a sword, and Mum, unarmed. He thought for a moment, then pointed the sword at Mum instead. Behind him, archers nocked arrows on to the strings of their bows, and

trained them on Mum and Dad.

Mum's eyes narrowed. Dad wafted his half a sword, and tried to stop his hand from shaking. The captain gave his own sword a showy twirl in the air.

'Oh, do get on with it!' said the king. 'I've got a feast to get to after this.'

'Right!' yelled Mum, fists clenched. 'You're first!' She took a single step towards the king, but Edward stepped between them.

'I don't suppose you can, I dunno . . . breathe fire or something, can you?' Frith asked Edward.

'No!' Edward sounded offended at the very idea. 'And even if I could, I wouldn't.'

'Archers, take aim,' said the captain.

'Your Majesty,' Dunstable said, urgently, 'I really think—'

'Now,' said Edward, 'if we can all just be reasonable . . .'

'Fire!' shouted the captain.

A blurry swarm of arrows flew to their target.

The crowd gasped. Spuggy screamed.

'Ow!' said Edward, head bowed, looking down with sad disappointment at the two dozen arrows sticking out of the folds of his flesh. He began plucking them out, wincing each time, dropping them to the ground. 'Well,

that's just *rude!*' He cast a grumpy stare at the soldiers in general, and the captain in particular, then to make his unhappiness absolutely clear, he wagged a finger at them.

'Don't just give up!' yelled the king. 'Shoot more arrows! Or use the big long pointy things. What are they called again?'

'Halberds, Your Majesty,' said Dunstable. 'But if I might suggest—'

'No! No, you may not! I've had just about enough of you, Dunstable! Questioning everything I command! I'm the king! You do as I say!'

'But, Your Majesty, with respect—'

'No!' The king picked out a pair of soldiers with a wave of his royal finger. 'You two, get him out of my sight. Throw him in the dungeon, and I'll deal with him later.'

As Dunstable was led away, the king returned his attention to Edward, with the Carters peeking out from behind him, and Cabbage still barking furiously by his feet.

'Oh, for goodness' sake, can someone at least shut that dog up? He's driving me mad!'

'Archers!' shouted the captain, and the archers took reluctant aim at Cabbage.

'Don't do that,' said Edward.

'Cabbage!' yelled Spuggy. 'Come here, boy. Come on.'

'Cabbage!' called Dad. 'Be a good boy and be quiet, and don't get shot with arrows.'

'He'd better not get swearing shot,' said Mum, and glared at the archers, several of whom began to shake.

Cabbage, with his eyes fixed on the king, stretched out his body, bared his teeth, and let out a low, sinister growl.

'Aim,' said the captain, with a distinctly unmilitary quaver in his voice.

'No!' said Spuggy and Frith.

'Cabbage, don't!' said Dad.

But Cabbage did. Growling and snarling, he bolted towards the king.

'Fire!' shouted the captain, and the archers let fly a fresh volley of arrows.

Cabbage dodged with ease the few arrows that came anywhere near him, and leaped at the king with a rasping snarl, hitting him hard in the chest.

The crowd gasped.

The king fell backwards into the mud.

Cabbage, delighted with a job well done, gave a happy

woof of triumph, then peed on His Majesty's boots.

The king climbed to his feet, and found that his crown had fallen off.

Cabbage ran a cheeky circle around his feet.

The king kicked him, hard, sending him yelping through the air to land at Edward's feet.

The crowd gasped again.

'You really shouldn't have done that,' said Edward in a reasonable voice.

'Boo!' said someone in the crowd.

'You really swearing shouldn't!' seethed Mum.

Spuggy ran to Cabbage and knelt beside him.

'Boo!' said another voice in the crowd. And another.

'Stay where you are!' The captain placed himself in front of the king.

'Arthur, darlin'?' said Mum.

'Yes, dear?' said Dad.

The booing swelled to a roar. Mum had to shout to be heard.

'You take the fella in the stupid hat. I'll deal with the rest of them.'

'Mum!' said Frith, as archers aimed, and soldiers with halberds and swords advanced from all sides. 'I don't think . . .'

And then everything went quiet.

CHAPTER 37

THE SILENCE DID NOT last for long. Almost at once it turned to screaming.

The crowd were all looking one way, so Frith looked that way too, and saw a gigantic figure, the height of ten men, striding through a gap in the stands, wearing a knotted blanket for a hat.

'Right,' said the Big Wise Head, stepping over to the centre of the field, and sending soldiers running in terror. 'What's going on here, then?' He knelt, and lowered his head close to the ground, addressing the king. 'Perhaps you could enlighten me, Your Majesty?'

'Certainly,' blustered the king, attempting a dignified pose. 'I was, as

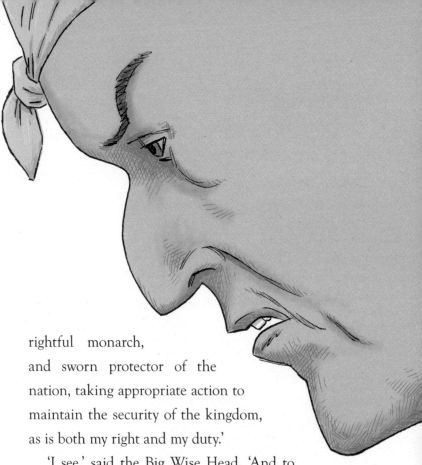

rightful monarch,
and sworn protector of the
nation, taking appropriate action to
maintain the security of the kingdom,
as is both my right and my duty.'

'I see,' said the Big Wise Head. 'And to
do this you were going to – let me guess – have
these fine citizens killed, were you?' He wafted a
hand at Edward and the others.

The king looked him straight in the eye.

'Fine citizens? These four are dangerous enemies of
the kingdom. Spies sent from the lands to the north.
And as for the monster—'

'Monster?' said the Big Wise Head. 'He's no monster!'

He pointed a gigantic finger at the king. '*You're* the monster!'

'He did kick that dog,' said a small voice in the crowd, and there was a hum of agreement.

'How dare you!' said the king, pointing an angry (but much smaller) finger back at the Big Wise Head. 'That's treason! I'll have you executed!'

'You can try.' The Head smiled. 'But you'll have to get past this squirrel first.'

A familiar-looking squirrel hopped down from behind one of the Big Wise Head's ears.

'And if you try anything,' said the Head, 'he *will* turn you into a frog.'

The king looked puzzled.

The king looked at the squirrel.

The squirrel looked at the king.

The king shouted at the handful of remaining soldiers: 'By order of the king, kill—'

And then the squirrel did a funny little dance and squeaked.

And there was a puff of smoke.

And the king turned into a carrot.

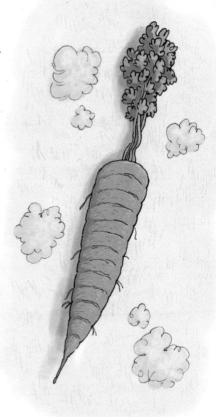

There was a long, surprised silence.

'I thought you said a frog,' said Frith.

'Yes,' said the Big Wise Head. 'He's a bit out of practice. And he's a squirrel, which doesn't help. Now . . .' The Head turned his attention to the captain, and the soldiers cowering behind him. 'Your king just ordered that my friends here be put to death. But your king is now a carrot. So, what you need to ask yourself is this: do you want to stay loyal to a carrot? If you do, then you'll

295

have me and the squirrel wizard here to deal with.' The squirrel nodded defiantly. 'Or you *could* just walk away.'

The captain thought for a moment.

'Your Majesty,' he said to the carrot. 'I believe that you may have had a change of heart and would now wish to pardon these prisoners and release them. But if I'm wrong, then speak your will and I shall, of course, loyally obey your command.'

The carrot didn't say anything.

'Thank you, Your Majesty,' said the captain. 'Your mercy is an example to us all.' The captain sheathed his sword, bowed to the carrot, and led the soldiers swiftly away.

Frith watched them go, and allowed herself to think, for the first time in quite a while, that maybe she wasn't going to die after all. Then she looked out at the crowd.

'What about that lot?' she said.

'I'll have a word,' said the Big Wise Head.

The Big Wise Head stood, and the crowd fell silent.

'People of the kingdom, please be calm. I understand that your king invited you all here promising you spectacular entertainment. As he has just been turned into a carrot by a magical squirrel, I think you will have to agree that, in that respect at least, he has been true to his word. But it is my sad duty to tell you that in many other

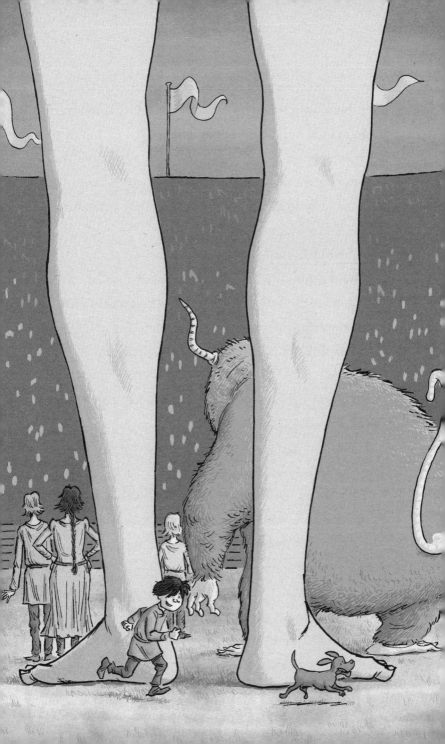

ways your king has *not* been honest with you. He claimed that this family' – he pointed down at the Carters – 'are a threat to the safety of the kingdom. But, in fact, they are good, honest folk.

'And your king claimed that this creature from the Thornville woods is a monster.' Edward gave a little wave.

'He said that he ate your cattle.'

Edward shook his head.

'He did not. The king's men stole your cattle to provide feasts at the palace. Your king said that this innocent creature ruined your crops.'

Edward shook his head again.

'He did not. The king's men took them. The king blamed him for the lack of fish because he peed in your rivers . . .'

Edward looked embarrassed and whistled innocently. The Big Wise Head chose not to notice.

'But, again, the king's men took fish from the rivers for the king's own table. And he didn't care if his people were starving. And still he took more and more taxes from you, to pay – so he said – for a war with the armies of the north lands.' The Big Wise Head paused, looking round the arena at the rapt crowd. 'But there is no war! The people in the north lands are peace-loving and kind. They have no army.'

The crowd gasped.

'You have been lied to, and robbed, by your king for many years,' the Big Wise Head continued.

'*And* he kicked that dog!' called out a voice from the crowd.

'But no more.' The Head smiled at the crowd. 'From this day on, you are at peace, and you are free. Go now, and live your lives well.'

A voice called out, though the words were lost in the general hubbub of the crowd.

'Please,' said the Big Wise Head. 'I think someone has a question. Allow me to hear it. Thank you. What was it you said, madam?'

A woman near the top of one of the stands stood up.

'That's all very well,' she yelled. 'But could you please put some clothes on? You're frightening my daughter.'

CHAPTER 38

Luckily, there were a lot of very big flags flying around the arena, which the Big Wise Head tied into a make-shift loincloth while the crowds drifted away, chattering excitedly. When he was done, he knelt down next to Frith and the others, and reached down a hand to let the squirrel jump onto it.

'So, is he,' said Frith, pointing at the squirrel, 'the wizard who cursed you for two thousand and . . . what was it?'

'Two thousand and sixty-four years. Yes. Apparently, he's felt terrible about it ever since. But he couldn't find me to put things right. Rubbish wizard, *and* a terrible sense of direction.'

The squirrel squawked and jumped and danced about a bit while the Big Wise Head watched carefully.

'He says thank you for the map, by the way.'

'He's . . . very welcome,' said Frith. 'And thank *you* both for saving us!'

'Ah, we didn't save you. I don't think the army stood much of a chance against your mother anyway. But it probably was less messy this way.'

There was a polite cough, and the Head turned to see the Duke of Dunstable, and the two soldiers who had been escorting him to the dungeon.

'Excuse me,' said one of them, 'we were wondering . . . Oh, hello there, miss. Nice to see you again.'

'Oh, yes. Hello again,' said Frith to Stan, and gave Charlie a wave.

'Sorry to bother you, oh Big Wise Head,' said Stan, 'but we were wondering if you could help us.'

'The thing is,' said Charlie, 'we were ordered to put

the Duke here in the dungeon. Only, now the king is a carrot, we're not entirely sure if we still should. And being as 'ow you're so wise, we thought you might have a view on the subject.'

The Big Wise Head smiled.

'Dunstable?' he said.

The Duke nodded.

'I've heard about you,' said the Head.

'Really?'

'Oh yes! There's a jackdaw called Colin who speaks

very highly of you indeed. Brave, resourceful, clever, kind . . .'

'That sounds about right,' said Stan.

'That's why we'd rather not throw him in the dungeon, see?' said Charlie. 'We thought maybe the king, what with being a bit, um . . .'

'Carroty,' said Stan.

'Yes, with him being so carroty now, maybe he could use a bit of help running the country.'

'So, we wondered if you thought it might be a good idea for the Duke here to lend a hand?'

'That would be very wise indeed.' The Head looked over at His Majesty the carrot, lying on the ground nearby. 'If His Majesty has no objection?'

The king said nothing.

'Well, that's settled then.' The Big Wise Head smiled at Dunstable. 'Good luck.'

'So we're going to have a carrot for a king now?' said Dad, and thought for a moment. 'Well, I don't suppose he can be any worse than he was before.'

'I swearing well hope not,' said Mum. 'Now, darlin', put down that swearing sword before you do yourself a mischief.'

'Good idea,' said Stan, eyeing the broken sword distastefully.

'What is it?' tutted Charlie. 'Alexander's of Westminster?'

They shook their heads.

'Poorly balanced,' said Stan.

'Inadequately tempered,' said Charlie.

'Shoddy,' they both said together.

Dad dropped the half a sword into the mud. Then, finding himself with both arms free, he wrapped them round Frith in a tight hug.

'Now, Dunstable,' said the Big Wise Head. 'I suspect that the king is quite likely to want to make a lot of changes to improve life for his subjects from now on?'

'I'm sure you're right.'

'But he lacks the funds to make that happen?'

'I fear that the coffers are almost empty.' Dunstable cast a wary eye at the carrot, and lowered his voice. 'He has been, at times, quite imprudent.'

'Yes. Well, I might be able to help with that. Draw up some plans, and I'll see you tomorrow.' Then to Frith he said: 'I have to go back to the well. Could you come with me?'

Dad answered for her.

'Yes, we can head that way. What do you say, Spuggy? Are you ready to go home?'

Spuggy released his grip on Cabbage, who sprang away, fully recovered from His Majesty's kick, and set off running in mad zigzags.

'Home!' grinned Spuggy. 'Oh yes!'

'Right then,' said Dad. 'Let's . . .' He looked off to one side in alarm. 'Cabbage! Drop it!' he yelled. 'Put the king *down*!'

It took a while to catch Cabbage, and then to persuade him to release His Carroty Majesty from his jaws. But once they had, Dad gathered everyone together again ready to depart.

'Come on then, Carter family, let's . . .' Then he trailed off, noticing Spuggy looking frantically about the field.

Spuggy gave him an imploring look, close to tears.

'Dad!' he said. 'Where's Edward?'

CHAPTER 39

SPUGGY WAS CRYING SO much that he was in danger of washing his face clean.

'He won't have gone far,' said Dad.

'But you don't know that!' wailed Spuggy. 'Maybe the soldiers took him! And I didn't even notice. And now they're going to . . . to kill him. And he'll think I didn't care! And I do care!'

'Don't worry, love,' said Mum. 'We'll find him.'

'But how? How will we find him?'

'Ahem!' said the Big Wise Head. 'I believe I might be of some use here.'

'Of course!' said Dad. 'You can use all your cleverness and wisdom to work out where he's gone.'

'Or you can talk to the birds, and get them to look for him,' said Frith.

'Or,' said Mum, 'he could stand up?'

'Yes,' said the Head. 'I thought I'd try that first.' He stood up, turned his head one way, then the other, then pointed. 'He's just leaving through the gates, out into the Barren Wasteland.'

They hurried to the marketplace, picked up Geraldine and the cart, and set off. With the Big Wise Head keeping them on course they soon caught sight of Edward, mooching slowly ahead of them. A shout from Spuggy made him stop, turn, and amble back towards them.

'Why did you just *go*?' demanded Spuggy, leaping down from the cart before it had properly come to a stop.

'You were with your family, so I didn't want to get in the way.' Edward shuffled his feet and stared at the ground.

'And are you all right?' Frith joined Spuggy walking beside Edward. 'All those arrows!'

Edward brushed the question away with a wave of his hand. 'Oh! The little pointy sticks? They don't bother me. I have very thick skin.'

'Well, I was *worried!*' Spuggy gave Edward's thick skin a punch.

'I'm sorry. But . . . I realized I didn't really belong, and I didn't want to make a fuss, so I thought I'd just . . . go.'

'What do you mean, *you don't belong?*' Spuggy grumbled. 'I'm your friend. I'm your *best* friend! Of course you belong.'

'That's very nice of you,' said Edward. 'But you're a family. Of humans. And I'm . . .' He looked away. 'I'm a monster, aren't I?'

'No!' said Spuggy.

'I am,' said Edward. 'I'm a monster, and I didn't even know. But that's why you've always told me to stay away from other people, isn't it?'

'No, I—'

'And that's what you thought, isn't it?' Edward turned to Frith. 'That's why you ran away from the cave.'

'No, I, er . . .'

'And that's what everyone in the city thought. I'm a monster. Who needs to be got rid of.'

'No,' said Frith.

'No!' said Spuggy.

'Yes,' said the Big Wise Head.

They all stopped walking and looked up at him.

'Yes. That's what they all *thought*. But they had been lied to, and they were wrong.' He knelt down. 'These two know better.' Spuggy and Frith nodded vigorously. 'And I know better. And all the birds of the woods know better.' He smiled at Edward. 'And you should know better too.'

'And that's the wisest being in the land telling you that,' said Frith. 'So you'd better believe it.'

Spuggy sat on the back of the cart, chattering happily to Edward walking behind. Frith stood on the Big Wise Head's shoulder and marvelled at the view.

'This is *great*!' she said. 'I can see so much more nothing from up here.'

'Are you complaining?' said the Big Wise Head. 'Because all I have to do is shrug and . . .'

'No, I'm very grateful, really. Up this high I can probably burn in the sun a bit faster too.' Frith leaned in against the Head's neck and gave it an affectionate pat. 'Really, though. Thank you. You really did save us.'

'That's OK,' said the Big Wise Head. You sort of saved me too, even if it was accidentally. And I'd already heard from a swallow that you were in trouble. I would have got to you sooner, but the wizard took a few goes to lift the curse even this much. I was a cat for a while, you know.' The Big Wise Head shivered at the memory. 'Horrible! Then a mole. And then a potato.'

'A potato? Really? What was that like?'

'Oddly peaceful. Anyway, then I got to be me, but still this big, and I thought that was close enough. It's a *bit* odd, but . . .'

'But the view is amazing,' said Frith.

'Yes. And it meant I could get to the city a lot faster.'

Frith looked over at the squirrel, who was sitting on top of the Big Wise Head's knotted blanket hat. 'How did he end up being a squirrel, anyway? Was *he* cursed by a rival wizard or something?'

'He did it to himself.'

Frith thought about this. 'How come?' she said. 'I get that his magic is, um . . . a bit hit and miss now *because* he's a squirrel. But when he was human . . . What happened?'

The Big Wise Head looked puzzled.

'I don't know!' he said, with wonder in his voice. 'I am the Big Wise Head, and I don't know the answer to your

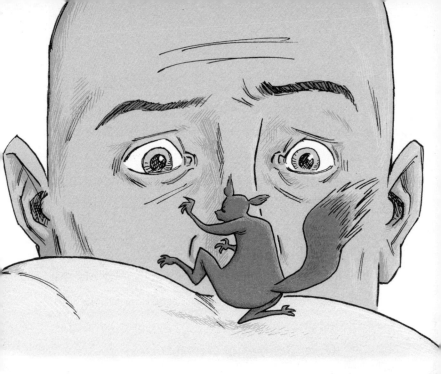

question! How wonderful!' He smiled. 'Wizard, how did you end up being a squirrel?'

The Head lifted up a hand and the squirrel jumped on to it, then turned a circle, squeaked, and danced, and gestured, while the Head observed him closely.

'Mm hmm . . . Yes . . . I see . . . He says that he has some very wise advice to offer *me*.'

'Oh yes,' said Frith. 'What's that, then?'

The squirrel jigged and squawked and squeaked some more.

'He says,' said the Head, 'never do magic when you're drunk.'

They stopped when they reached the well. There was a deep hole in the ground, where The Big Wise Head had been. Mum yelled and swore at Spuggy when he leaned over the edge of it to look in. The Head led Frith over to the well, then he pushed and pulled at the circular wall around it until he had cleared it away, and there was nothing left but another deep hole in the ground.

'What did you do that for?' said Frith.

'You'll see,' said the Head, and lay down on the ground, and reached into the well until his whole arm had disappeared.

Then he pulled his clenched fist back out, and tipped a huge mound of glistening wet coins on to the ground.

'Oh!' said Frith.

The Big Wise Head pulled out the rest of the coins he had been paid during the two thousand and sixty-three years of his curse, and added them to the pile.

'That,' said Frith, 'is a lot of coins!'

'I suppose so,' said the Big Wise Head. 'And I want you to have' – his gigantic hand reached over to the mountain of cash – 'this one.' He plucked a single coin from the top and handed it to Frith. 'Money back for the question you asked,' he explained. 'And the rest I shall donate to the king.'

'You're going to give all that money to a carrot?'

'Yes. But I expect he'll spend it wisely. The Duke of Dunstable will have some ideas about how to make life better for everybody. And the king won't say no to any of them.'

It was too late to get back to Thornville before dark, so they stayed the night. They built a fire, with the Head lying curled around it to keep the wind off, and they ate what little food they had, and they talked into the night.

'Oh, hey,' said Frith when it was late and dark and she was nodding towards sleep. 'What should we call you now? We can't call you the Big Wise Head now you're a whole gigantic person.'

'I suppose not,' said the Big Wise Head. 'And I'm not sure I really want to be wise any longer either.' He thought a little. 'Maybe I should just use my name from before I was cursed,' he said.

'Oh yes?' said Frith. 'What was that then?'

'Nigel,' said the Big Wise Head. 'Nigel Small.'

The fire crackled softly. Orange embers floated up on swirls of smoke into the night.

'You should probably sleep on it,' said Frith.

CHAPTER 40

FRITH WAS THE LAST to wake up, even though dawn was still breaking. Mum and Dad were loading the cart, and the Big Wise Head was cawing in conversation with the crow on his palm. Frith went over to join Edward and Spuggy, who were kicking dust onto the embers of the fire.

'I, um, wanted to say sorry,' she said to Edward without looking at him. 'You were right. I did think you were a monster.'

'That's OK,' said Edward.

'To be fair, you *are* very big, with horns, and lots of pointy teeth. And there were all these rumours about there being a monster in the woods. So, I think most people would have made the same mistake . . .'

'I didn't,' said Spuggy.

'No. You didn't, did you?' Edward stopped kicking

317

dust, and struck a thoughtful pose. 'Why didn't you?'

'I think it was because . . . well . . . I think you just reminded me of . . . me.'

Frith looked at her scruffy little brother. Then she looked at Edward, five times Spuggy's height, with his tail, and horns, and many, many teeth.

'You were sitting in the woods, on the autumn leaves,' said Spuggy. 'And you looked . . . You looked a bit sad. And lonely.' Spuggy kicked some more dust onto the fire, making it look like a very complicated task that required all his attention. 'Then I said hello, and you tried to run away but tripped over, and then we had a talk, and it was nice, and we were friends.'

'But . . .' Edward scratched his head with a long, clawed finger, 'you always told me never to talk to anyone else, and to stay out of sight. Because you knew that, whatever *you* thought about me, anyone else would see me as a monster.'

Spuggy looked horrified. 'Oh! No! It wasn't that!' He shook his head as if he was trying to make his brain rattle. 'I just wanted you all to myself. But I suppose now I'll have to share you with Frith.'

'Maybe a little bit,' said Edward, smiling. 'But not much. Not after everything you told me about her.'

'Hang on a minute,' said Frith. 'What . . . ?'

'Although, I have to say she doesn't seem *quite* as bad as you made out.'

'Eh? What did he . . . ?' Frith cast an angry look at Spuggy who quickly turned his eyes away. 'Ah, never mind. Actually, probably a lot of it *was* true,' she said. 'I've not been a very good big sister.' She thought she might try to be a better one, just a bit, from now on. But she decided she definitely wasn't going to say so out loud. 'Anyway,' she said to Edward, 'I'm really glad I got to find out I was wrong about you.'

'I'm glad too,' said Edward.

Using his blanket hat as a purse, the Big Wise Head gathered up the coins, and set off back to the city to give them all to the Duke of Dunstable, except for the one or two he was going to spend on having some very big clothes made.

'Goodbye forever,' he said, without looking down at Frith.

'Thank goodness,' said Frith, only looking up after he'd passed by.

'That was a bit rude,' said Spuggy. 'He could have said a proper goodbye.'

'I think,' said Dad, wandering over from the cart, 'that he's just not very good at goodbyes. I imagine he's been a bit lonely, all the time he's spent here on his own. So, maybe that makes it quite hard.'

'A *bit* lonely?' said Mum. 'It's a wonder he didn't go off his swearing nut! I daresay he'll want to spend some time in the city with lots of people now he's got the chance.'

'I suppose,' said Frith.

'At least until he realizes that being with people drives you just as swearing mad as being alone.'

'Thanks very much,' said Dad. 'And what about you, Edward?'

'What about me?' Edward looked puzzled.

'Are you going to go home, and live alone in the woods, and just see Spuggy once in a while? Or would you like to come with us to the village?'

'Do you . . . ? Do you think that would be all right?'

'All right?' said Mum. 'It'll be better than just swearing all right. It'll be swearing brilliant! I can't wait to see the look on Bill Simpson's face for a start.'

Edward looked uncertain.

'Oh, pleeease

come to the village,' said Spuggy, aiming his best wide-eyed pleading expression at him. 'Pleeease.'

'I suppose,' said Edward. 'I suppose I could come and take a look. If you're sure.'

He looked at each of them in turn, and they were all sure.

So, they climbed aboard the cart, and Dad took up the reins.

'Home, Geraldine,' he said, and off they rolled.

Frith leaned in against Dad.

'Sorry we disappeared like that and made you and Mum worried,' said Frith.

'That's OK,' said Dad.

'*I* wasn't worried,' Mum called from the back. 'I'm worried now we've got you both back! Swearing nuisances!'

Frith ignored her.

'And sorry I lost the gold coins. Or one of them anyway. Well, I lost one, then spent the other one, but then I got it back again.'

'That's OK,' said Dad.

'But obviously we'll take the one you have, and you can chop firewood every day until you're an old woman to pay us back for the one you lost,' said Mum.

'Oh, yes,' said Frith. 'And I lost the axe. Sorry.'

'Actually, *I* lost the axe,' said Edward. 'I was trying to

get it back to Frith but—'

'Never mind,' said Mum. 'We'll blame Frith anyway.'

'And we'll buy a really good new one from James the smith,' said Dad.

'And you'll chop wood with it until you're a *very* old woman to pay us back for the gold coin you lost *and* the price of an axe,' said Mum.

'OK, Mum,' said Frith.

They rode on for a while, each of them smiling to themselves.

'Do you think we'll ever see the Big Wise Head again, Dad?' said Frith.

'I don't know, love. Maybe. What do you think?'

'I don't know.' Frith stared off into the distance, her eyes following the flight of a bird in the sky ahead of them, hovering, then swooping, then climbing, and looping, and gradually drawing closer. 'I hope so.' The bird glided effortlessly over their heads. Frith wasn't sure, but she thought it was a red kite. 'I think, probably, yes.' She snuggled into Dad's side again.

'Are you looking forward to being home, kiddo?'

'S'pose,' said Frith. 'A bit.'

'Looking forward to chopping all that wood, I'll bet,' said Mum.

'Absolutely,' said Frith.

Then Dad started singing, quietly to himself, at first, without even realizing he was doing it, then a little louder. And then Cabbage started howling along, and an argument started up about whether this was an improvement or not. And somewhere, unseen in the distance, a very lost squirrel did a funny little dance and squeaked, and there was a puff of smoke, and something or other

happened. But whatever it was didn't matter, for now, because Frith, and Spuggy, and Mum, and Dad, and Cabbage, and Edward, were arguing, and complaining, and shouting at each other.

And they were going home.

And they were already home.

And they were as happy as could be.

ACKNOWLEDGEMENTS

This book was written and illustrated by me, so I get my name on the front as if it's All My Own Work. But really, it's a team game, so I'd like to thank a bunch of the good people who played on my side for this one.

My thanks, then, to the guv'nor David Fickling for editing and directing early on, and to mighty Anthony Hinton for the long haul beyond; and to the tireless Alison Gadsby for designing. Thank you for your skills, your patience, your care and your understanding.

Thank you to Julia Bruce for copy editing, and to Sam Burt for proof reading. Thanks, too, to the rest of the team at DFB HQ: Bron, Phil, Liz, Fraser, Rosie, Meggie, Rachel and Kate, doing all the Other Stuff that I couldn't do in a million years.

My lovely dad died in the latter stages of this book's creation, and that made family matter even more than usual. Respect, thanks and love, then, to Mum, Mike and Andy.

Deepest gratitude and love to Pam and to Mila, for seeing me through this and so much more.

And thanks to Dad. Sorry you didn't get to read this one. I miss you.